Practice Book 1

Cornelsen English Grammar

English Edition
Große Ausgabe

Cornelsen

Cornelsen English Grammar: Practice Book 1

Erarbeitet von Jennifer Seidl, M.A., München *sowie* Prof. Hellmut Schwarz, Mannheim

in Zusammenarbeit mit der Englischredaktion Filiz Bahşi (verantwortliche Redakteurin), Michael Ferguson (Projektleitung), Dr. Marion Kiffe, Maria Larscheid *sowie* Bettina Schaschke, Jennifer Schrübbers (Assistenz)

Beratende Mitwirkung Mervyn Whittaker, Bad Dürkheim

Illustration Eva Muszynski, Berlin

Umschlaggestaltung Knut Waisznor

Layout Katharina Wolff-Steininger

Technische Umsetzung Ilona und Ingo Ostermaier *sowie* Eva Baumgart-Catania, Peter Richter, Eva Schmidt

Für die Sekundarstufe II gibt es ebenfalls ein Übungsbuch:
Cornelsen English Grammar. Practice Book 2,
ISBN 978-3-464-06312-5

Bildquellen: argus Fotoarchiv, Hamburg (Frischmuth: S. 115 Malerin); Gary Barber, Dallas/TX (S. 150 Cafeteria u. American Football); John Birdsall, Nottingham (S. 157); www.britainonview.com (S. 32; S. 76 oben u. unten links; S. 101); Jan Chipps, London (S. 80); CINETEXT, Frankfurt a. M. (S. 15 rechts); Corbis, Düsseldorf (Tom Stewart: S. 42; Mitchell Gerber: S. 88; Richard T. Nowitz: S. 85); Corel Library (S. 57 alle bis auf Strand u. Hotel mit Pool; S. 76 unten Mitte u. unten rechts; S. 150 Baseball); Cornelsen Archiv (S. 150 Wolkenkratzer); dpa, Frankfurt a. M. (S. 115 Architektin u. Fremdenführerin; S. 150 Inline Skater u. Stretched Limo; S. 152); Format, London (Joanne O'Brian: S. 115 Krankenschwester); Getty Images, Gauting (V.C.L.: S. 115 Verkäufer); International Stock, New York (Laurie Bayer: S. 150 Mädchen im Auto; Bill Stanton: S. 150 Cheerleaders); Maria Larscheid, Berlin (S. 15 links); Mauritius, Berlin (SST: S. 115 Sekretärin; Rosenfeld: S. 115 Elektriker); Peter Peitsch/peitschphoto.com (S. 115 Schauspieler); Schapowalow, Hamburg (Weisser: S. 163 unten); Skjold Stock Photographs, Saint Paul/MN (S. 44; S. 64; S. 163 oben; S. 166); Bob Strong, New York (S. 150 Kiosk); Thomas Willemsen, Stadtlohn (S. 115 Straßenarbeiter); Zefa, Hamburg (S. 57 Strand; S. 57 Hotel mit Pool; S. 98)
Nicht alle Copyrightinhaber konnten ermittelt werden; deren Urheberrechte werden hiermit vorsorglich und ausdrücklich anerkannt.

www.cornelsen.de

1. Auflage, 6. Druck 2008/06

Alle Drucke dieser Auflage sind inhaltlich unverändert und können im Unterricht nebeneinander verwendet werden.

Druck: CS-Druck CornelsenStürtz, Berlin

ISBN 978-3-464-06311-8

Inhalt gedruckt auf säurefreiem Papier aus nachhaltiger Forstwirtschaft.

Inhaltsverzeichnis Contents

The article – *Der Artikel*

The adjective and the adverb – *Das Adjektiv und das Adverb*

Quantifiers – *Mengenbezeichnungen*

Pronouns and question words – *Pronomen und Fragewörter*

Conditional sentences – *Bedingungssätze*

Relative clauses – *Relativsätze*

Indirect speech – *Die indirekte Rede*

Hinweise zur Benutzung des Practice Book

Liebe Schülerinnen und Schüler,

sicherlich habt ihr Fragen zu eurem Cornelsen English Grammar: Practice Book (PB). Wir haben uns überlegt, welche das sein könnten, und versucht, euch die richtigen Antworten zu geben.

1 *Wozu dient das PB?*

Das *PB* hat zwei Hauptfunktionen. Ihr könnt damit
- überprüfen, wie gut ihr bestimmte Kapitel der englischen Grammatik beherrscht, und diejenigen
- wiederholen und üben, in denen ihr Wissenslücken entdeckt habt. Das *PB* hilft euch also vor allem dann, wenn ihr eure Grammatikkenntnisse **selbst testen**, **festigen** und eventuelle **Schwachpunkte beseitigen** wollt. Besonders nützlich ist es in Wiederholungsphasen, z. B. vor und nach der Leistungsmessung, insbesondere in Verbindung mit einer Schulgrammatik. Das *PB* bezieht sich eng auf die *Cornelsen English Grammar (CEG)*, kann aber natürlich auch mit jeder anderen Grammatik verwendet werden.

2 *Was enthält das PB?*

Wie euch das Inhaltsverzeichnis zeigt, besteht das *PB* aus 14 Kapiteln, die in ihrer Reihenfolge der *CEG* entsprechen. Allerdings werden im *PB* manchmal zwei Kapitel, die in der *CEG* getrennt behandelt werden (z.B. *Adjektiv/Adverb*), zu einem Kapitel zusammengefasst. Aber auch das Gegenteil kann der Fall sein: So wird das *CEG*-Großkapitel *Satzgefüge* im *PB* in drei Einzelkapitel *(Bedingungssätze, Relativsätze, die indirekte Rede)* aufgeteilt. Die parallele Verwendung von *CEG* und *PB* ist sehr einfach: Im *PB* wird grundsätzlich auf die Paragrafen der *CEG* hingewiesen, auf die sich die Testsätze und Übungen beziehen. Solltet ihr die Bezeichnungen für bestimmte grammatische Phänomene vergessen haben, so könnt ihr sie in der *CEG* (S. 230-234 bzw. im Register S. 235-247) oder in der Grammatik, die ihr gerade benutzt, nachschlagen.

3 *Wie sind die einzelnen Kapitel aufgebaut?*

Die Kapitel sind in ihrer äußeren Form alle gleich aufgebaut, sodass ihr euch leicht zurechtfinden werdet. Jedes Kapitel umfasst die beiden Teile *Test* und *Exercises*.

a *Der Test*

Mithilfe der ca. 30-35 Testsätze pro Kapitel könnt ihr herausfinden, wie gut ihr die Form und den Gebrauch bestimmter grammatischer Erscheinungen beherrscht. Damit ihr das möglichst genau feststellen könnt, ist der *Test* in unterschiedlich aufgebaute Teilabschnitte gegliedert: Es gibt *Multiple choice*- und Einsatzübungen sowie Übersetzungen von Satzteilen und ganzen Sätzen und den festen Bestandteil *Spot the mistakes*, bei dem ihr die Fehler in den bereits formulierten Sätzen entdecken und korrigieren sollt. Wenn ihr den *Test* bearbeitet habt und umblättert, findet ihr unter der Überschrift *Correct yourself* die Lösungen. Unterhalb der Lösungen steht der sogenannte *Exercise finder*: Links stehen die Nummern der Testsätze, in der Mitte die entsprechenden Paragrafen in der *CEG* und rechts die Nummern der *Exercises*, welche die in den Testsätzen behandelten grammatischen Probleme gezielt üben.

Exercise finder

Sentences	CEG	Exercises
1, 11, 25	▶ 41c	▶ 7a

b *Die Exercises*

Ebenso wie die *Tests* bieten auch die *Exercises* mehrere Varianten von Übungstypen, sodass ihr genügend anregendes Material zum Wiederholen der unterschiedlichen Grammatikbereiche finden werdet. Die *Exercises* sind in vielen Fällen in a- und b-/c-Teile untergliedert, wobei die b-/c-Teile meistens für selbstständige Transferleistungen stehen. Rechts neben der Überschrift wird bei jeder

Exercise das behandelte grammatische Phänomen konkret benannt. Die dazugehörigen *CEG*-Paragrafen sind ebenfalls angegeben ▶ **2, 3**. Die Lösungen der *Exercises* sind im separat eingelegten *Key to the exercises* enthalten.

4 *Wie kann man sinnvoll mit dem PB arbeiten?*

Ihr könnt das *PB* sehr flexibel nutzen. Wenn ihr aber seine Vorzüge voll ausschöpfen wollt, ist der folgende Weg am sinnvollsten:

Test → **Correct yourself** → **Exercise finder** → **Exercises** → **CEG**/Schulgrammatik
↳ **CEG**/Schulgrammatik

a *Zur Arbeit mit den Tests:*

Die Testaufgaben, die zum ausgewählten Grammatikkapitel gehören, werden in Stillarbeit gelöst. Ihr schreibt eure Lösungen der Reihe nach auf ein Blatt Papier, blättert anschließend um und überprüft anhand des *Correct yourself*-Teils, ob ihr Fehler gemacht habt. Es empfiehlt sich, eine als falsch markierte Lösung durch die richtige zu ersetzen. Versteht ihr eine Lösung nicht, könnt ihr gleich die *CEG* heranziehen. Den entsprechenden *CEG*-Paragrafen findet ihr im *Exercise finder*. Ihr könnt auch zuerst die als fehlerhaft gekennzeichneten Sätze mit der Zuordnung im *Exercise finder* vergleichen. Im Anschluss kann die dort angegebene *Exercise* gelöst werden und bei Bedarf der entsprechende *CEG*-Paragraf hinzugezogen werden.

b *Zur Arbeit mit den Exercises:*

Im *Exercise finder* könnt ihr auf einen Blick sehen, wie viele Fehler ihr pro Grammatikparagraf gemacht habt. Bei mehr als einem Fehler solltet ihr in jedem Fall die Übung, auf die verwiesen wird, schriftlich lösen und anschließend deren Richtigkeit – eventuell in Partnerarbeit – mithilfe des *Key to the exercises* überprüfen. Wenn ihr bei eurer Korrektur viele Fehler entdeckt, solltet ihr noch einmal eure Grammatik zurate ziehen und ein paar Tage später sowohl Testsätze als auch Übung(en) wiederholen.

Andere Arbeitswege:

Neben der hier skizzierten Methode gibt es zahlreiche Varianten, z.B.
- könnt ihr das betreffende Grammatikkapitel bereits vor dem Lösen der Testsätze durcharbeiten.
- könnt ihr nur die Testsätze ohne die nachfolgenden *Exercises* lösen.
- könnt ihr die *Exercises* unabhängig von den Testsätzen, eventuell aber in Verbindung mit der *CEG* bearbeiten.

Welchen Weg ihr auch immer wählt: Wir wünschen euch viel Erfolg und Spaß bei der Arbeit!

Jennifer Seidl & Hellmut Schwarz

Abkürzungen

aux.	→ *auxiliary/-ies*	perf.	→ *perfect*	quest.	→ *question/s*
demonstr.	→ *demonstrative*	pl.	→ *plural*	rep.	→ *reporting*
inf.	→ *infinitive*	pos.	→ *positive*	sent.	→ *sentence/s*
neg.	→ *negative*	prep.	→ *preposition/s*	sim.	→ *simple*
obj.	→ *object*	pres.	→ *present*	sing.	→ *singular*
part.	→ *participle/s*	progr.	→ *progressive*	sub.	→ *subject*

The sentence/Word order

A **Complete the sentences using a verb in the negative form or in the question form.**

1 Selima is using the computer, but she … the scanner.
2 Pete has bought some comics. … a computer magazine too?
3 Liz and Jan like my new jeans, but they … my new jacket.
4 Jan has got a brother, but she … a sister.
5 Mike phoned this afternoon, but he … last week.
6 I know Jane likes dogs, but … cats too?
7 Jerry has cleaned his bike, but he … his dad's car yet.
8 Mum made a cake yesterday. … biscuits as well?
9 I know you watch science fiction films, but … comedy shows too?
10 David knows a lot about history, but he … much about physics.

B **Make questions from the statements. Begin with a question word.**

11 Vicky is going to Ibiza in August.
12 Pam always phones Jane on Saturdays.
13 Sally and Rob have gone to their grandmother's in Scotland.
14 Ali visits his uncle every week.
15 Nathan doesn't like Jane because she always wants to borrow money.
16 Herschel discovered the planet Uranus in 1781.
17 Tom and Dave are listening to some old cassettes.
18 Todd didn't give in his English project because he hadn't finished it.

C **Complete the dialogue with a question tag, a short answer or the correct verb form after *so …/neither …***

A: Becky has got a new computer, (19) …?
B: Yes, (20) … And so (21) … Liz.
A: You know a lot about computers, (22) …?
B: No, (23) … Not really. But neither (24) … Liz. We're not experts.

D **Translate the German parts into English.**

25 *(Auf wen wartest du?)* … For me? Well, I'm here.
26 *(Bleibt da. Bewegt euch nicht.)* … I won't be long.
27 *(Worüber redet ihr?)* … Not about exams, I hope.
28 *Ich habe Anna einige CDs geliehen.* (lend)
29 If the weather's fine this afternoon, *(können wir Rad fahren)*.

E **Spot the mistakes. There is one mistake in each sentence (pair).**

30 Someone has stolen my purse. Shall I report it the police?
31 Just a moment. I'd like to ask you something, so go not away.
32 I gave to Laura those old music magazines.
33 My mother doesn't like body piercings. – Mine also not.
34 Although Jane all her pocket money spends, she always has enough for the disco.
35 We don't understand this maths problem. Can you explain it us again?

The sentence/Word order

? Correct yourself

A 1: *is not using/isn't using* 2: *Has he bought* 3: *do not like/don't like* 4: *has not got/hasn't got* 5: *did not phone/didn't phone* 6: *does she like* 7: *has not cleaned/hasn't cleaned* 8: *Did she make* 9: *do you watch* 10: *does not know/doesn't know*

B 11: *When is Vicky going to Ibiza?* 12: *Who always phones Jane on Saturdays?* 13: *Where have Sally and Rob gone?* 14: *Who does Ali visit every week?* 15: *Why doesn't Nathan like Jane?* 16: *What did Herschel discover in 1781?* 17: *What are Tom and Dave listening to?* 18: *Why didn't Todd give in his English project?*

C 19: *hasn't she?* 20: *she has.* 21: *has* 22: *don't you?* 23: *I don't.* 24: *does*

D 25: *Who are you waiting for?* 26: *Stay there. Don't move.* 27: *What are you talking about?* 28: *I have lent Anna some CDs. / I have lent some CDs to Anna.* 29: *we can go cycling.*

E 30: *... Shall I report it to the police?* 31: *..., so don't go away.* 32: *I gave Laura those old music magazines./I gave those old music magazines to Laura.* 33: *... – Neither does mine.* 34: *Although Jane spends all her pocket money, ...* 35: *... Can you explain it to us again?*

Exercise finder

Sentences	CEG	Exercises
1, 3, 4, 5, 7, 10	▶ 3	▶ 1
2, 6, 8 ,9	▶ 5a/b	▶ 2, 4a, 5
11, 13	▶ 5a	▶ 3
12, 14, 16	▶ 6	▶ 7, 8, 9
15, 18	▶ 5b/d	▶ 4b
17, 25, 27	▶ 5e	▶ 6
19, 22	▶ 11	▶ 12
20, 23	▶ 7b	▶ 10
21, 24, 33	▶ 10b	▶ 11
26, 31	▶ 13a/b	▶ 13
28, 32	▶ 20a/b	▶ 15
29, 34	▶ 16b	▶ 14
30, 35	▶ 20d	▶ 16

1 Pop group of the month

positive/negative statements; aux./main verbs ▶ 2, 3

	Gina	Jerry	Trish	Rick
Born in	Bristol	London	Bristol	Brighton
Likes	surfing	shopping	shopping	tap dancing[1]
Been to	USA, 1999	Japan, 2000	USA, 1999	France, 2000
Wants to	get a film role	become a pop star	sing in a musical	top the charts

a Look at the picture and read the information about the band *TNT*. The statements below are not correct. Can you correct them with a negative (modal) auxiliary, as in the example? Use short forms.

Example: Jerry was born in Bristol.
*He **wasn't** born in Bristol. He was born in London.*

1 Trish and Gina are the same age.
2 Rick has been to Australia.
3 Gina can play the drums.
4 Trish would like a film role.
5 Gina and Trish have been to Peru.
6 Rick has got a tattoo on his left arm.
7 Gina and Trish were born in London.
8 Jerry is 18.

b The following statements about the pop band are wrong too. Can you correct them, this time with a negative form of *do*? Use the short forms *don't*, *doesn't* or *didn't*.

Example: Jerry comes from Brighton.
*He **doesn't** come from Brighton. He comes from London.*

1 Gina and Trish come from Leeds.
2 Rick plays the drums.
3 Trish went to Australia in 1999.
4 Rick likes surfing.
5 Gina flew to the USA in 2000.
6 Rick and Gina play the drums.

c Here's some more information about *TNT*. Complete the sentences with negative verb forms. Sometimes you need forms of *do*, sometimes you don't. Use either the simple present or the simple past.

Example: Trish (not – be) a member of the band two years ago.
*Trish **wasn't** a member of the band two years ago.*

1 Jerry (not – be) very good at school.
2 Rick and Trish (not – do) any sport.
3 Gina (not – have got) a driving licence[2].
4 Trish and Jerry (not – like) each other three years ago.
5 Rick (not – be able to) swim.

1 tap dancing *Stepptanz* 2 driving licence *Führerschein*

2 *Quick questionnaire: TV* *yes/no* questions; aux./main verbs

▶ 4, 5a/b

a Can you do without TV, or is it a big part of your life? Answer the questionnaire and find out. First, complete the questions.

Complete questions 1-5 with an auxiliary, e.g. *is*, *have*, *would*, *can*, etc.

Example: ***Can*** you name two German and two American soap operas?

Complete questions 6-10 with *do/does* (simple present) or *did* (simple past).

Example: ***Did*** you see all your favourite programmes last week?

Then complete questions 11-15 with either *do/does/did* or other auxiliaries.

		YES (*Be honest!*)	NO
1	*... you name two music channels?*	☐	☐
2	*... television an important part of your daily routine?*	☐	☐
3	*... you ever watched TV instead of doing something else with others?*	☐	☐
4	*... you able to relax better with TV than with a book?*	☐	☐
5	*... you like to have a TV set in your room?*	☐	☐
6	*... TV take up more than 30% of your free time?*	☐	☐
7	*... you watch more than three videos last week?*	☐	☐
8	*... you spend more time watching TV than doing your homework?*	☐	☐
9	*... you record[1] more than five programmes last week?*	☐	☐
10	*... it seem as if something is missing if the TV set is broken?*	☐	☐
11	*... you got a favourite programme that you hate to miss?*	☐	☐
12	*... your parents think you watch too much TV?*	☐	☐
13	*... you name four chat shows?*	☐	☐
14	*... you surf the channels when you're bored?*	☐	☐
15	*... you watch TV every day last week?*	☐	☐

Now count the *yes* answers and check your score.

0-5: You're fully in control. You live your life instead of watching others do it. Good!
6-10: Be careful! TV seems to be your favourite form of entertainment. What about sports and hobbies?
11-15: Danger of addiction[2]! There's more to life than television – or is there? Be more critical and don't become passive!

b Work with a partner. Ask your partner the completed questions and count the *yes* answers. Then check his/her score. Does your partner agree with the result?

1 record [rɪˈkɔːd] *aufnehmen* 2 addiction *Sucht*

3 *Sea, sand and sun* **word order: *yes/no* quest., quest. with a quest. word; aux.** ▶ 4, 5a

a Angela is spending her summer holidays with Yasmin. Yasmin shows her some pictures of her best friends. Angela wants to know what they are doing in their holidays. Write Angela's questions, as in the examples.

Examples: Yasmin: Megan is going to summer camp.
Angela: (Pat?)
*And Pat? **Is she going** to summer camp?*
Yasmin: Carol has been to Ibiza.
Angela: (Ben?)
*And Ben? **Has he been** to Ibiza?*

Yasmin:
1 Sarah is going to Italy. (her boyfriend?)
2 Brian would like to go sailing. (Mark?)
3 Jan has gone to Mallorca. (her brother and sister?)
4 Mel is staying at home. (her parents?)
5 Tom can afford[1] to go to Florida. (his girlfriend?)

b Angela wants to know more. She asks questions with a question word. What are her questions? Use *when, where, why* and *how*. Sometimes there is more than one possible question.

Example: Yasmin: Gil is touring California.
Angela: ***When is he** touring California?*
***How is he** touring? By car or by bus?*

Yasmin:
1 Sally is going to Ireland.
2 Mark would like to stay at home.
3 Jill and Luke are flying to Tunisia.
4 Ian is touring Wales.
5 We are going trekking.

1 afford *sich leisten*

4 *New friends* word order: *yes/no* questions, quest. with a quest. word; main verbs ▶ 4, 5b/d

a You are staying in England with your pen pal Peter. He takes you to a party and introduces you to Tahira, Cathy, Kim, Max and Rob.
Ask Peter questions about his friends with *do/does* (simple present) and *did* (simple past).

Examples: Peter: Max lives in Woodstock.
(Ask about Rob.)
You: ***Does Rob live** in Woodstock too?*
(Ask about the others.)
You: ***Do the others live** in Woodstock too?*
Peter: Tahira went to the USA last year on an exchange programme.
(Ask about Cathy.)
You: ***Did Cathy go** to the USA too?*

Peter:
1 Tahira likes discos. (Ask about Cathy and Kim.)
2 Cathy went to the disco last night. (Ask about Rob.)
3 Rob plays football for the school team. (Ask about Max.)
4 Kim passed her GCSEs last year. (Ask about the others.)
5 Max buys a lot of CDs. (Ask about Kim and Cathy.)
6 Tahira and Kim collect clothes for Oxfam[1]. (Ask about Cathy.)

b Now you are talking to Tahira, Cathy, Kim, etc. You want to know more details about what they tell you, so you ask them questions with a question word. Use the simple present and the simple past. Be careful, some of your questions are negative (as in example 2). To make your questions sound natural, begin them with *Oh? …*, *Really? …*, *Great! …* or *Well, …*

Examples: Max: I take karate lessons. (where?)
You: *Really? **Where do you take** (karate) lessons?*
Max: But I didn't go to my training yesterday. (why?)
You: *Oh, **why didn't you go** to your training?*

1 Kim and Rob: We sometimes go to the Internet café. (when?)
2 Cathy: I don't like the Internet café. (why?)
3 Rob: Max and I play squash. (how well?)
4 Tahira: I go to a fitness club, but I didn't go last night. (why?)
5 Rob: I saw a good film last night. (which film?)
6 Tahira: I bought some cool posters yesterday. (where?)
7 Kim: I don't go out during the week. (why?)
8 Max and Rob: We want to start a band. (what kind of …?)

1 Oxfam = Oxford Committee for Famine Relief, British charity organization which helps poor countries

5 *An e-mail to New York* word order: *yes/no* questions; aux./main verbs ▶ 4, 5a/b

Kerstin has written an e-mail to an e-pal[1] in New York. Unfortunately, she is not very good at asking questions in English, so they are in German. She needs some help. Can you translate her questions into English for her before she sends the mail?
Here's a hint: read the English sentences before and after the German sentences carefully. They sometimes give help with vocabulary and sentence structure.

Hi, Kelly!
I found your e-mail address on an e-pals web site. I see you would like to write to someone in Germany.
My name is Kerstin and I'm from Hamburg. I'm seventeen and I still go to school. Gehst du noch zur Schule? I've got a brother called Michi. Hast du Geschwister?
In my free time I like to meet my friends. We sometimes go to a disco, or we just hang around[2] in town. (1) Magst du Discos? I've got a pet hamster called Jo-Jo. (2) Hast du ein Lieblingstier?

I've never been to the USA. (3) Bist du schon mal in Deutschland gewesen? (4) Möchtest du vielleicht nach Hamburg kommen? There's lots to see and do here. New York must be an exciting city. (5) Siehst du manchmal Filmstars auf der Straße?

I quite like school. Some of our teachers are fun, but some are pretty awful. (6) Sind deine Lehrer nett? (7) Lernst du Deutsch in der Schule? I'm learning English and French. I don't know what I want to do after school. (8) Weißt du, was du nach der Schule machen willst? (9) Willst du auf die Uni gehen? Perhaps I'll go to university to study journalism.

(10) Kannst du mir etwas über deine Schule und deine Freunde erzählen? Perhaps you can send me a photo of you and your best friends. (11) Möchtest du ein Foto von mir haben? If you would, I'll send you one with my next e-mail.

I hope we can be friends. (12) Wirst du meine Mail beantworten? I hope you will. You can write in English or German – or both.

Kerstin

Examples:

Do you still **go** to school?

Have you got any brothers or sisters? / **Do you have** any brothers or sisters?

1 e-pal *E-Mail-Freund/in* 2 hang around *herumhängen*

6 *What are they talking about?* **prepositions in quest. with a quest. word** ▶ 5e

Liz and Tim are exchanging news about friends. Liz is on a train, so the reception[1] on her mobile is sometimes bad. When Liz and Tim don't hear each other clearly, they ask questions with a question word. What are their questions? Be careful with the prepositions. Look where they stand.

1 Liz: That new boy at the youth club comes from Devon.
2 Tim: We listened to some old *Metallica* CDs yesterday.
3 Liz: Janet spends all her money on clothes and fashion mags.
4 Tim: Beth's parents were away, so she looked after her little brother last week.
5 Liz: Melanie writes to six pen pals.
6 Tim: My parents have gone to Scotland for two weeks.
7 Tim: They flew to Edinburgh yesterday.
8 Liz: Nicola is going out with her ex-boyfriend again.
9 Liz: Mick has paid for the rock festival tickets.

7 *Tricky translations* **subject/object questions** ▶ 6

a A friend who goes to a different school needs help with some English homework. He asks you. Compare the sentence pairs. Which translation is correct?

Example: *Wer hat dich vom Bahnhof abgeholt?* a) Who did you pick up at the station?
Answer: b) b) Who picked you up at the station?

1 *Wer rief dich an?* a) Who phoned you? b) Who did you phone?
2 *Wen schlägt Dave immer beim Tennis?*
a) Who does Dave always beat at tennis? b) Who always beats Dave at tennis?
3 *Was verursachte den Unfall?*
a) What did the accident cause? b) What caused the accident?
4 *Wer sah Jim Bentley?* a) Who saw Jim Bentley? b) Who did Jim Bentley see?
5 *Was tötete die Katze? Eine Maus oder einen Vogel?*
a) What killed the cat? b) What did the cat kill?

b Now translate these pairs into English.

1 Wer hat dich eingeladen? Wen hast du eingeladen?
2 Wer kennt dich? Wen kennst du?
3 Wen magst du? Wer mag dich?

1 reception *Empfang*

8 *Write a quiz* **word order: quest. with a quest. word; main verbs; subj./obj. quest.** ▶ 5b, 6

You are writing a history quiz about famous people. Who did what, and when? Here are some facts about four famous men and women. Make three quiz questions about each person, with *who, when, what,* as in the example.

Example: Isaac Newton discovered the force of gravity[1] in 1665.
***Who discovered** the force of gravity?*
***When did Newton discover** the force of gravity?*
***What did Newton discover** in 1665?*

1 Mary Anderson invented the windshield wiper[2] in 1903.
2 Levi Strauss made the first pair of jeans in 1850.
3 Alexander Fleming discovered penicillin in 1928.
4 Robert Watson-Watt developed a radar system in 1935.

9 *Lord Manley* **quest. with a quest. word; aux./main verbs; subj./obj. questions** ▶ 5a/b, 6

Lord Manley has been found dead in his country house, killed with his own hunting rifle[3]. It looks like suicide[4], but his housekeeper[5], Mrs Danvers, feels sure that it was murder. Chief Inspector Watson and his sergeant ask her some questions. Later in his office, Watson discusses the housekeeper's statements with his sergeant. What are Watson's questions? Begin with *who* or *what*. Be careful: sometimes you need *did*.

Examples: Sergeant: According to[6] the housekeeper, something was worrying Lord Manley.
Watson: ***What was worrying** him?*
Sergeant: He phoned somebody late at night.
Watson: ***Who did** he **phone** late at night?*

Now continue. These are the sergeant's notes:

According to Mrs Danvers (housekeeper):

1 *Something had made Lord Manley nervous.*
2 *He tried to contact somebody urgently.*
3 *Somebody came to the house after dark.*
4 *He went to see somebody after supper.*
5 *Something made a strange noise in the night.*
6 *Somebody had had a motive to kill him.*
7 *He kept something in his safe.*

1 force of gravity *Schwerkraft* 2 windshield wiper *Scheibenwischer* 3 hunting rifle *Jagdgewehr* 4 suicide *Selbstmord* 5 housekeeper *Haushälterin* 6 according to *laut, nach*

10 *Julia's week* ***yes/no*** **questions: short answers**

▶ 7b

a It's Thursday today. Here's Julia's diary for this week.

Mon	*Rained all day.* ☹ *Went to town, bought cool new shoes!* ☺ *No homework!* ☺ *Guitar lesson (instead of Tuesday!).* ! *Mick phoned.* ! ☺ *Sarah and Jill phoned. Dad went to Rome on business.* *Super weather. (Some people have all the luck ...)*
Tue	*Late for school. Mum's birthday – so I made a super quiche for supper.* *Tasted really great.* ! *Mick phoned* ! *Dad phoned from Rome.* *Letter from my penfriend.* ✉
Weds	*Mick didn't phone. Why???? Judo - 6.30 as always. Rained again.* ☹ *Washed the dishes for Mum. Went cycling with Amy.* *Did French homework. Yuck!*
Thurs	*???? Will anything exciting happen?*
Fri	*Disco 8.30*
Sat	*Cinema with Mick* ☺ ☺ ☺
Sun	*???? Boring as always ...*

What does the diary tell us about Julia? Use short answers, as in the examples. Be careful with the tenses.

Examples: Has Julia got plans for Friday evening?
Yes, she has.
Does she go to judo on Thursday?
No, she doesn't.

1 Is Julia doing anything on Sunday?
2 Does she sometimes help at home?
3 Is there going to be a party at the weekend?
4 Did any of Julia's friends phone on Tuesday?
5 Has she got any plans for Thursday evening?
6 Did her boyfriend phone her on Wednesday?
7 Is her boyfriend's name Mick?
8 Did Julia do any homework on Sunday?
9 Was it her Mum's birthday on Wednesday?
10 Did she go shopping on Monday?
11 Can Julia cook?
12 Does she usually have her guitar lesson on Mondays?

b Now work with a partner. Look at Julia's diary again. Take turns to ask and answer questions which are not in part a). Write and answer three questions each.

Examples: You: ***Did Julia buy*** *a pair of shoes on Tuesday?*
Partner: ***No, she didn't.***
Partner: ***Is she learning*** *French?*
You: ***Yes, she is.***

Key to the exercises Practice Book 1

Cornelsen
English
Grammar

English Edition
Große Ausgabe

Cornelsen

The Sentence/Word order

1 Pop group of the month

a 1 They aren't the same age. Trish is older.
2 He hasn't been to Australia. He's been to France.
3 She can't play the drums. She can play the guitar.
4 She wouldn't like a film role. She'd like to sing in a musical.
5 They haven't been to Peru. They've been to the USA.
6 He hasn't got a tattoo on his left arm. He's got one/a tattoo on his right arm.
7 They weren't born in London. They were born in Bristol.
8 He isn't 18. He's 21.

b 1 They don't come from Leeds. They come from Bristol.
2 He doesn't play the drums. He plays the guitar
3 She didn't go to Australia in 1999. She went to the USA in 1999
4 He doesn't like surfing. He likes tap dancing.
5 She didn't fly to the USA in 2000. She flew to the USA in 1999.
6 They don't play the drums. They play the guitar.

c 1 wasn't 2 don't do 3 hasn't got 4 didn't like 5 can't/isn't able to

2 Quick questionnaire: TV

a 1 Can/Could 2 Is 3 Have 4 Are 5 Would 6 Does 7 Did 8 Do 9 Did 10 Does
11 Have 12 Do 13 Can/Could 14 Do 15 Did

3 Sea, sand and sun

a 1 And her boyfriend? Is he going to Italy?
2 And Mark? Would he like to go sailing?
3 And her brother and sister? Have they gone to Mallorca?
4 And her parents? Are they staying at home?
5 And his girlfriend? Can she afford to go to Florida?

b 1 How is she going (to Ireland)? By car or by plane? / When is she going (to Ireland)?
2 Why would he like to stay at home?
3 When are they flying (to Tunisia)?
4 When is he touring Wales? / How is he touring? By car or by motorbike/bus?
5 Where/When are you going trekking?

4 New friends

a 1 Do Cathy and Kim like discos too?
2 Did Rob go to the disco too?
3 Does Max play football for the school team too?
4 Did the others pass their GCSEs (last year) too?
5 Do Kim and Cathy buy a lot of CDs too?
6 Does Cathy collect clothes for Oxfam too?

b 1 Great! When do you go (there/to the Internet café)?
2 Really? Why don't you like it/the Internet café?
3 Oh, how well do you play (squash)?
4 Well, why didn't you go (to the fitness club last night)?
5 Oh, which film did you see (last night)?
6 Really? Where did you buy them/the posters?
7 Well, why don't you go out during the week?
8 Great! What kind of band do you want to start?

5 *An e-mail to New York*

1 Do you like discos? 2 Have you got/Do you have a favourite pet? 3 Have you ever been to Germany? 4 Would you (perhaps) like to come to Hamburg (perhaps)? 5 Do you sometimes see film stars on the street? 6 Are your teachers nice? 7 Are you learning/Do you learn German in/at school? 8 Do you know what you want to do after school? 9 Do you want to go to university? 10 Can you tell me something about your school and your friends? 11 Would you like to have a photo of me? 12 Will you answer my mail?

6 *What are they talking about?*

1 Where does he come from? 2 What did you listen to (yesterday)? 3 What does she spend all her money on? 4 Who did she look after (last week)? 5 How many pen pals does she write to? 6 How long have they gone for? 7 Where did they fly to (yesterday)? 8 Who is she going out with (again)? 9 What has he paid for?

7 *Tricky translations*

a 1 a 2 a 3 b 4 a 5 b

b 1 Who invited you? Who did you invite? 2 Who knows you? Who do you know?
3 Who do you like? Who likes you?

8 *Write a quiz*

1 Who invented the windshield wiper in 1903? When did Mary Anderson invent the windshield wiper? What did Mary Anderson invent in 1903?
2 Who made the first pair of jeans in 1850? When did Levi Strauss make the first pair of jeans? What did Levi Strauss make in 1850?
3 Who discovered penicillin in 1928? When did Alexander Fleming discover penicillin? What did Alexander Fleming discover in 1928?
4 Who developed a radar system in 1935? When did Robert Watson-Watt develop a radar system? What did Robert Watson-Watt develop in 1935?

9 *Lord Manley*

1 What had made Lord Manley nervous?
2 Who did he try to contact urgently?
3 Who came to the house after dark?
4 Who did he go to see after supper?
5 What made a strange noise in the night?
6 Who had had a motive to kill him?
7 What did he keep in his safe?

10 *Julia's week*

a 1 No, she isn't. 2 Yes, she does. 3 No, there isn't. 4 Yes, they did. 5 No, she hasn't. 6 No, he didn't. 7 Yes, it is. 8 No, she didn't. 9 No, it wasn't. 10 Yes, she did. 11 Yes, she can. 12 No, she doesn't.

11 *After school chat*

a 1 Cindy – Lisa 2 Simon – Mark 3 Daniel – Sue 4 Katie – Sally 5 Ron – Kim 6 Alice – Jenny 7 Vicky – Ellen 8 Laura – Matt

b 1 So do I. 2 Neither does mine. 3 So would mine. 4 Neither can I. 5 So did I. 6 Neither do we.

c 1 So do I. 2 So would I. 3 Neither do mine. 4 Neither have we. 5 Neither did I. 6 So am I.

12 *Party talk*

1 aren't you? haven't I? 2 weren't you? wasn't it? 3 is she? didn't she? 4 has it? isn't there? 5 haven't they? did it? 6 doesn't it? isn't he? 7 does he? is it? 8 don't they? doesn't he? 9 will you? can we? 10 will you? do we?

13 *Just do it!*

1 Well, don't tidy it. Watch TV instead.
2 Well, don't do it. Send some e-mails instead.
3 Well, don't learn it. Take biology instead.
4 Well, don't drink it. Have/Drink cocoa instead.
5 Well, don't go to the party. Go to a disco instead.
6 Well, don't eat them. Have/Eat some fruit instead.

14 *My neighbourhood*

a 1 I still don't know all the people who live in our new street.
2 –
3 When it rains, her mother takes us to school in the car.
4 … If she calls, my mother makes her a cup of coffee.
5 Her children make a lot of noise before they go to bed.
6 When the boys from number 10 pass our house, they throw things in the garden, …
7 –
8 … He complains because I play my music too loud.

15 *Jingle bells*

a 1 it to him him a Christmas dinner. 2 my boyfriend a photo of me in a frame. 3 it to him 4 grandmother some new slippers. 5 some new socks for Uncle Ron 6 beautiful Christmas cards to all my friends. 7 all mine beautiful e-mails.

b 1 No, she isn't. She's giving the new slippers to grandmother.
2 No, she isn't. She's making the cake for Uncle Ron.
3 No, he isn't. He's sending e-mails to all his friends.

4 No, she isn't. She's giving the photo to her boyfriend.
5 No, she isn't. She's sending cards to all her friends.
6 No, she isn't. She's going to cook the Christmas dinner for Uncle Ron.

c 1 Who is Mrs J. buying the slippers for?
2 Who is Mrs. J. cooking the Christmas dinner for?
3 Who is Jane sending the Christmas cards to?
4 Who is Nick getting the socks for?
5 Who is Nick sending e-mails to?

16 *A bike theft*

1 the situation to you. 2 it to him 3 the thief to us 4 him to you 5 your statement to Constable Scott. 6 a piece of advice to you

Modal auxiliaries and be, have, do

Modal auxiliaries

1 *What can they do?*

a 1 Chris can't swim, but he can dive.
2 Mike can play the guitar, but he can't play the drums.
3 Max can't use the Internet, but he can burn CDs.
4 Sarah can't windsurf, but she can waterski.
5 Megan can dance, but she can't sing karaoke.

2 *Ben's accident*

a 1 couldn't/wasn't able to 2 can/is able to 3 will be able to 4 won't be able to 5 couldn't/wasn't able to 6 be able to 7 haven't been able to

3 *What does it mean?*

1 … are allowed to park …
2 … are not allowed to play …
3 … is allowed to stand …
4 … are not allowed to feed the animals.
5 … are not allowed to take photographs …
6 … is allowed to park there.

4 *House rules*

a 1 She was allowed to have a shower every day.
2 She was not allowed to take food up to her room.
3 She was allowed to use the washing-machine only once a week.
4 She was not allowed to stick posters on the walls.
5 She was allowed to use the telephone only in an emergency.

6 She was allowed to make hot drinks only in the kitchen. / She was not allowed to make hot drinks in her room.

b 1 Were you allowed to have visitors?
2 Were you allowed to have male visitors/boys in your room? / Were boys allowed to visit you?
3 How often were you allowed to have a bath?
4 Were you allowed to eat in your room? / Were you allowed to take food up to your room?
5 When were you allowed to play music?

5 *Staying with a host family*

1 Mrs Ashton, may/could I cook vegetarian food for myself, please?
2 Dan, can I go to the football match with you?
3 Mr Ashton, may/could I have a key just for one night, please?/… could you give me a key …?
4 Ted, are you allowed to cross the road when the light is red?
5 Can/Could I see your poster collection?
6 Ted, are we allowed to use a dictionary in the exam?

6 *A cheeseburger, please*

a 1 has to be clean every day.
2 must be polite to customers.
3 has to wear his cap all the time.
4 have to get the orders right first time.
5 must work quickly without chatting.

b 1 have to 2 has to 3 have to 4 must 5 must

7 *Hard work*

a 1 Lee had to put up a lamp. 2 Kim had to repair the bookshelves. 3 Lee had to repair the wardrobe. 4 Lisa had to sew some curtains. 5 Ross had to clear away some old boxes. 6 Lisa had to clean the carpet.

b 1 didn't have to repair them.
2 didn't have to clean it.
3 didn't have to wash them.
4 didn't have to make new ones.
5 didn't have to buy a new one.

8 *Sue says*

1 mustn't break them.
2 needn't pay for them.
3 mustn't lose it.
4 needn't watch it.
5 mustn't forget (it).
6 mustn't fail it.
7 needn't get up early.
8 needn't walk.

9 *Trouble at home*

a 1 Lucy's father shouldn't criticize her boyfriend.
2 Lucy should tidy her room.
3 Lucy shouldn't make big phone bills.
4 Lucy should offer to do things in the house.

5 Lucy's parents should find time to listen to her.
6 Lucy shouldn't think only of herself.
7 Lucy should think about her future.
8 Her parents should get to know her friends.
9 Lucy should get up earlier at weekends.

b 1 You ought to try harder in school/try to get good marks/show them what you can do.
2 You ought to tell them that you're not happy/ask them to listen to you/ask them for advice.
3 You shouldn't refuse to do everything he tells you. / You ought to ask him if what he wants is really important.
4 You ought to tell them that you want to talk seriously/tell them why you're not happy.
5 You shouldn't leave home until you earn enough money. / You ought to tell your parents and see what they say.

10 *Requests, offers, suggestions*

a 1 Shall we go for a hamburger?
2 Would you like a cola? / Can I get you a cola?
3 Can/Will you bring my CDs back tomorrow, please?
4 Can/Could I borrow your sleeping bag for the weekend, please?
5 Can't/Couldn't we go on Friday instead?
6 Would/Could you show me how to download this information, please?
7 Can't we meet at the Internet café in the High Street?
8 Can/Could I help you to carry the bags/shopping?

b 1 Shall we go for a pizza?
2 Can/Could I help you to carry the books?
3 Could/Would you help me with my computer, please?

11 *Clothes shopping*

1 won't 2 might 3 must 4 can't 5 must 6 may 7 will

12 *Mobile phones – yes or no?*

1 needn't 2 should 3 can 4 couldn't 5 was able to 6 mustn't 7can't 8 might not 9 have to 10 may

Be, have, do

13 *Learning English*

a 1 there was 2 there is 3 there will be 4 There are 5 there were 6 there won't be

b 1 How many Italian students are there now? There's one.
2 How many Swedish students were there last month? There weren't any.
3 How many Russian students will there be next month? There will be three.
4 How many Chinese students were there last month? There was one.
5 How many French students will there be next month? There won't be any.

c 1 There is 2 there were 3 there will be 4 There are 5 there have always been 6 there will be 7 Is there?

14 *Daily routines*

a 1 Jeff has a shower after work
2 Tony has breakfast at 8.15.
3 Both boys have a break in the morning.
4 Tony has a sleep after school.
5 Both boys have dinner at 7.30.

b 1 Tony doesn't have a
2 Jeff doesn't have
3 The boys don't have
4 Tony doesn't have a
5 The boys don't have

c 1 Do you sometimes have a bath? Yes, I do. I usually have a bath on Sundays.
2 Did you have a shower this morning? Yes, I did. I had a shower before breakfast.
3 Did you have lunch in town last week? Yes, I did. I had a pizza on Wednesday.
4 Do you have a hot dinner every evening? No, we don't. We often have sandwiches.
5 Did you have fun the last time you went to the disco? Yes, I did. We had a good time.

15 *Doing things*

a 1 Oh good. I see you've done the shopping.
2 First the good news. It says I'm doing well in sports.
3 Mum's not here, so I have to do the housework today.
4 We did a test in the maths lesson.
5 Shh! I have to concentrate. I'm doing my homework.
6 I'm just doing my hair. I hope you'll like it.

The tenses of the full verbs

Full verbs

1 *Spelling check*

a -s: buys, comes, enjoys, says, walks
-es: does, goes, misses, mixes, teaches, washes, watches
-ies: carries, cries, flies, studies, tries

b is, has, goes, flies, wishes, travels

c preferring, coming, offering, controlling, swimming

d lying, rising, fitting, hurrying, promising, travelling

2 *Check your forms*

a hurried, watched, dried, wished, chatted, phoned, cooked, robbed, planned, enjoyed, invited, dropped

b met, grew, meant, caught, brought

c simple past: stole, wrote, broke, was, did, forgot
past participle: seen, swum, drunk, driven

d seen – saw, stole – stolen, swum – swam, wrote – written, drunk – drank, broke – broken, was – been, did – done, driven – drove, forgot – forgotten

e 1 done 2 stolen 3 broken 4 written 5 been 6 seen

3 *Simple or progressive?*

a A3 B4 C6 D5 E1 F2

b 1 s 2 p 3 p 4 s 5 s 6 p

4 *Quick and easy*

a state verbs: know, prefer, believe, contain, recognize, need, suppose, seem, want

5 *Meet Chris*

a 1 know 2 want 3 don't like 4 go 5 is doing 6 is learning 7 is working 8 seems 9 love 10 prefer 11 don't watch 12 doesn't ask 13 sees 14 are taking 15 go 16 don't watch

Present and past

6 *Meet Mike*

1 leave 2 does 3 wants 4 gets up 5 stops 6 buys 7 reads 8 know 9 chat 10 tell 11 catches 12 misses 13 takes 14 hurries 15 arrives 16 get 17 give 18 passes 19 tries 20 looks forward to 21 plan 22 says

7 *When school is out …*

a 1 always go straight home. 2 usually meets friends. 3 often hang around in town. 4 never play football. 5 sometimes plays football. 6 sometimes goes for a hamburger. 7 often go for a hamburger. 8 usually phones some friends. 9 always phone some friends.

8 *Choose a pen pal*

a 1 Steve enjoys school. Kim and Josie don't enjoy school.
2 Kim and Steve enjoy parties. Josie doesn't enjoy parties.
3 Josie and Steve hate snakes and spiders. Kim doesn't hate snakes and spiders.

4 Kim and Josie hate homework. Steve doesn't hate homework.
5 Kim and Steve find shopping boring. Josie doesn't find shopping boring.
6 Kim and Josie find sightseeing holidays boring. Steve doesn't find sightseeing holidays boring.

9 *A barbecue*

a 1 is playing 2 are dancing. 3 are lying 4 are serving 5 is grilling 6 is eating 7 is carrying 8 is enjoying

b 1 The music isn't playing now.
2 The teenagers aren't dancing now.
3 Ali and Sam aren't lying on the grass now.
4 Katie and Jenny aren't serving food now.
5 Sanjay isn't grilling chops and sausages now.
6 The teenagers aren't enjoying the barbecue now.

10 *Summer jobs*

a 1 Luke is serving petrol at a local garage until September.
2 Roger and Pete are cleaning stables at a riding school for three weeks.
3 Sharon and Kim are doing restoration work in old churches for five weeks.
4 Lynn is working on a dig in Scotland until the end of August.
5 Scott and Ed are cleaning up old steam engines in Wales for the whole of the holidays.
6 Linda is looking after children at the local kindergarten for four weeks.

11 *Term time and holidays*

a 1 practises the guitar.
2 On Fridays he plays football.
3 On Saturday mornings he helps his father.
4 On Saturday evenings he goes to the youth club.
5 On Sunday mornings he sleeps until luch time.
6 On Sunday evenings he does his homework.

b 1 practises the guitar, but now he's sitting in a café with friends.
2 It's Friday. David usually plays football, but now he's playing computer games.
3 It's Saturday morning. David usually helps his father, but now he's shopping in town.
4 It's Saturday evening. David usually goes to the youth club, but now he's dancing at the disco.
5 It's Sunday morning. David usually sleeps until lunch time, but now he's cycling with friends.
6 It's Sunday evening. David usually does his homework, but now he's enjoying an evening at the cinema.

12 *Mini-dialogues*

1 Is she still phoning 2 is watching 3 is going 4 is she going? 5 Do you know? 6 always goes 7 is working 8 usually works 9 don't pay 10 am meeting 11 are doing 12 is coming 13 is working 14 doesn't work 15 are you coming 16 are practising 17 Are you bringing 18 are you making 19 know 20 make 21 always bring 22 am going

13 *Consequences*

a 1c 2f 3e 4h 5a 6b 7j 8d 9g 10i

14 *Have you ever …?*

a 1 I have never eaten Mexican food.
2 I havn't done a bungee jump yet.
3 I have spoken English on the telephone once or twice.
4 I have never been on television.
5 I have often failed a test or exam.
6 I haven't seen a snake yet.
7 I have never won a prize.
8 I haven't put up a tent yet.
9 I have made lasagna once or twice.
10 I have stayed up all night once or twice.
11 I have often gone to Italy.

15 For *or* since?

a for: a long time, several years, weeks, two months
since: last week, last Tuesday, we left school, my birthday, I visited him in hospital, 1998

c 1 have lived here for four/… years.
2 have known him since 1998/…
3 have been here for four days.
4 has had it since 1999/…
5 have worked here for seven months.
6 hasn't been there since 2000/…

16 *What have they been doing?*

a 1 Because he has been working at the computer. 2 Because she has been chopping onions.
3 Because they have been walking in the woods. 4 Because she has been lying in the sun.
5 Because he has been oiling his bike. 6 Because they have been watching a horror movie.

17 *Evening classes*

a 1 Jason. He's been doing it for three months.
2 Beth and Anita. They've been taking the course since April.
3 Jerry. He's been learning it since September.
4 Ben and Megan. They've been doing the course for six months.
5 Jason. He's been learning it since March.
6 Beth. She's been taking the course for four months.
7 Anita. She's been learning it since February.
8 Megan. She's been taking the class since April.

18 *Describe the pictures*

1a has been repairing 1b has repaired
2a have played 2b have been playing
3a has been learning 3b has learnt
4a has snowed 4b has been snowing

19 *What did you do, and when?*

a 1 Last Saturday I slept until noon.
2 We all met for the first time two years ago.
3 My best friend didn't phone me yesterday.
4 Last week I didn't go to the gym.
5 My mother bought me a new pair of trousers yesterday afternoon.
6 On my last birthday I had a big party.
7 We didn't go dancing last Friday.

8 In my last holidays I met some really interesting people.
9 A week ago a friend of mine came to visit me.
10 My parents didn't go out last night.

b 1 I brushed my teeth this morning. 2 I phoned my best friend last week. 3 I bought something new three days ago. 4 I went to a party four months ago. 5 I listened to the news yesterday evening. 6 I helped at home last Sunday.

20 *A weekend in London*

a 1 I didn't buy 2 we didn't take 3 we didn't go 4 she didn't look round 5 we didn't get 6 We didn't eat 7 They didn't visit 8 we didn't walk 9 She didn't shop 10 he didn't see

b 1 They didn't stay at the Ritz. 2 Tim didn't buy any souvenirs. 3 Unfortunately, they didn't see Prince William. 4 Anna didn't visit the Tower. 5 John and Mel didn't go to a pub. 6 Mel didn't do a bus tour.

21 *The story of Fred*

a 1 found a lottery ticket on the street. 2 won £100.000 in the lottery. 3 ate at Gino's. 4 bought some new skis. 5 flew first class to Switzerland. 6 broke his right arm and his left leg.

b
1 still felt very happy.
2 Fred and Heidi fell in love.
3 After three weeks Fred left hospital.
4 He was rich, so he gave Heidi a big diamond ring.
5 As soon as Fred could walk, they got married.
6 After the wedding they went on a long honeymoon to the Bahamas.
7 The sun shone every day.
8 Unfortunately, Fred spent all the lottery winnings.
9 When they were back at home again, Fred sold his expensive skis.
10 With the money he bought fifty tickets for the next lottery.

22 *Boyfriends*

a
1 Did you wear your new jeans? – No, I didn't.
2 Did you go to a disco? – Yes, we did.
3 Did you like it? – Yes, I/we did.
4 Did you see anybody we know? – No, I didn't.
5 Did Terry take you home in his car? – Yes, he did.
6 Did he ask you out again? – No, he didn't.

b
1 What did you buy?
2 How much did they cost?
3 Where did you go in the evening?
4 What film did you see?
5 When did you get home?
6 When did you do your homework?
7 Why didn't you do it?

23 *A letter*

a 1have had 2 has been 3 hasn't rained 4 have been 5 went 6 met 7 could 8 didn't have to 9 danced 10 has fallen 11 have also made 12 haven't met 13 have taken 14 was 15 Did you have 16 Did you meet 17 left 18 got

24 *Visitors to Germany*

1 Have you been to other countries?
2 Have you been to Berlin?
3 When were you there? / When did you go there?
4 What did you see there?
5 Did you like it there?
6 Which other cities have you also visited?
7 Have you been to Cologne?
8 Did you see the famous cathedral?
9 Where did you go last weekend?
10 To Munich? Did you see the football match last Saturday?

25 *Chat before school*

1 got 2 Has she written 3 hasn't had 4 left 5 phoned 6 arrived 7 Have you seen 8 have just arrived. 9 has already gone 10 have already looked 11 hasn't arrived 12 lent 13 still hasn't paid 14 have bought 15 did you buy 16 did they cost? 17 bought 18 haven't worn 19 bought. 20 wore 21 have worn

26 *What were they doing?*

a At number 2 Mr Johnson was reading a newspaper, and Mrs Johnson was writing a letter.
At number 3 Mrs Todd was baking a cake.
At number 4 Kate and David were playing loud music/were listening to loud music.
At number 5 Mr Carter was drinking a glass of wine. His dog was sleeping in his basket.
At number 6 the Taylors were playing cards (with some friends).
At number 7 Mrs Sutton was washing her hair. Toby was going to bed.

b 1 I was doing my homework at six o'clock yesterday evening.
2 At seven o'clock this morning I was having a shower.
3 At 11.30 last night I was watching the end of a really exiting film.
4 I was still having lunch at two o'clock yesterday afternoon.

27 *Accidents*

a 1 Mrs Baxter burnt her hand when she was taking a cake from the oven.
2 Mr Granger hurt his back when he was moving the furniture.
3 Billy hurt his leg when he was playing football.
4 Mr Simpson bumped his head when he was cleaning out the attic.
5 Mrs Walker cut her finger when she was chopping onions.
6 Kate fell off her bike when she was riding to school.

28 *Jenny's story*

a 1 noticed 2 was watching 3 got off 4 was raining 5 was blowing 6 looked 7 was 8 was cycling 9 felt 10 was still thinking 11 was crossing 12 heard 13 was following 14 began 15 was beating 16 felt 17 was sleeping. 18 felt 19 rang 20 dropped

29 *A bad day …*

a 1 He was late for the first lesson because he had missed the bus to school.
2 He couldn't buy anything to eat in the break because he had forgotten his wallet.
3 He failed the French test because he hadn't learnt any grammar.
4 He couldn't play football in the sports lesson because he had left his football boots at home.
5 He missed his favourite sports programme because he had forgotten to set the video recorder.
6 His girlfriend was very angry because she had seen him flirting with another girl in the break.
7 He couldn't phone the other girl because he had lost the phone number.
8 He couldn't go out in the evening because he hadn't done his homework.

30 *What had they been doing?*

a 1 had been waiting for his girlfriend/friends for an hour.
2 had been painting the kitchen/room all afternoon.
3 had been shopping all day.
4 had been dancing non-stop at the disco.
5 had been waiting at the bus stop in the rain.
6 had been training with weights/doing weight training for an hour.
7 hadn't been listening to the teacher. / had been thinking of her boyfriend.

Ways of expressing future time

31 *A class trip*

a 1 I expect the hotel will be
2 it certainly won't be
3 I hope we won't have to
4 I'm sure it will be
5 I hope the teachers won't bore
6 I suppose Mr Jones will talk
7 Perhaps there won't be
8 I'm sure there will be
9 I suppose the whole trip will be
10 I think most of us will have

32 *A helping hand*

1 All right, I'll tell him. 2 OK. I won't play it. 3 Well, I'll lend you mine.
4 Don't worry, I won't break them. 5 Well, I'll help you. 6 All right. I won't tell her.
7 OK. I won't eat them now. 8 All right. I won't lose them.

33 *Future jobs*

a 1 Pete is going to become a mechanic.
2 Zoe is going to play professional tennis.
3 Dave and Ted are going to study information technology.
4 Jane is going to learn graphic design.
5 Jill is going to become an actress.
6 Luke and Simon are going to work in a research laboratory.
7 Sally is going to open a fitness club.
8 Sue and Ann are going to work in the fashion industry.
9 Will is going to study space technology.
10 Brian is going to work in tourism.

34 *What's going to happen?*

a 1 is going to drop the books.
2 is going to break.
3 is going to crash into the tree.
4 is going to rain.
5 is going to sink.
6 is going to walk into the road sign.

35 *Money talk*

2 am going to, will 3 will, will, won't 4 is going to, will, will 5 Are you going to, won't

36 *Are you doing anything tonight?*

a 1 Tim is coming at seven-thirty.
2 I'm washing my hair tonight.
3 Paul and I are playing computer games.
4 I'm writing letters tonight.
5 I'm going to the sports centre with Ed.
6 Ann and I are doing our history project.
7 Mick is picking me up at seven.
8 I'm going for a pizza with Dave.

37 *A study trip*

1 leaves/starts 2 stop 3 arrives 4 stay/sleep 5 tour/visit/go to 6 take/go on/do 7 climb
8 visit/tour/go to

38 *At this time tomorrow ...*

a 1 won't be sitting in my office. I'll be lying on the beach.
2 won't be studying for exams. I'll be working as a model.
3 won't be doing homework. I'll be riding my new motorbike.
4 won't be watching a stupid film. We'll be giving our first concert.

b 1 I'll be studying for a test. / I won't be studying for a test.
2 I won't be doing my homework.
3 I'll be sitting in school. / I won't be sitting in school.
4 I'll be dancing at the disco.
5 I'll be having a party. / I won't be having a party.
6 I'll be watching TV. / I won't be watching TV.

39 *Saving up*

1 After two months Kim will have earned £270.
2 After three months Luke will have saved £330.
3 After three months Kim will have spent £150.
4 After six months Luke will have earned £900.
5 After six month Luke will have spent £240.
6 By the end of the year Luke will have saved £1320.
7 By the end of the year Kim will have saved £1020.

40 *Kate's birthday*

a 1 will rain 2 am going to have 3 will be 4 won't rain 5 are coming 6 am inviting 7 are going to have 8 is going to play 9 will be celebrating 10 will be doing 11 will have left 12 will have got 13 is giving 14 will be

The passive

1 *Quick puzzle: which state?*

L A R N A C F I O I California

2 *What's done in school?*

a 1 The classrooms are cleaned every day.
2 I think the windows are washed once a month.
3 The classroom furniture is dusted every day.
4 The waste bins are emptied every day.
5 I think the floors are polished every week.
6 The staff room is cleaned every day.
7 The school dustbins are emptied once a week.
8 The school building is probably painted every five years.
9 In summer the grass is cut every week.
10 The fire alarm is probably tested twice a year.

3 *Test yourself: where and when?*

1 The Summer Olympics 2000 were held in Sydney, Australia
2 Coca Cola was invented in Atlanta nearly 100 years ago.
3 Queen Elizabeth II was crowned in Westminster Abbey in 1953.
4 The film *Titanic* was produced in Hollywood from 1994-97.
5 Madame Tussaud's wax museum was opened in Baker Street, London, in 1835.
6 *The Beatles* were discovered in Liverpool in 1961.
7 John Lennon was shot in New York in 1980.
8 The first lawn tennis championships were played in Wimbledon in 1877.
9 The theme park *Disneyland* was set up in Anaheim, California, in 1955.
10 The first Levi jeans were made in San Francisco in 1850.

4 *What's in the news?*

1 A man has been hit by a falling tree in Woodland Road.
2 A new sports centre has been opened in Elm Street.
3 Two youths have been arrested for drunk driving.
4 Beech School chemistry lab has been destroyed by a fire.
5 Some teenagers have been injured on the motorway.
6 A policeman has been fined for speeding.

5 *Before and after*

1 had been cleaned 2 had been washed up 3 had been moved 4 had been put back 5 had been taken away 6 had been thrown away 7 had been emptied 8 had been polished 9 had been watered 10 The cans and cigarettes/The rubbish in the big plant pot/under the big plant had not been thrown away.

6 *Wedding preparations*

1 The invitations will be sent off on Monday.
2 The band will be booked on Tuesday.
3 The wedding dress will be picked up on the 18th.
4 The flowers will be ordered on the 20th.
5 The taxis will be booked on the 21st.
6 The cake will be ordered next week.

7 *School dos and don'ts*

a 1 Litter should be put in bins.
2 Food and drinks cans should not be left in classrooms.
3 Bicycles must not be left in front of the school gates.
4 Walkmans may be used in the breaks only.
5 Sports equipment must be taken back to the gym after use.
6 Mobile phones may not be taken to an exam.
7 Toilets and showers should be kept clean at all times.
8 Wet clothing must not be hung on radiators.

8 *Writing a report*

1 First, parents and visitors were welcomed by the head teacher, Mrs F.D. Fox.
2 Then the school song was sung by the school choir.
3 Afterwards a speech was given by the head teacher on the successes of the past year.
4 Prizes and certificates were awarded by Mr J. Rolls from the Education Department.
5 Mr Rolls was thanked by Mrs Fox for the support and cooperation of the Education Department.
6 Then the programme of events and activities was announced by two sixth-form pupils.
7 Parents and visitors were shown round the school by pupils.
8 Food and soft drinks were sold by pupils and teachers.

9 *An exciting day*

1 We were asked to study the script.
2 We were advised to read it aloud.
3 I was nervous, so I was told to relax and just be natural.
4 We were given some stage instructions.
5 I was told not to look into the camera.
6 Leo was asked to speak a bit louder.
7 Well, after it was all over we were/everybody was thanked for taking part.
8 We were paid our expenses for the day.
9 Before I left, I was shown into the casting agent's office.
10 ... I was offered a small part in a new soap opera.
11 And I was promised the chance of a bigger part in their next project.

10 *It is said ...*

a 1 It is believed that ... 2 It is said that ... 3 It is thought that ... 4 It is expected that ... 5 In Britain, it is thought that ... 6 It is said that ...

b 1 Prince William is believed to be the most popular Royal. 2 The British are said to be a nation of tea-drinkers. 3 The British are thought to be bad at learning foreign languages. 4 Britain is expected to introduce the euro soon. 5 The Prime Minister is thought to have improved education. 6 British people are said to be great animal lovers.

11 *The Tower of London*

1 was started 2 was completed 3 have been witnessed 4 was used 5 be feared 6 is said 7 were murdered 8 be crowned 9 were beheaded 10 is said 11 be haunted 12 was executed 13 being imprisoned/having been imprisoned 14 was also kept 15 is used 16 be viewed 17 is not recommended 18 are kept 19 are answered 20 have been told 21 can be taken 22 be bought 23 be reached 24 is visited 25 will be visited

The infinitive and the gerund

The infinitive

1 *What are your teachers like?*

a 1 us to be 2 us to listen to 3 us to do 4 us to bring 5 us to talk 6 us not to copy 7 us to stick 8 us not to eat

b They allow us to work in groups.
They don't allow us not to do our homework.
They don't allow us to use our mobiles.

2 *He wants her to meet him*

a 1 to go to the cinema with him tomorrow.
2 her to meet him after school.
3 her to phone him.
4 her to give him an answer.
5 her to miss the party on Friday.
6 her to meet his friends.

3 *A message on the answer phone*

a 1 She wants Luke to phone Mr Briggs.
2 She tells him to give Mrs Hill the parcel that's in the hall.
3 She would like him to take the bottles to the bottle bank.
4 She tells him not to forget the dentist's at five.
5 She would like Katie to turn the oven on at six.

6 She tells her to put the meat pie in at 6.15.
7 She wants her to peel the potatoes.
8 She would like Katie and Luke/them both to take Spike for a walk.

4 *Who's the first?*

I'm always the last to get up at weekends. My brother is always the last to watch TV during the week. My sister is usually the first to have a shower in the mornings. My father is usually the only one to go to bed early. Etc.

5 *There's nothing to do*

1 to go 2 to do 3 to listen to. 4 to read. 5 to chat to 6 to watch 7 to eat 8 to do.

6 *Moving*

a 1 The box is too big for her to lift.
2 The carpet is too heavy for him to carry.
3 It's impossible for them to push the sofa through the door.
4 It's impossible for them to move the cupboard.
5 The picture is too high for him to reach.
6 The TV set is too heavy for her to lift.

7 *I don't know how to do it*

a 1 how to 2 what to 3 how to 4 where to 5 who to 6 where to 7 what to 8 where to 9 how to 10 how to

8 *Why*

a 1 to get/keep fit 2 to ask for some holiday brochures / to get some information / to book a holiday 3 to learn to ride / to take riding lessons 4 to meet others / to surf and chat 5 to listen to/buy CDs

b 1 to talk about their problems / just to go on TV / to have fun arguing
2 to get a better job qualification
3 to meet people with the same interests / to play their favourite sport
4 to surf and to chat / to find information.
5 to win money / to have fun / to be on TV / to show what they know

9 *I'd rather go somewhere hot*

a 1 let's 2 would rather 3 Why not 4 would rather 5 why not 6 would rather 7 had better 8 rather than 9 let's 10 rather than

10 *A welcome visit*

1 lets 2 lets 3 doesn't make 4 lets 5 don't make 6 let 7 makes 8 makes 9 don't let 10 makes 11 don't let 12 let

11 *Rachel's story*

a 1 I noticed a dark girl come in five minutes later.
2 I heard the blond girl ask the assistant another question.
3 I saw the dark girl go to the perfumes.
4 I noticed her pick up a large bottle of Calvin Klein.
5 I saw her put it in the inside pocket of her jacket.
6 I heard her say to the blond girl '…'
7 I saw them walk past the cash desk.
8 I watched them leave the shop with the stolen perfume.
9 I saw them get into a car across the road.
10 I saw it drive off immediately.

12 *A whizz-kid*

1 to 2 to 3 to 4 – 5 to 6 to 7 to 8 – 9 – 10 – 11 to 12 – 13 to 14 to 15 to 16 to 17 – 18 – 19 to 20 – 21 to

13 *Future plans*

a 1 to, to, – 2 to, to, to 3 –, –, to, to, to, to 4 to, to, to, to. 5 to, to, to, – 6 –, –, –, to, to

The gerund

14 *Rick's hobbies*

a I think Rick's hobbies and interests are:
1 jogging 2 travelling 3 boxing 4 cycling 5 skiing 6 riding 7 inline skating 8 drawing 9 filming 10 writing e-mails.

15 *Meet Claire*

a 1 trying 2 travelling, 3 meeting 4 making 5 smoking. 6 going 7 catching 8 eating 9 getting up 10 being 11 cutting, 12 wearing 13 asking 14 modelling 15 doing

16 *I don't remember doing it*

a 1 to ask 2 to bring 3 putting 4 feeling 5 to look. 6 asking 7 to put 8 to tell 9 buying 10 telling 11 talking 12 to put

17 *Judy, her family and friends*

1 He's famous for telling stupid jokes.
2 She's excited about going out with a cool sixth-former on Friday.
3 She's crazy about entering karaoke competitions.
4 I'm sorry about not sending my cousin a birthday card last week.
5 She's proud of being the best disco-dancer in the class.
6 I'm pretty bad at dancing.
7 He's glad about moving to London soon.
8 She's really interested in learning how to program.
9 She's good at cooking foreign food.
10 I'm a bit worried about not passing some of my GCSEs.
11 We were disappointed about not winning the football match.
12 He's used to working late (quite a lot).
13 He's tired of getting up early for his Saturday job.
14 I'm a bit angry about not getting an invitation to Sue's party.

18 *Make sentences*

a 1 I don't believe in working too hard.
2 My best friend sometimes complains about having too much homework.
3 I always look forward to going on holiday.
4 I never dream about becoming rich and famous.
5 My friends sometimes worry about not passing exams.
6 My best friend doesn't always feel like going out.
7 I can't concentrate on doing my homework.
8 I sometimes apologize for making a mistake.
9 My friends sometimes talk about not having enough money.
10 I never think about leaving school.

19 *Ben*

a 1 by washing people's cars. 2 instead of staying in. 3 in spite of not feeling well. 4 without working harder. 5 for finding her some Internet addresses. 6 before going to bed.

20 *Exam tips*

1 It's worth starting early with your revision.
2 It's hopeless learning everything the night before.
3 It's no use staying up late to learn.
4 It's a waste of time learning grammar rules by heart.
5 You can't help making a few careless mistakes.
6 There's no point writing more than necessary.
7 It's no good copying from your neighbour.
8 Remember – it's no fun marking bad tests.

21 *No, thank you*

1 to drive 2 driving 3 go 4 go 5 walking 6 going 7 seeing. 8 going 9 paying.
10 going out 11 staying 12 to go 13 asking 14 thinking 15 to go out

22 *A day trip*

1 to spend a quiet day by a lake.
2 doing that if it's too cold.
3 go for a ride on the London Eye. … to do in a group.
4 going shopping in London? … seeing a musical.
5 to go to Windsor Castle?
6 having/spending a day in Oxford / going to Oxford for the day.
7 to wait and see what the weather is like.

The participle

1 *Reading habits*

a 1e 2a 3f 4d 5g 6b 7h 8c

b 1 bored 2 boring 3 interested 4 interesting 5 surprising 6 frightening 7 frightened 8 exciting 9 confusing. 10 confused. 11 excited 12 disappointing 13 fascinating 14 amazing 15 man-eating 16 disappointed.

2 *A party*

1 Who's the girl standing alone in the corner?
2 Who's the boy talking to the girl with the punk hairstyle / with the short skirt?
3 Who are the boys sitting on the floor?
4 Who's the girl wearing the long dress?
5 Who's the boy playing the guitar?
6 Who are the two boys smoking cigarettes?
7 Who's the girl dancing with the boy in the white T-shirt? / Who are the boy and the girl dancing in the middle of the room?
8 Who are the girls looking at the CDs?
9 Who's the girl holding the (cola) bottle?
10 Who's the boy eating the big plate of sandwiches?

3 *On the way home*

1 He heard someone's parrot talking.
2 He smelt someone's dinner burning.
3 He heard a boy playing the violin.
4 He noticed a man shaving.
5 He saw a boy kissing his girlfriend.
6 He heard a man and a woman quarrelling.
7 He saw a man having a bath.
8 He listened to a girl practising karaoke.

4 *Don the punk*

a 1 He has had his hair cut short.
2 He has had his hair dyed blond.
3 He has had his nose pierced.
4 He has had his arms tattooed.
5 He has had contact lenses fitted.

5 *The Grand Canyon*

1 Driving along the South Rim, we ... 2 Taking a photo, Tony ... 3 Hiking down into the Canyon, we ... 4 Having seen the film, we... 5 Having asked the price of helicopter tours, Tony ... 6 Getting on the mule, Gina ... 7 Having been in the saddle for a few hours, we ... 8 Watching the sunset over the Canyon, we ... 9 Having rafted down the Colorado for three days, we ... 10 Having camped in the Canyon for a week, we ...

6 *Learning to drive*

1 ..., feeling nervous, Tom ... 2 Not having learnt the Highway Code, he ...
3 ..., not having seen the sign. 4 ..., driving too fast he ... 5 Having gone to bed late, he ...
6 ..., not having noticed a red light, he ... 7 Not being used to the gears, he ...
8 ..., having left the handbrake on, he ...

7 *Bad luck*

1 Getting out of the shower, Vince ... 2 Having forgotten her purse, Gina ...
3 Not having finished his project, Leo ... 4 Not knowing the way to the job centre, Vanessa ...
5 Eating his school lunch, David ... 6 Having lost the number, Jerry ...
7 Having played badly for two hours, Ed ... 8 Lifting weights, Marc ... 9 Being tired, Ann ...
10 Not having taken his boots to school, Greg ...

8 *What were they doing?*

1 Dave was just leaving the house, talking on ... 2 Phil was jogging in the park, listening to ... 3 Jan was putting bottles in the bottle bank, helped by ... 4 Vanessa was walking to the station, carrying ... 5 Steve was driving down East Street, playing ... 6 Lou was crossing a busy road, helping ... 7 Lisa and Beth were chatting in a café, having ... 8 Paul and Ed were fighting on the football field, cheered on by ...

9 *Describe the pictures*

1 – 2 – 3 when 4 while 5 – 6 when/while

10 *Fly the Eye*

1 taking 2 speaking 3 Seeing 4 admiring 5 Taking/Having taken 6 being 7 designed 8 speaking 9 Measuring 10 weighing 11 Talking 12 buying/having bought 13 boarding. 14 staring 15 looking forward 16 given

11 *The creator of Sherlock Holmes*

1 Known for being untidy and rebellious, he was often punished.
2 Being interested in writing, he became editor of the school magazine.
3 He left school at sixteen, having passed /after passing his university entrance exam.
4 Before university he spent a year at a school in Austria, improving his German.

5 Not having much money for university, he had to take jobs.
6 Not being very successful as a doctor, he decided to try writing.
7 Finding that he could make more money with books, he gave up medicine.
8 His first collection of stories, called *The Adventures of Sherlock Holmes*, made him famous.
9 But having become tired of his hero, Doyle officially killed him off in 1894.
10 But his readers complained, refusing to believe that Holmes was dead.
11 He wrote a story involving Holmes in a secret mission for the government during war time.
12 He died of a heart attack in 1930, having become one of the world´s best paid authors.

The noun

1 *Puzzles with plurals*

a men feet teeth knives parties potatoes

b mice roofs discos watches children grown-ups crossroads

2 *Clothes*

a a pair of white jeans, a trouser suit, a pair of blue trousers, an anorak, a pair of overalls and a red jacket

b some pyjamas, a white blouse, some Bermuda shorts and some leggings.

3 *Packing*

1 these 2 some. 3 is 4 this 5 one. 6 pairs of 7 are 8 them. 9 pair 10 pair of
11 some 12 are 13 are 14 pairs of 15 are 16 them. 17 they are. 18 are 19 doesn't
20 are 21 them.

4 *Richard's school*

a 1 class 2 is 3 choir 4 meets 5 team 6 are 7 group 8 performs 9 band 10 have
11 police 12 have

b Nouns that always have a plural verb form: cattle, people, police.

5 *What has Emma bought?*

1 some orange juice 2 some soap 3 some cornflakes
4 some coffee 5 some chewing gum 6 some stamps 7 some chocolate
8 some batteries 9 some toothpaste 10 a birthday card
11 a magazine 12 some video cassettes

6 *At the corner shop*

a I'd like a packet/box of chocolate biscuits, a large bar of milk chocolate, a box/packet of *After Nine* mints, a jar of strawberry jam, a large carton/bottle of orange juice, a tube of *Everclean* toothpaste, six cartons of fruit yoghurt, two cans of vegetable soup, a bottle of tomato ketchup, a kilo bag of sugar, 400 grammes of cheese, a litre of milk.

7 *Poor Amy*

a 1 some advice. 2 some information 3 some homework 4 some shopping 5 some damage 6 a cupboard, some furniture 7 some luggage 8 a job

b 1 Mother: There's some washing to do. Amy, can you help me, please?
2 Brother: Can you help me to move some equipment into the garage?
3 Mother: Amy, there's some housework to do. Can you clean the windows?

8 *Quick check*

Correct: 4, 5, 7
Corrected: 1 black hair 2 some good news / a piece/bit of good news
3 two pieces/bits of information 6 much homework 8 some cool music 9 That's (some) useful advice. / a useful piece/bit of advice. 10 Walking up the hill was hard work.

9 *A crossword puzzle*

a 1 news 2 damage 3 traffic 4 plastic 5 homework 6 progress 7 work

b some weather, a piece of/a bit of news/some news, some/a bit of damage, some traffic, some/a piece of plastic, some/a piece of/a bit of homework, some/a bit of progress, some/a bit of work

10 *Cathy's family and friends*

a 1 He is Sally's brother. He is the Smiths' son. He is James's best friend.
2 They are the Wilsons' neighbours.
3 She is James's sister. She is the Wilsons' daughter.
4 He is the boys' football coach. He is Tom and James's football coach.
5 She is the Smiths' dog. She is the neighbours' dog.
6 She is Mrs Wilson's sister. She is the children's aunt. She is Cathy and James's aunt.
7 He is Sally and Tom's uncle.
8 He is William's son. He is Sally and Tom's cousin. He is Mr and Mrs Wilson's nephew.

b Can be left out: 1, 3, 4, 5, 6 ('shop' last three times).

11 *A visit to the cinema*

a 1 works of famous English-speaking authors 2 last term's report 3 today's maths homework 4 yesterday's newspaper? 5 name of the cinema. 6 end of the High Street, 7 twenty minutes' walk, 8 beginning of the film. 9 captain of our school football team 10 Andy's sister.

b 1 at the end of the week. 2 on his cousin Meg's birthday. 3 *The Secret of the Thirteenth Floor* 4 her father's car. 5 the name of the pizzeria, the name of the street.

The article

1 *Mini-dialogues*

a 1 milk 2 the milk 3 cola. 4 milk. 5 health 6 The pizza 7 pizza 8 Pizza 9 the pasta 10 pasta 11 history. 12 the history 13 life 14 the life 15 People 16 the people

2 *Tony's e-mail*

1 – 2 – 3 the 4 the 5 – 6 – 7 the 8 the 9 the 10 – 11 – 12 – 13 The 14 – 15 the 16 – 17 –

3 *A visitor from England*

a 1 What would you like for lunch?
2 Which sports do you do in (the) summer? / What kind of sport do you do in (the) summer?
3 Shall we go to the cinema on Friday evening?
4 Would you like to visit a few friends with me in the afternoon?
5 Would you like to see a football match on Saturday?
6 Is your birthday in August?

b 1 – 2 the 3 the 4 – 5 –, – 6 the 7 – 8 – 9 (the)

4 *Correct the mistakes*

Correct: 4, 5, 7
Corrected: 1 … most of the time. 2 … half the time. 3 Both (the) tyres … 6 … twice the amount. 8 … all the time. 9 … for half the price. 10 … double the size …

5 *What are their jobs?*

I think … Sharon is an architect. Jane is a nurse. Laura is a tour guide. Emma is a secretary. Tim is an actor. Jerry is a shop assistant. Nick is an electrician. Lucy is an artist.

6 *How often? How much? How fast?*

1 £15 a night. 2 30 miles an hour. 3 £1.99 a kilo. 4 £5.99 a bunch. 5 four hours a day. 6 £7.99 a bottle.

7 *Meet the Martins*

a 1 … a shower. … for breakfast. 2 … in bed. … got a headache … a temperature. 3 … to work. … by bus, … in a hurry, … by car. 4 … to school. … in class. As a rule … 5 … to the cinema, … on TV 6 … After school, … the piano, … the guitar for a change

b 1 on TV? 2 listen to the radio? 3 for breakfast? 4 go to school? 5 by bus? 6 to the cinema? 7 in bed? 8 after school? 9 to town? 10 have dinner?

The adjective and the adverb

The adjective

1 *My best friend*

a younger/older, fatter/thinner, taller/smaller, fairer/darker, better at/worse at …, more musical, tidier, more athletic, more practical, fitter, more easy-going

b the youngest/the oldest, the fattest/the thinnest, the tallest/the smallest, the best at …/the worst at …, the most musical, the tidiest, the most athletic, the most practical, the fittest, the most easy-going

2 *Eating in London*

1 oldest 2 most traditional 3 cheapest. 4 quickest. 5 biggest 6 coolest 7 best 8 most inexpensive 9 hottest (die schärfsten …) 10 tastiest 11 trendiest 12 most typical 13 worst

3 *Mini-dialogues*

1 nearest 2 next 3 further/farther 4 latest 5 latest 6 last 7 nearest 8 next 9 further 10 last 11 farther/further 12 older/elder 13 older

4 *Compare the cars*

1 as expensive as 2 more luxurious than 3 more powerful than 4 as comfortable as 5 less stylish than 6 easier to park than 7 cheaper to run than 8 less economical than 9 more reliable than 10 less environment-friendly than 11 noisier than 12 as modern as

5 *Add a word*

a 1 girl 2 woman/girl 3 – 4 persons/people. 5 – , – 6 persons/people 7 people 8 man 9 boys 10 –

b 1 The bad thing 2 The best thing 3 The worst thing 4 The crazy thing 5 The funny thing

The adverb

6 *Check your forms*

a truly simply happily publicly basically cheerfully

b Adjectives: dull, fantastic, friendly, reliable, silly
Adverbs: nicely, politely, shyly, stupidly
Adjectives and adverbs: early, fast, hard, late

7 *A first date*

1 nervously 2 politely 3 patiently 4 slowly 5 loudly 6 angrily 7 carefully 8 carelessly

8 *A phone call*

a 1 terribly 2 fast, not fast enough 3 wait long 4 hard 5 right 6 rained heavily today 7 late 8 daily

9 *At the zoo*

1 high. 2 hard 3 wrong. 4 right 5 nearly 6 hardly 7 fairly 8 highly 9 freely. 10 most 11 mostly 12 pretty

10 *Describe the pictures*

1 They feel really comfortable. 2 It smells delicious. 3 It sounds awful. 4 He doesn't look friendly. 5 Ben's medicine tastes bitter. 6 Sarah's room looks untidy. 7 The pupils don't seem/look interested. 8 … because it gets dark early in winter.

11 *I'll do things better*

a 1 She's going to behave better in class.
2 She's going to do her homework more regularly.
3 She's going to try harder in tests.
4 She's going to go to bed earlier.
5 She's going to come home more punctually.
6 She's going to write more neatly.
7 She's going to work faster in class.
8 She's going to listen to the teachers more.
9 She's going to concentrate better in class.
10 She's going to help more at home.

12 *At the disco*

1 (This week) Janet and Michelle really enjoyed their disco evening (this week).
2 (In the *Insomnia*) They often meet interesting people (in the *Insomnia*).

3 There are usually lots of students there at the weekend. / Usually there are lots of students there at the weekend. / At the weekend there are usually lots of students there.
4 In fact, they met two rather nice boys.
5 The music had just stopped for a few minutes, when two boys came up and asked them politely/and politely asked them if there was a phone.
6 Luckily, the disco wasn't very full, so they didn't have to shout loudly.
7 (Soon) They were (soon) chatting excitedly about everything and nothing.
8 Of course, they danced several times too.
9 They all decided to meet in the shopping mall the next day.
10 (Perhaps) They will (perhaps) meet again at the disco next week. / Next week they will perhaps meet again at the disco.

13 *Correct the mistakes*

Correct: 5, 9, 11
Corrected: 1 My brother never goes to bed ... 2 Tony speaks German quite well. 3 Sandra quietly closed the door ... 4 I'll see you there at six o'clock. 6 I have never been to Dublin. 7 Jane carefully locked the door ... 8 We have already decided ... 10 I really must go now. 12 I always clean my room ...

14 *Oh dear!*

a 1 lazy 2 thoroughly. 3 well 4 correctly. 5 practical 6 early. 7 tired 8 well 9 sore 10 terribly. 11 Unfortunately, 12 extremely 13 friendly 14 badly, 15 fast 16 slowly 17 busy. 18 angrily

15 *Marie's family*

1: nice, angry, nicely, angrily 2: intelligent, stupid, intelligently, intelligent, stupidly
3: serious, excited, excitedly, seriously 4: good, badly, well, good, bad

Quantifiers

1 *We need some butter*

a They will have to buy some flour, some fresh cream, some lemons and some dark chocolate. They won't need to buy any milk, any margarine, any sugar or any walnuts.

b 1 any 2 some 3 any. 4 any 5 some. 6 any 7 any 8 some 9 some? 10 any 11 any 12 any?

2 *A walking tour*

I think we should take some maps, some water, some food, some matches, some binoculars, some sunglasses, some sunscreen and some sticking plasters.
I don't think we should take any magazines, any umbrellas, any school books or any CDs.

3 *After the party*

a 1 There are a lot of meatballs.
2 There aren't many sausages. / There are only a few sausages.
3 There isn't much potato salad. / There's only a little potato salad.
4 There's a lot of popcorn.
5 There aren't many grapes. / There are only a few grapes.
6 There isn't much bread. / There's only a little bread.
7 There aren't many strawberries. / There are only a few strawberries.
8 There isn't much chocolate pudding. / There's only a little chocolate pudding.

b 1 a few 2 a lot of 3 a lot of 4 much 5 many 6 a few 7 a little 8 a lot of

4 *A letter from Bournemouth*

1 every 2 Every 3 each 4 each 5 every 6 each 7 each 8 any. 9 each. 10 any

5 *Opinions*

1 That's not true. Not all the boys I know are intelligent.
2 That's not true. Not all teenagers spend their parents' money. Some do jobs to earn their own money.
3 That's not true. Not all the boys I know are good at technical things. Some girls are better.
4 That's not true. Not all the girls in my class work hard.
5 That's not true. All the pupils in my class work quite hard at school and at home.
6 That's not true. Not all the boys I know are better with computers than girls .
7 That's not true. Not all the teenagers I know waste money with their mobiles.
8 That's not true. Not all the boys I know like sports. Girls are often better.

6 *What will you have?*

a 1 neither 2 either 3 none. 4 All 5 Either. 6 Neither. 7 No 8 both 9 either/both. 10 both

7 *I've looked everywhere*

1 everybody, 2 nobody 3 nowhere. 4 somebody 5 anybody 6 somewhere.
7 something 8 anything 9 anywhere? 10 everywhere 11 something 12 nothing

Pronouns and question words

Pronouns

1 We saw them

1 him 2 him 3 her 4 them? 5 it 6 it 7 us. 8 them, 9 us. 10 me 11 you, 12 you.

2 A visit to an English family

1 they 2 her. 3 she 4 them. 5 It 6 you. 7 They 8 them 9 She 10 it 11 She

There are six different translations for Sie/sie.

3 The German 'man'

a 1 They 2 You/One 3 You/One 4 They 5 You 6 They 7 They 8 You/One 9 you/one 10 They

4 What a mix-up!

1 yours 2 mine 3 my 4 her 5 yours 6 hers 7 our 8 theirs 9 his 10 your 11 my 12 his 13 my 14 mine

5 Happy families

1 of his own 2 his own 3 of her own 4 of her own 5 her own 6 of their own 7 their own 8 of his own 9 of her own 10 their own 11 of their own 12 their own

6 Describe the pictures

a 1 She has taken off her shoes. 2 He has bumped his head. 3 They have put on their coats. / They are putting on their coats. 4 The cat has hurt its paw. 5 'Put the money in your pocket.' 6 'I think I have broken my arm.'

7 Did you enjoy yourself?

a 1b 2c 3d 4e 5a

b 1 – 2 – 3 myself 4 – 5 – 6 myself 7 himself 8 themselves 9 – 10 yourself 11 themselves 12 – 13 himself 14 – 15 – 16 –

8 *Teach yourself*

1 each other 2 each other 3 himself 4 ourselves 5 yourself 6 myself 7 each other 8 themselves 9 each other 10 herself 11 yourselves 12 themselves

9 *Mini-dialogues*

a 1 Those 2 these 3 this 4 that
5 these 6 this 7 that 8 those 9 these
10 this 11 this 12 that 13 those 14 that 15 This

10 *He's already got one*

He's (already) got
1 a leather one from his sister 2 an expensive German one from his father 3 a new American one 4 some high-quality Japanese ones 5 a waterproof Swiss one 6 four mega-size ones 7 three new ones 8 a valuable antique one from his grandmother

Question words

11 *Are you a typical teenager?*

a 1 Where 2 When 3 How long 4 Who 5 How many 6 How much 7 How 8 How often 9 What 10 What 11 Why 12 Whose

12 *A strange dream*

1 What was making a terrible noise? 2 Who heard you shouting? 3 What were you afraid of? 4 Who were you running to? 5 Who did you see following you? 6 What was holding you back? 7 Who tried to help you? 8 Who shouted your name? 9 What grabbed you from behind? 10 Who did you recognize?

13 *A computer theft*

1 Which door was not locked?
2 Which pupils heard something?
3 Who knew that the school had (got) new computers?
4 Who did you see running away?
5 Who phoned/called the police?
6 Which policeman/police officer did you speak to?
7 Which pupil/Which of the pupils informed the headmaster?
8 Which of you can describe the men?

14 *Shoe shopping*

a 1 What 2 Which 3 What 4 Which 5 Which 6 Which 7 What 8 Which 9 Which 10 What

15 *A bad connection*

1 Where did you go last night? 2 Who did you see at the disco? 3 What/Who didn't he mention? 4 Who was he with? 5 How did he look? 6 Who asked you for your telephone number? 7 When/What time did you go home? 8 What did you realize when you got home? 9 What had you forgotten? 10 Whose/How many/Which videos did you watch again?

16 *A local hero*

a 1 Which match was your best last season?
2 How long have you been team captain?
3 How many hours/How long do you train every day?
4 When/What time do you usually start training?
5 What time /When do you normally get up?
6 How tall are you?
7 How much do you weigh?
8 Where do you come from originally?
9 Who is your biggest fan?
10 How many fan letters do you get every week?
11 Where do you go at the weekends? / What do you do at the weekends?
12 What do you do in your free time?
13 Why are you so popular?
14 Which team/Who do you think will win the European Cup?

Conditional sentences

1 *A trip to Edinburgh*

1 when 2 If 3 when 4 if 5 If 6 If 7 when 8 if 9 when 10 if

2 *What will happen if ...?*

a 1 If I don't go to bed until after twelve, I'll get up late.
2 If I get up late, I won't catch the school bus.
3 If I don't catch the school bus, I'll have to walk.
4 If I have to walk, I won't arrive on time.
5 If I don't arrive on time, I'll make the teacher angry.
6 If I make the teacher angry, I'll get extra homework.
7 If I get extra homework, I'll have to stay in tomorrow night.
8 If I have to stay in tomorrow night, I'll miss the rock concert.
9 If I miss the rock concert, I'll lose the fifteen pounds for the ticket. – I think Dan will decide (not) to go to the disco

3 *An exchange pupil*

a 1 If it's warm enough at the weekend, we could go on a bike tour.
2 If you like parties, you could meet all my friends on Friday night.
3 If the weather's bad on Saturday, we could look round the shopping mall.

4 If you are interested in history, we could go to the town museum.
5 If my best friend has time, she could come and meet you this afternoon.
6 If you understand enough German, we could watch some videos.
7 If you play tennis, my brother could play with you.
8 If you like Italian food, we could have a pizza at my favourite pizza restaurant tonight.

4 *What parents say*

a 1 ..., you (will) get toothache/they (will) go bad.
2 If you go to bed too late, ... / If you don't get enough sleep, ...
3 ... you don't/won't know where your things are. / ... it looks/will look terrible
4 If you watch too much TV ... / If you sit at the computer for hours ...
5 You (will) have to do more work at home ... / You (will) miss things ... / You won't/don't know how to do the work ...
6 ... if you go out so much / ... if you spend it all every month.
7 You (will) feel hungry ... / You can't/won't be able to concentrate in class ...
8 ... if you go out too often. / ... if you spend too much time with friends.

5 *If I won the lottery ...*

a 1 If Justin won ..., he would buy a motorbike.
2 If Tariq won ..., he would put the money in the bank.
3 If Selima won ..., she would go on holiday to Australia.
4 If Maggie won ..., she would buy presents for her family.
5 If Pete won ..., he would invite all his friends to a big party.
6 If Jill won ..., she would buy a horse and learn to ride.

6 *It would be cheaper*

1 went 2 would see 3 stayed 4 wouldn't need 5 booked 6 wouldn't pay 7 would get
8 booked 9 would be 10 took 11 asked 12 would say

7 *Living in the USA*

a If we lived in America, we could visit some national parks.
..., I could watch baseball matches.
..., my sister could learn to drive.
..., I could rollerblade on the pavements.

b ..., I/my brother might learn to play American football.
..., I might drive to school in my own car/drive myself and my friends to school.
..., I/my brother might be in a baseball team.
..., I might be very interested in sports.
..., we might do lots of extra-curricular activities.
..., I might join a drama group.
..., I might spend most of the day in school.
..., I might get a weekend job.
..., I might not understand everything at first.
..., I might not have good grades/ I might have better grades.

8 *Giving advice*

1 If I were you, I would join a sports club or a youth club. / …, I would invite some of your classmates to your house. / …, I would try to get to know them better.
2 If I were you, I would look for another girlfriend. / …, I would say nothing and see what happens.
3 If I were you, I would get some help from a friend. / …, I talk to a teacher about your problems.
4 If I were you, I would tell your form teacher about the problem.
5 If I were you, I would be honest and tell your parents. Everybody loses things.

9 *It wouldn't have happened if …*

a 1 If Sue hadn't done her homework in the bus, it wouldn't have been full of mistakes.
2 If Pete hadn't left his wallet in a snack-bar, it wouldn't have disappeared.
3 If Peggy hadn't given in her English project late, she wouldn't have got a bad mark.
4 If Owen hadn't forgotten Julie's birthday, she would have gone to the disco with him.
5 If Sanjay had locked his bike, it wouldn't have been stolen.
6 If Sean had told Diane the truth, she wouldn't have dumped him.
7 If Beth hadn't lost Ben's CDs, he wouldn't have got angry.

10 *Friday 13th*

a 1 had not met 2 would not have gone 3 had not left 4 would not have disappeared 5 would have had 6 had not lost 7 had not given 8 would have had 9 would not have got 10 had taken 11 had not got 12 would not have caught

11 *A hundred years ago*

a If I had lived a hundred years ago, I would have lived with my parents too.
…, probably I would have got married very early.
…, I wouldn't have gone to school by bus.
…, maybe my family would have been very poor.

b If I had lived a hundred years ago, I couldn't have gone to university because it would have been too expensive.
…, I couldn't have studied computer science.
…, I couldn't have gone on holiday with my friends.
…, I couldn't have travelled by plane.

12 *A walking trip*

1 had put on 2 weren't 3 wouldn't have come 4 don't see 5 looked after 6 don't find 7 will have to 8 wouldn't go 9 I'll phone 10 I'll say 11 had known 12 would have asked

Relative clauses

1 *A holiday in Italy*

1 They are the girls who went on holiday with Nicole. / They are the girls who have just come back from Italy with Nicole.
2 Giorgio was the son who came home in the middle of the night on his motorbike.
3 *Casa Giovanni* was a restaurant which served very good seafood.
4 Peppino was the dog who always barked loudly when Giorgio came home.
5 Tim and Markus were two young Germans who were also staying at the guesthouse.
6 The *Mamma Mia* was a disco which the girls always went to in the evenings.
7 Andy and Rob were teenagers from Ireland who went to the *Mamma Mia* every night too.
8 *Gina's* was a boutique which sold trendy teenage clothes.
9 *La Fiorentina* was an ice-cream parlour which sold fantastic ice-cream.

2 *I like people who …*

… people/boys/girls who/that …
… places/discos/parties/jokes/films/holidays that/which …

3 *People at a barbecue*

1 That's Steve, the boy whose girlfriend has just left him.
2 That's Rob, the boy who's good with computers.
3 That's Sarah, the girl whose brother is often on TV.
4 That's Kim, the girl who's just got a place at Oxford University.
5 That's Sylvia, the girl whose moped was stolen last week.
6 That's Justin, the boy who's just bought a motorbike.
7 That's Tariq and Sanjay, the boys whose family comes from India.
8 That's Melanie and Pam, the girls whose father has just lost his job.

4 *Where's the ketchup?*

a 1 Where's that red felt-tip ( ) I found yesterday?
2 Where's that new exercise book ( ) I bought for French?
3 What did I do with those e-mail addresses ( ) Jan gave me?

b 1 Where's the bottle of coke that was in the fridge?
2 Where's the piece of apple pie ( ) I didn't eat at lunch?
3 Who's eaten the crisps ( ) I bought this morning?
4 Where are the videos ( ) I put on the TV?
5 Where's the new computer magazine ( ) Dad brought home?
6 Where's my black T-shirt that needs washing?
7 Where are the new batteries ( ) I bought yesterday?

5 *Write the clues*

a Across: 6 It is something you pack clothes in. 7 It is something you sleep in (indoors). 9 It is something you laugh at. 10 It is something you write with.
Down: 1 It is something you sit on. 2 It is something you drink from/out of. 4 It is something you put a letter in. 5 It is something you cut with. / They are things you cut with. 6 It is something you wash your hair with. 8 It is something you sleep in (outside/outdoors).

b 1 It's something you look through. 2 It's something you take photographs with. 3 It's something you put flowers in.

6 *Old classmates*

1 He was the boy who always beat me at sports.
2 She was the girl ( ) nobody liked.
3 They were the boys who sang in the church choir.
4 She was the girl who never stopped talking.
5 She was the girl ( ) I often quarrelled with.
6 He was the boy ( ) I used to sit next to.
7 He was the boy ( ) you helped with maths.
8 He was the boy ( ) you once had a big fight with.
9 They were the girls who were always up for a laugh.

7 *A youth hostel trip*

a 1 where 2 (who/that) 3 (that) 4 which 5 (that/which/where) 6 (that/which) 7 (that/which) 8 where 9 (who/that) 10 whose 11who/that 12 why 13 when 14 (that/which)

Indirect speech

1 *A phone call*

a 1 He says perhaps he can borrow his brother's car.
2 He says if not, you will have to go to the cinema on the bus.
3 He says the film starts at eight-thirty.
4 He says he'll phone again in half an hour.
5 He says he will have to borrow ten pounds from you for the cinema tickets.

2 *Keeping fit*

a 1b 2a 3d 4c 5e
b 1 told 2 says 3 hasn't told 4 said 5 is telling

3 *Weekend plans*

a 1 Pat said she was going on a bike tour with the youth club.
2 Dave said he worked at the supermarket all day on Saturdays.
3 Beth said she had already spent all her pocket money.
4 Phil said he felt too tired to go out because he had studied for a maths test till one in the morning.
5 Joy said her cousins from Plymouth were coming.
6 Brian said he didn't want to do anything.
7 Jan said she had been ill on Tuesday and Wednesday, so she had to do a lot of homework at the weekend.
8 Robin said a friend had invited him to his house for the weekend.

b 1 Nazreen said she might go to Bristol with her parents.
2 Sean said he would probably go to visit his girlfriend in Brighton.
3 Selima said she could only go somewhere on Saturday afternoon.
4 Max said he wouldn't have time to go out until Sunday evening.
5 Vicky said she couldn't promise, but she would try to meet Trish for a pizza on Saturday.
6 Barry said he might not be at home all weekend.

4 *A class discussion*

a 1 He said pupils didn't take it seriously enough.
2 She said she had once fallen off the parallel bars and had broken a tooth.
3 He said school sport was a waste of time.
4 She said she had hated gymnastics since her accident.
5 She said she had never had a good mark for PE.
6 He said two lessons a week weren't enough.
7 He said he liked outside sports in summer, but didn't like running in circles in the gym in winter.
8 She said she would never be good at PE, so she got bad marks.
9 He said exercise and movement were important for teenagers.
10 She said she was the best tennis player in their club.

5 *When do I become an adult?*

She wrote that she could get married at 16 but that she couldn't vote until she was 18. At the cinema she already had to pay for an adult ticket, but she wasn't allowed to watch adult films. She wrote that she couldn't buy cigarettes or alcohol until she was 18, but she could drive a car at 17. On the bus and tube she started paying adult fares at 15. She already paid the adult fare on a plane. She wrote that airlines gave reductions to children under 12, which meant that she was an adult at 13 … She wrote that in the States she couldn't gamble in a casino until she was 21 and that she couldn't rent a car in her name until she was 25. She wrote that the age when she became an adult seemed to depend on where she was sitting.

6 *Poor Hannah*

Hannah said: 1 'We have been going out for about two months. 2 There's just one problem – he's from Bangladesh. 3 The problem will be my parents. 4 They will never accept him. 5 I don't know how I am going to tell them because they are narrow-minded. 6 It can cause a lot of trouble in the family. 7 I have never had a coloured boyfriend before. 8 My father may/might even tell me to stop seeing him. 9 But I can't give him up. 10 He's the nicest boyfriend I have ever had.'

7 *A first meeting*

Mark to a friend:
1 She told me (that) she was born in Chicago.
2 She said (that) they lived there until she was twelve.
3 She said (that) she thinks they will go back one day.
4 She told me (that) she hasn't lived in London very long.
5 She said (that) she is taking her driving test next week.

Nicole to a friend:
6 He said (that) he has been to the States twice.
7 He told me (that) he went to San Francisco last year.
8 He said (that) he'll probably go to New York this year.
9 He said (that) he loves shopping in the States.
10 He said (that) he'll show me his photos tomorrow.

8 *Scenes from a soap opera*

1 Donna threatened to leave Jeff if he didn't end the affair with Maria.
2 Jeff promised Donna that he would not see her again.
3 Troy advised Josh to forget Lauren.
4 But Josh admitted that he had fallen in love with her.
5 Kay invited Vince to stay to dinner.
6 Vince explained (to her) that he couldn't because Melissa was waiting for him at home.

9 *The first day at work*

a 1 ... who the boss was. 2 ... which computer system the firm used.
3 ... who could show her round. 4 ... where the photocopier was.
5 ... how the fax machine and the scanner worked.
6 ... who she could ask for help. 7 ... when the lunch break was.
8 ... what time everybody went home.

10 *I asked how much the rent was*

a 1 I asked when I had to pay the rent.
2 I asked how many other students lived in the house.
3 I asked if there were any rules about visitors or noise.
4 I asked if I had to share the bathroom and kitchen.
5 I asked where the nearest tube station was.
6 I asked if there was a telephone for students to use.
7 I asked if I could use the washing-machine.
8 I asked who I should contact if there was a problem.
9 I asked if I would be allowed to paint or decorate the room.
10 I asked if there was anywhere to park my bicycle.

b How much is a room for two people per night?
Are all the rooms with shower or bath?
Is a full English breakfast included in the price?

11 *What did he ask them to do?*

a 1 He asked Suzi to clean the hamster's cage.
2 He asked her not to give the hamster too much food.
3 He asked his father to bring him some computer magazines.
4 But he asked him not to bring old ones.
5 He asked Ed to do his paper round for him.
6 He asked Paul to phone him every day and tell him all the news.
7 He asked Dan to write down all the homework.
8 He asked his mother not to let anybody go into his room.

12 *What the policeman said*

a 1 He told us not to keep money … 2 He told us not to walk around on our own at night. He advised us to share … 3 He advised us to sit with others in the tube or train. He told us not to sit alone in a carriage. 4 He advised us to stay near crowds if we were alone. 5 He told us not to count money in public places. 6 He told us not to walk through … 7 He told us to watch out for pickpockets … 8 He advised us not to put cameras in pockets. 9 He advised us not to wear expensive … 10 He told us to dial …

13 *Going au pair*

1 Mrs Hill wanted to know if Gina could cook and if she would mind cleaning. She asked her if she could start in August.
2 Mrs Hill told Gina that there was a family in Bordeaux with three children. She explained that the father was often away on business, so the mother needed help with the children. She added that she had had good reports about the family from other au-pairs. They would treat Gina well. She mentioned that the mother didn't speak much English. She told Gina that she would have her own room and she could go to school three times a week, and that the boys were three and five.
3 Gina told Mrs Hill that she had stayed with a penfriend in Paris for a week. She explained that she wanted to get a job in France, so she needed a lot of practice. She told Mrs Hill that she had had a lot of experience with children. She also said she wasn't keen on housework, but she wouldn't mind it if she had enough free time. She added that she could cook a few simple things.
4 Gina asked Mrs Hill if she would have her own room. She also wanted to know how much free time she would get, and how old the boys were.
5 Mrs Hill told Gina to let her know next week if she wanted the job.

11 *After school chat* **inversion: *so/neither do I*, etc.** ▶ 10b

a Some 6th form pupils are chatting to their friends after school. Who is each person talking to? Match the statements to the comments, as in the example.

Example: Ann: I'd like to go somewhere exciting, like California. → Rachel: So would I.
Ann is talking to Rachel.

b Rachel and Ann are still talking about holidays. What comments does Rachel make? Begin with *so* or *neither*.

Ann:	Rachel:
1 I like sailing.	… I.
2 My brother doesn't like crowded beaches.	… mine.
3 My parents would like to go camping.	…
4 I can't surf or waterski.	…
5 I got a great suntan[2] last summer.	…
6 We don't like places where it's too hot.	…

c Now make comments to the statements that are true for you.

1 I hate homework.
2 I would like to have a pen pal in the States.
3 My parents don't like my music.
4 We haven't got a pet.
5 I didn't go out last night.
6 I'm looking forward to the next holidays.

1 be keen on *sehr gern mögen* 2 suntan *(Sonnen-)Bräune*

12 *Party talk* **question tags**

▶ 11, 12

Karen's parents are away, so she has decided to have a party. Friends have brought friends, so Karen doesn't know everybody. Complete the mini-dialogues with the missing question tags. Mind the tenses.

Examples: Alan: These sandwiches look good, ***don't they***? I think I'll take a few more.
Karen: Yes, but you'll leave some for the others, ***won't you***?

1 Chris: You're Karen, ...? Karen: That's right.
Chris: I've seen you somewhere before, ...? Where was it?
Karen: Probably at my last party.
2 Karen: You were at Mandy's party last Friday, ...?
Ben: Yes, that's right. It was a bit boring, ...? I left early.
3 Sasha: Debbie isn't coming, ...?
Gary: No, she said she had to babysit, ...? Or was that yesterday?
4 Mindy: Where's the cola? Surely it hasn't all gone, ... ? I'm thirsty.
Karen: There's some more over there in the corner, ...?
5 Alan: Those sausages have all gone, ...?
Karen: I think you're right. That didn't take long, ...?
6 Alice: The last bus goes at about twelve, ...?
Laura: Yes, but Jeff's taking us home in his car, ...? I'll ask him.
7 Karen: Jeff doesn't like parties much, ...?
Nick: No, he prefers discos. But this one isn't bad, ...?
8 Sita: Kim and Alan seem to be enjoying the party, ...?
Rob: Well, Alan always enjoys himself, ...?
9 Kim: Oh, great! *Puddle of Mudd!* Turn the music up a bit, ...?
Karen: Well, we can't make it much louder, ...? It's deafening[1] already.
10 Sanjay: Tell me when you're leaving. You won't go without me, ...?
Don: Well, actually, I'm about to leave now. We don't have to say Goodbye to everyone, ...?

13 *Just do it!* **imperatives**

▶ 13a/b

Jenny is giving her family and friends some advice. She is using negative and positive imperative forms, as in the examples.

Examples: Sister: I hate these fatty sausages. I prefer vegetables.
Jenny: *Well, **don't eat** them. **Have/Eat** some vegetables instead.*
Brother: I don't feel like doing my maths. I'd like to go out.
Jenny: *Well, **don't do** it. **Go out** instead.*

1 Brother: I hate tidying my room. I'd like to watch TV.
2 Sister: I don't feel like doing my French homework. Sending e-mails is more fun.
3 Simon: I don't like learning chemistry. I'd rather take biology next year.
4 Eve: This coffee's awful. It's too strong. I prefer cocoa.
5 Helen: I've got to go to Diana's party. Discos are more fun.
6 Sister: I don't like these sweet biscuits. I'd rather have some fruit.

---
1 deafening *ohrenbetäubend*

14 *My neighbourhood* **word order: main/subordinate clauses** ▶ 16

a Here's part of an exercise that your English teacher is correcting. The exercise is: 'Write about the people in your new neighbourhood.' Can you see the mistakes? Look at the word order. Are the verbs in the right place? Write the wrong sentences again, with the correct word order.

Example: I was sad when we moved because I all our neighbours liked.
*I was sad when we moved because **I liked** all our neighbours.*

1 I still don't know all the people who in our new street live.
2 Luckily, I know a girl who goes to our school.
3 When it rains, takes us her mother to school in the car.
4 Mrs Bayer, our next-door neighbour, is quite nice. If she calls, makes my mother her a cup of coffee.
5 Her children make a lot of noise before they to bed go.
6 When the boys from number 10 our house pass, they throw things in the garden, like chocolate papers and cans.
7 The dog at number 12 always barks when the paperboy comes.
8 Mr König, our neighbour on the other side, isn't very friendly. He complains because I my music too loud play.

b Now write three sentences about the people in your neighbourhood, one each with *who*, *when* and *because*. Be careful with the word order.

15 *Jingle bells* **word order: position of indirect object** ▶ 20a/b/c

a Jane, her brother Nick and their parents are discussing what to give their friends and relatives for Christmas. Complete the sentences with the words in brackets. Do not change the order. Add *to* or *for* where necessary, as in the examples.

Examples: Mrs J.: I'll make (Uncle Ron – his favourite cake).
I'll make ***Uncle Ron his favourite cake***.
Mr J.: But you can't send (it – him) by post.
But you can't send ***it to him*** by post.

1 Mrs J.: Then we'll take (it – him) on Christmas Day. And when he visits us, I'll cook (him – a Christmas dinner).
2 Jane: I'm going to give (my boyfriend – a photo of me in a frame[1]).
3 Nick: Well, I'm glad you're going to give (it – him) and not to me.
4 Mrs J.: I'm going to buy (grandmother – some new slippers[2]).
5 Nick: I'm going to get (some new socks – Uncle Ron) because sometimes he's got smelly feet ...
6 Jane: I shall write (beautiful Christmas cards – all my friends).
7 Nick: And I shall send (all mine – beautiful e-mails). It's cheaper.

1 frame *Rahmen* 2 slippers *Hausschuhe*

b Answer with *to* or *for*, as in the example.

Example: Is Nick getting grandmother the socks?
No, he isn't. He's getting the socks **for** *Uncle Ron.*

1 Is Mrs J. giving Uncle Ron new slippers?
2 Is Mrs J. making grandfather a cake?
3 Is Nick sending his grandparents e-mails?
4 Is Jane giving Nick a photo?
5 Is Jane sending cards to her family?
6 Is Mrs J. going to cook Uncle Peter a Christmas dinner?

c Now ask questions with *who*, like this:

Examples: Mrs J. – make – cake?
Who *is Mrs J. making a cake* ***for****?*

Jane – give – photo?
Who *is Jane giving the photo* ***to****?*

1 Mrs J. – buy – slippers?
2 Mrs J. – cook – Christmas dinner?
3 Jane – send – Christmas cards?
4 Nick – get – socks?
5 Nick – send – e-mails?

d What did you *give/buy/get/send* the following people for Christmas or birthdays last year?

1 your parents 2 your brother/sister 3 your grandparents 4 your best friend

Examples: *I* ***gave*** *my mother a scarf for her birthday.*
For Christmas I ***got*** *my father something for the car.*

16 *A bike theft* [1] **word order: indirect object with *to***

▶ 20d

Jerry is at the police station. Complete his conversation with the police officer. Put the words in brackets in the correct order and add *to* where it is necessary.

Example: Jerry's new BMX bike has been stolen. He's going to report (police – theft).
He's going to report *the theft* **to** *the police.*

1 P.O.: How did it happen? Did you leave your bike unlocked?
Jerry: Well, I'll explain (situation – you).
2 P.O.: What does the bike look like? Tell Constable Scott, will you?
Jerry: All right. I'll describe (him – it) as well as I can.
3 P.O.: Could you point out (thief – us) if we showed you some photographs?
4 Jerry: Oh, yes. My friend and I saw him close up. We could describe (you – him) in detail.
5 P.O.: Good. Then you can dictate (your statement [2] – Constable Scott). He'll take it down.
6 P.O.: And might I suggest (you – a piece of advice) in future? Never leave an expensive bike where you can't see it. You might not see it again.

1 theft *Diebstahl* 2 statement *Aussage*

Modal auxiliaries and be, have, do

A Which modal is correct?

1 Julie (had to/must) do her homework again yesterday because it was so untidy.
2 We (shouldn't/weren't allowed to) take photos in the palace, so we got some postcards.
3 Jill had an accident last week, but fortunately she (didn't have to/needn't) go to hospital.
4 I need some money. I (have to/must) go to the bank this afternoon.
5 Try the blue trousers on. They (can/might) fit better than the black ones.

B What would you say? Make offers, suggestions, requests, or ask permission in the following situations. Use modals. Sometimes there is more than one possible answer.

6 You're hungry. Make a suggestion to a friend. '... go for a quick snack somewhere?'
7 You need some money. Ask a friend. '... lend me five pounds until tomorrow?'
8 You would like to borrow a friend's magazines. Ask her. '... borrow these magazines?'
9 A little boy is carrying a heavy bag. Offer to help him. '... carry the bag for you?'
10 You want to make a phone call from someone's house. Ask politely. '... use your phone, please?'

C Spot the mistakes. There is one mistake in each sentence (pair).

11 I was late for school this morning. I missed the bus, so I must walk.
12 I've got a high temperature, so I needn't go out today, I'm afraid.
13 I'm sorry, but you are not able to smoke here.
14 If you don't feel well, you shall see a doctor.
15 You mustn't help me this time, thanks. I can do the exercise myself.

D Translate the German clauses in brackets into English.

16 *(Wir mussten nicht lange warten)* ... because there wasn't a queue.
17 *(Ich durfte nicht ausgehen)*... because I hadn't finished my homework.
18 *(Es könnte später regnen)*..., so put your anorak on.
19 *(Du darfst nicht über das Geschenk reden.)* ... It's a surprise.
20 *(Ann konnte nicht gehen)* ... for three weeks after her accident.
21 *(Ich werde viel sparen können)* ... next month. I'm getting money for my birthday.
22 *(Dürfen wir die Hausaufgaben später abgeben?)* ... We all need more time.

E Complete the conversation with suitable modals in the correct tense. Sometimes more than one verb is possible.

A: (23 you) ... to go to the disco next Saturday?
B: I'm not sure. We (24) ... go to my cousin's for the weekend. Why weren't you at the party last night?
A: I (25) ... go because I (26) ... babysit for the neighbours again. But they are very nice to me. I (27) ... to watch TV and play all their CDs, even computer games. I usually (28) ... make the little boy something to eat, but I (29) ... wash up or clean the kitchen. You (30) ... try babysitting too. It's a good way to earn extra pocket money.

F Translate the German sentence parts in brackets using a form of *be*, *have* or *do*.

31 *(Ich dusche immer)* ... before breakfast.
32 *(Gibt es ein chinesisches Restaurant)* ... in your part of town?
33 *(John machte seine Hausaufgaben nicht)* ..., so the maths teacher is angry.
34 *(Wann esst ihr sonntags zu Mittag?)* ... – Usually between one and two.
35 *(Es waren keine großen Äpfel im Supermarkt)* ..., so I didn't buy any.
36 *(Wer hat gestern eingekauft?)* ... Nobody gave me the change.

Modal auxiliaries and be, have, do

? Correct yourself

A 1: *had to* 2: *weren't allowed to* 3: *didn't have to* 4: *must* 5: *might*

B 6: *Shall we* 7: *Will you/Can you/Could you* 8: *Can I* 9: *Shall I* 10: *May I/Could I*

C 11: *... so I had to walk.* 12: *... so I mustn't go out ...* 13: *... you are not allowed to ...* 14: *... you should/ought to see a doctor.* 15: *You needn't help me ...*

D 16: *We didn't have to wait long* 17: *I wasn't allowed to go out* 18: *It might rain later* 19: *You mustn't talk about the present.* 20: *Ann couldn't/wasn't able to walk* 21: *I will be able to save a lot* 22: *May we/Could we give in the homework later?*

E 23: *Will you be able* 24: *may/might* 25: *couldn't/wasn't able to* 26: *had to* 27: *am allowed* 28: *have to* 29: *needn't/don't have to* 30: *should/ought to*

F 31: *I always have a shower* 32: *Is there a Chinese restaurant* 33: *John didn't do his homework* 34: *When/What time do you have lunch on Sundays?* 35: *There weren't any big apples at the supermarket* 36: *Who did the shopping yesterday?*

Exercise finder

Sentences	CEG	Exercises
1, 11, 26	▶ 41c	▶ 7a
2, 17	▶ 39d	▶ 4
3, 16	▶ 41c	▶ 7b
4, 28	▶ 41a	▶ 6
5, 18, 24	▶ 47a/b	▶ 11
6, 7, 9	▶ 43, 45	▶ 10
8, 10, 22	▶ 39b	▶ 5
12, 15, 19, 29	▶ 41a	▶ 8, 12
13, 27	▶ 39a	▶ 3
14, 30	▶ 42a	▶ 9, 12
20, 21, 23, 25	▶ 37c/d/f	▶ 1, 2, 12
31, 34	▶ 55	▶ 14
32, 35	▶ 52a	▶ 13
33, 36	▶ 57	▶ 15

1 *What can they do?* **ability:** ***can, could, be able to***

▶ 36, 37a-d/f

a What *can they do*? What *can't they do*?

Example: *Tina* ***can't speak*** *Italian, but she* ***can speak*** *English.*

windsurf ▪ ~~speak English~~ ▪ dive ▪ burn CDs ▪ play the guitar ▪ sing karaoke ▪ waterski ▪ dance ▪ use the Internet ▪ ~~speak Italian~~ ▪ swim ▪ play the drums

b What *could* and *couldn't you do* in the past? Use ideas from a) or your own ideas. Write three sentences with *could* and *couldn't*, as in the examples.

Examples: *Last year I* ***could use*** *Winword, but I* ***couldn't download*** *files.*
When I was ten, I ***couldn't play*** *tennis but I* ***could play*** *football.*

1 Last year …
2 Two/Three, etc. years ago …
3 When I was ten/eight, etc., …

c What *will you be able to do* when you leave school? Write three sentences.

Examples: *I* ***will be able to get*** *a job.*
I ***will be able to enjoy*** *my free time without homework.*

2 *Ben's accident* **can, could, be able to: various tenses** ▶ 36, 37a/b/c/f

a Ben has had an accident and is in hospital. Matt, a friend, meets Ben's sister Jane.
Complete the dialogue with *can/could* or a form of *(not) be able to*. In some cases both forms are possible. Be careful with tenses, and use negative forms when necessary.

Examples: Matt: Steve told me that Ben's in hospital. I've been busy with exams so I ***haven't been able to*** visit him. I wanted to phone him, but I ***couldn't/wasn't able to*** find the number that Steve gave me. What happened to Ben?

Jane: He had an accident playing football and hurt his knee[1]. He (1) … walk after the accident, but his knee's much better now after the operation. He (2) … get out of bed without help now. He (3) … come home soon, probably next week, but the doctor says he (4) … play football again until next summer.

Matt: I once broke my right arm. It wasn't so bad because I (5) … do any school tests for a few weeks. But after a time it was nice to (6) … do everything normally again – even homework. Well, tell Ben I've been busy with exams so (7) … visit him up to now. I'll see him at home next week. Bye!

b Have you or somebody you know ever broken an arm, a leg, a finger, etc.? What *couldn't you/weren't you able to do*? Write three sentences.

Examples: *I once broke my right thumb[2]. I **couldn't write** very well. I **wasn't able to play** ball games and I **couldn't use** the computer. I **wasn't** even **able to fasten** my buttons.*

3 *What does it mean?* **permission, prohibition: *be allowed to*; present** ▶ 38, 39a

You are visiting an English family in Cornwall. Their little boy is just four, so he can't read yet. When you are out with him, he asks you what the signs say. Can you explain to him what they mean using *is/are (not) allowed to …*? Parts of the sentences are done for you.

The sign means that …

Example: you … take your dog into the supermarket.
you ***are not allowed to*** take your dog into the supermarket.

Continue:
The sign means that …
1 only hotel guests … in the car park.
2 children over twelve … there.
3 nobody … in the bus.
4 visitors to the zoo …
5 you … in the museum.
6 everybody …

1 knee *Knie* 2 thumb *Daumen*

4 *House rules* **be allowed to: simple past, will-future** ▶ 38, 39d/e

a Angela has just returned from a year as an au pair in the USA. Unfortunately, her host family was rather strict. This notice was in her room.

House rules for au pairs

No parties.
No music after 9 pm.
Visitors only on Sundays (only two visitors - no male visitors please).
Please do not stick posters on the walls.
Use the telephone only in an emergency.
Showers every day, baths twice a week.
For personal clothing use washing-machine once a week only.
Please do not take food up to your room.
Please make hot drinks only in the kitchen.

Free day: Sunday Free evening: Saturday
(Please do not come home later than 11 pm.)

Thank you

Poor Angela. What was *she (not) allowed to do*? Write sentences as in the example:

Example: Music?
She ***was allowed to play*** *music only before nine pm.*
Or: *She* ***was not allowed to play*** *music after nine pm.*

1 Showers?
2 Food?
3 Washing-machine?
4 Posters?
5 Telephone?
6 Drinks?

b Angela's friends asked lots of questions about her stay. Here are her answers. What were their questions? Sometimes you need a question word. Use *when* or *how often*.

Example: A.: Parties? No, unfortunately. Not at all. Q.: ***Were*** *you* ***allowed to have*** *parties?*

1 A.: Yes, but not more than two girls.
2 A.: No, no boys at all.
3 A.: Twice a week, but showers daily.
4 A.: No, I wasn't. No food in my room.
5 A.: Only until nine o'clock at night.

c Imagine that you are going to have an au pair girl in your family next year. Write six sentences. What *will she be allowed to do* (three sentences)? What *won't she be allowed to do* (three sentences)?

Examples: *She* ***will be allowed to eat*** *with the family.*
She ***won't be allowed to drive*** *my parents' car.*

invite friends to her room
stay out all night
have a bath any time
eat with the family
stay in bed all day
drive your parents' car
use the phone whenever she wants
use your computer for e-mails
make calls on your mobile phone
borrow all your CDs
go out every evening
borrow your bike

5 *Staying with a host family* **request: *can, could, may, be allowed to*** ▶ 39b

Imagine you are in Brighton doing an English course. Your course teacher's name is Ted. You are staying with a family as a paying guest. The Ashtons are friendly and helpful. Dan, their son, is your age. You want to be polite. How would you ask permission[1] in the following situations? Use *can, could, may* or a form of *be allowed to*. Sometimes there is more than one suitable form.

Examples: You would like to invite a friend home after school. Ask Mrs Ashton.
Mrs Ashton, ***may/could I invite*** *a friend home after school, please?*
You have borrowed Dan's bike. But is it against English traffic regulations[2] to ride it on the pavement? Ask Ted.
Ted, ***are you allowed to ride*** *a bike on the pavement here?*

1 You don't want to eat meat. Ask Mrs Ashton if you can cook vegetarian food for yourself.
2 Dan and some friends are going to a football match on Saturday. You'd like to go with them. Ask Dan.
3 You are invited to a party which may go on until midnight. You would like to have a key, just for one night. You're not sure what the Ashtons will say. Ask Mr Ashton.
4 You've seen pedestrians[3] crossing the road when the light was red. People don't usually do that in Germany. Is it against the law in Britain? You're unsure. Ask Ted.
5 You've heard that the boy next door has a great collection of pop star posters. You'd like to see them. You've only met the boy once, but ask him.
6 There's going to be an English exam soon. You'd like to know if you can use an English dictionary in the exam. Ask Ted about it.

6 *A cheeseburger, please* **strong obligation: *must, have to*** ▶ 40, 41a

a Craig has got a holiday job in a fast food restaurant. His manager is strict. The employees have to do what he says. Complete the sentences with *have to/has to* or *must*, as in the examples.

Examples: The manager said to Craig: 'You must be on time every morning.'
So Craig ***has to be*** *on time every morning.*
The employees have to follow the manager's instructions.
The manager said: 'You ***must follow*** *my instructions.'*

1 The manager said to Craig: 'Your uniform must be clean every day.'
So Craig's uniform …
2 The employees have to be polite to customers.
The manager said to them: 'You …'
3 The manager said to Craig: 'You must wear your cap all the time.'
So Craig …
4 The manager said to the employees: 'You must get the orders right first time.'
So the employees …
5 Craig has to work quickly without chatting.
The manager said to him: 'You …'

1 ask permision *um Erlaubnis bitten* 2 traffic regulations *Verkehrsvorschriften* 3 pedestrian *Fußgänger*

b One evening Craig tells some friends about his job. Complete the conversation with *must*, *have to* or *has to*.

Craig: Well, I really ***must*** go to bed now. I ***have to*** get up at six-thirty.
Mark: Why so early?
Craig: Well, I (1) … start work at seven-thirty – making breakfasts. But that's nothing. One of the boys lives out of town, so he (2) … leave home at six. The manager is strict and not very nice. We all (3) … do exactly what he says.
Kate: Well, in that case we (4) … go now and let you go to bed. We'll see you tomorrow.
Craig: Sure. You really (5) … come and see me at work. I'll make you some special double burgers when the manager isn't looking.

7 *Hard work* ***must, have to*****: simple past; positive/negative**

▶ 41c

a Last year the students Ross, Kim, Lee and Lisa rented an old house. When they moved in, they *had to do* some work.
Look at the pictures. What *did the students have to do* in their rooms?

Use: clean ▪ clear away[1] ▪ ~~paint~~ ▪ put up ▪ repair (2×) ▪ sew[2] ▪ bookshelves ▪ carpet ▪ curtains[3] ▪ lamp ▪ old boxes ▪ ~~walls~~ ▪ wardrobe

Example: *Kim* ***had to paint*** *the walls.*

b The students *didn't have to repair* everything in the house. Make negative sentences with *have to* in the simple past, like this:

Example: The kitchen walls looked all right, so they (paint) …
… ***didn't have to paint*** *them.*

1 The kitchen cupboards were in order, so they (repair) …
2 The carpet in the living-room wasn't dirty, so they (clean) …
3 The bathroom tiles were clean, so they (wash) …
4 There were some nice curtains in Kim's room, so she (make) …
5 The bed in Lee's room was quite comfortable, so he (buy) …

1 clear away *aufräumen* 2 sew *nähen* 3 curtain *Gardine, Vorhang*

8 *Sue says* ***mustn't, needn't***

41a

What does Sue say to her friends and family in the following situations? Use *mustn't* or *needn't* and a suitable verb from the list:

~~be late~~ ▪ lose ▪ pay for ▪ get up early ▪ fail ▪ break ▪ forget ▪ watch ▪ walk ▪ ~~wash~~

Examples: To her boyfriend: The main film starts at 8.30. Let's go.
We ***mustn't be** late.*
To her mother: These jeans are clean, mum.
*You **needn't wash** them.*

1 Be careful with my fossils, you two. You …

2 The tickets for the match are free. We …

3 I've got the money for the class trip in my pocket. I …

4 The horror film on Channel Four tonight is stupid. You …

5 Sarah wants me to post this letter for her. I …

6 Janet's exam tomorrow is important. She …

7 Tomorrow's Saturday. Thank goodness. We …

8 I'll take you home on my motorbike, Mike. You …

9 *Trouble at home* **obligation: *should, ought to***

▶ 42a

a This is Lucy. She's sixteen and she's having problems at home. Probably both Lucy and her parents make mistakes and should try to change things. What *should* and what *shouldn't they* all *do* to improve the situation? Make sentences with *should* or *shouldn't* and the words in brackets, or use your own ideas.

Examples: Lucy's mother doesn't like her piercings. (be more tolerant)
*Lucy's mother **should be** more tolerant.*
Lucy's mother doesn't like the kind of clothes Lucy wears. (complain about)
*Lucy's mother **shouldn't complain about** Lucy's clothes.*

1 Lucy's father doesn't like her boyfriend. (criticize)
2 Lucy's room is in a terrible mess[1]. (tidy it up)
3 Lucy talks for hours on her mobile phone. (make big phone bills[2])
4 Lucy never helps with the housework. (offer to do things)
5 Her parents are too busy to listen to her problems. (find time)
6 Lucy plays loud music when her parents are trying to sleep. (think only of herself)
7 She does nothing for school and gets bad marks. (think about her future)
8 Her parents are not interested in her friends. (get to know)
9 At weekends Lucy stays in bed until the afternoon. (get up)

b What advice would you give Lucy? Make suitable sentences with *ought to* or *shouldn't*. Begin your sentences with *You …*

Examples: Lucy: My parents treat me like a child.
You: *You **ought to talk** to them/**show** them that you are not a child.*
Lucy: I get angry when my father criticizes me.
You: *You **shouldn't get** angry/**take** things so seriously.*

1 My parents are disappointed because I don't try hard in school.
2 They never have time for me.
3 My father is too strict. That's why I don't do what he tells me.
4 My parents don't take me seriously.
5 I'm thinking about leaving home.

c Work with a partner. Write a short paragraph about typical problems between pupils and teachers. Use *should/ought to* and *shouldn't*. What *should teachers and pupils do* to make the most of school time? What *shouldn't they do?*

Examples: *Some pupils talk in class. They **shouldn't disturb**[3] the lesson.*
*Some teachers get angry if you forget your homework. They **ought to be** more patient[4].*

1 mess *Durcheinander, Unordnung* 2 bill *Rechnung* 3 disturb *stören* 4 patient *geduldig*

10 *Requests, offers, suggestions* ***can, could, will, would, may, shall***

▶ 43-45

a You are staying in England with your penfriend for the summer holidays. How would you make suitable requests, offers or suggestions in the following situations? Choose from the modals in brackets. Sometimes two are suitable.

Example: You are shopping with your friend. You have forgotten your money. Ask your friend to lend[1] you ten pounds until tomorrow.
(would ▪ shall ▪ will ▪ may)
***Would/Will** you **lend** me ten pounds until tomorrow, please?*

1 You walk past a fast food restaurant with your friend. The hamburgers smell good and you're hungry. Make a suggestion.
(could ▪ won't ▪ will ▪ shall)
2 The boy next door calls, but your penfriend isn't at home. You have just put some cans of cola in the fridge. Offer the boy a cola while he's waiting.
(would ▪ may ▪ can't ▪ can)
3 A boy called Mick borrowed some of your CDs. You would like them back tomorrow. Ask him for them.
(can ▪ will ▪ may ▪ shall)
4 You'd like to go camping for the weekend with some friends. You haven't got a sleeping bag with you in England. The boy next door has one. Ask him if you can borrow it.
(can ▪ could ▪ will ▪ shall)
5 You and your penfriend are arranging a disco evening with some friends, but some of them can't go on Saturday. Suggest going on Friday instead.
(won't ▪ wouldn't ▪ can't ▪ couldn't)
6 Your penfriend lets you use his/her computer. You would like to download some information, but you're not quite sure how to do it. Ask him/her to show you.
(would ▪ could ▪ may ▪ shall)
7 You have chatted to someone interesting in an Internet chat room a few times. Suggest a meeting at the Internet café in the High Street.
(can't ▪ won't ▪ shouldn't ▪ needn't)
8 Your friend's mother is carrying some heavy bags of shopping. Offer to help her.
(can ▪ won't ▪ will ▪ could)

b Make a request, offer or suggestion to a friend in the following situations. If you think there is more than one possibility, write alternatives.

1 You would like to go for a pizza. Suggest it.
2 Your friend is carrying some heavy books. Offer to help.
3 You would like your friend to help you with your computer. Ask him/her.

1 lend *leihen*

11 *Clothes shopping* **probability, possibility** ▶ 47

Jane and Vicky are looking at clothes in a department store. Choose the correct modal.

Jane: Do you think these jeans ***will*** fit me?
Vicky: They ***might*** fit. You***'ll*** have to try them on.
Jane: What about this blue jacket? It's nice, but it's only size ten. I'm size 14.
Vicky: Oh, no. That (1 won't/couldn't) fit you. It looks much too small. Ask the shop assistant. She (2 can/might) have it in a bigger size.
Assistant: I saw a size 14 just an hour ago, and I haven't sold it. It (3 must/can) still be there.
Jane: But then, blue isn't really my colour. Look, I wonder how much this pullover costs. There's no price on it.
Vicky: Well, all the pullovers here are under 20 pounds, so it (4 can't/couldn't) be very expensive. The price tag (5 must/can) have fallen off.
Jane: I wonder where Helen is. She's late. She (6 may/should) have missed the bus. I expect she'll phone.
Vicky: Mmm. *(Her mobile rings.)* Oh, that (7 will/can) be her. Yes. Hi, Helen!

12 *Mobile phones – yes or no?* **modals: mixed exercise** ▶ 36-45, 47

In Britain, three out of four teenagers over 15 have a mobile. They're fun, trendy[1], adult – and dangerous? Read what Luke and Debbie think about mobiles. Complete their dialogue with the modals in the list. Before you begin, read the conversation through.

~~had to~~ ▪ can ▪ needn't ▪ was able to ▪ can't ▪ might not ▪
should ▪ couldn't ▪ mustn't ▪ have to ▪ may

Debbie: How many calls do you make on your mobile every day?
Luke: Too many. Last month my father ***had to*** pay my bill[2], because it was more than my pocket money. He wasn't pleased.
Debbie: Who do you call?
Luke: My friends, every evening.
Debbie: But surely you (1) … phone your friends on your mobile. That's really not necessary. You (2) … only use your mobile when you're not at home, and for important calls.
Luke: But my calls are important. They're usually about homework. And sometimes a mobile (3) … be really useful. Last week, a woman fell off her bike and broke her leg – right in front of me in Station Road. She (4) … stand up. I had my mobile with me, so I (5) … call an ambulance.
Debbie: I read that mobiles produce radiation[3]. Doctors say you (6) … make long calls at night because the radiation from the mobile makes your brain active, and then you (7) … sleep.
Luke: But mobiles (8) … be dangerous. The experts don't really know. Mobiles are good for text messaging too.
Debbie: Well, even that costs money, and I think text messaging is just a silly game. You (9) … have a lot of time and patience[4] to write a message.
Luke: You (10) … be right. But it's fun, isn't it?

1 trendy *angesagt, modisch* 2 bill *Rechnung* 3 radiation *Strahlung* 4 patience *Geduld*

13 *Learning English* **be used as a full verb: *there + be***

▶ 52a

a Rebecca teaches English to foreign students at a language school in Oxford. Complete what she says with *there + be*, in the necessary forms and tenses.

Examples: Hello. My name's Rebecca. Here's one of my EFL[1] classes. ***There are*** thirteen students on my present course. Last month ***there were*** fifteen, but next month ***there won't be*** more than ten or eleven.

The students come mainly from Europe, but last month (1) … even a girl from China. At the moment (2) … a boy from Iran, and next month (3) … two students from Japan. (4) … nearly always some students from Germany. Last month (5) … four in my group, but after summer (6) … any until the business courses start next October.

b Work with a partner. Ask and answer questions about the students and begin with *How many …?* Remember to use the correct tense of *be*.

Example: French – last month? (–)
You: ***How many*** *French students* ***were there*** *last month?*
Partner: ***There weren't*** *any.*

1 Italian – now? (1)
2 Swedish – last month? (–)
3 Russian – next month? (3)
4 Chinese – last month? (1)
5 French – next month? (–)

c Here's part of a brochure about Oxford, translated into German. Compare the English and German texts and fill in the missing English phrases with a form of *there + be*.

Example: In Oxford ***there is*** a course for everybody, whether pupil or top manager.

(1) … also a large variety of EFL language schools. Last year (2) … more language students in Oxford than ever before. Next year (3) … perhaps even more. (4) … courses of every kind, from beginners' courses to business seminars.
In Oxford (5) … a lot of language students from EU countries, but in the future (6) … more and more students from Eastern Europe and Asia.
(7) … perhaps an interesting course for you too?

In Oxford gibt es einen Kurs für jeden, ob Schüler oder Top-Manager.

Es gibt auch eine große Auswahl an EFL-Sprachschulen. Letztes Jahr waren in Oxford mehr Sprachschüler als je zuvor. Nächstes Jahr werden es vielleicht noch mehr sein. Es gibt Kurse aller Art, von Anfängerkursen bis hin zu Business-Seminaren. Es hat schon immer viele Sprachstudenten aus EU-Ländern in Oxford gegeben, aber in Zukunft werden es immer mehr Studenten aus Osteuropa und Asien sein. Gibt es vielleicht auch einen interessanten Kurs für Sie?

1 EFL *English as a Foreign Language*

14 *Daily routines* ***have*** **used as a full verb: activity verb**

▶ 55

a Tony and Jeff are brothers. Tony still goes to school and Jeff works as a trainee mechanic. Look at their daily routines.

	Tony	Jeff
a shower	8 o'clock (or later)	after work
breakfast	8.15	6.30
lunch	at school, 12.30	at the garage, 12.30
a break	11.00	9.30, 3.30
a sleep	after school	—
dinner	7.30	7.30

Say what you know about the two brothers using the activity verb *have*.

Example: Tony – shower
Tony ***has*** *a shower at eight o'clock.*

1 Jeff – shower
2 Tony – breakfast
3 Both boys – break – morning
4 Tony – sleep
5 Both boys – dinner

b Now look at the information again and complete the sentences about Jeff and Tony with *doesn't have/don't have*. Begin with *Jeff …*, *Tony …* or *The boys …*

Example: … shower before work.
Jeff ***doesn't have*** *a* shower before work.

1 … shower before eight o'clock.
2 … breakfast at 8.15.
3 … lunch before 12.30.
4 … break in the afternoon.
5 … dinner until 7.30.

c Ask a partner the following questions with the activity verb *have*. Use *Do you have …* (present tense) and *Did you have …* (past tense). Take turns to ask and answer.

Examples: you – lunch – at home?
Partner: ***Do you have*** *lunch at home?*
You: *Yes, I do, but sometimes I* ***have*** *a hamburger in town.*
you – party – on your last birthday?
You: ***Did you have*** *a party on your last birthday?*
Partner: *No, I didn't. I* ***don't*** *usually* ***have*** *a party on my birthday.*

1 you – sometimes – bath?
2 you – shower – this morning?
3 you – lunch – in town – last week?
4 you – hot dinner – every evening?
5 you – fun – the last time you went to the disco?

15 *Doing things* **do used as a full verb**

▶ 57

a What do you think the people in the pictures are saying? Match the speech bubble and the picture, then complete the bubble using an expression with *do* in its correct form.

Choose from: ~~do the dishes~~ ▪ do the housework ▪ do one's homework ▪ do the shopping ▪ do one's hair ▪ do well ▪ do a test

Example:

Oh, no! Who said it's my turn *to* ***do*** *the dishes*?

Shh! I have to concentrate[1]. I'm …

First the good news. It says I'm … in sports.

Oh, good. I see you've …

Mum's not here, so I have to … today.

I'm just … I hope you'll like it.

We … in the maths lesson.

b *Do you do* these things at home? You can use *sometimes*, *never*, *once*, etc. Write five sentences.

Examples: *I* ***don't do/never do*** *the washing*[2].
I once ***did*** *the cooking when mum was ill.*

1 do the washing
2 do the cooking
3 do the shopping
4 do the cleaning
5 do the ironing[3]

---

1 concentrate *sich konzentrieren* 2 do the washing *Wäsche waschen* 3 do the ironing *bügeln*

The tenses of the full verbs

A **Simple or progressive? Choose the correct form.**

1 What time (do you usually get up/are you usually getting up)?
2 My brother has got a holiday job this summer. He (works/is working) in a snack-bar.
3 I (walked/was walking) through the shopping mall when suddenly I met an old friend.
4 We (are often going/often go) camping to Italy in August.
5 I (have known/have been knowing) Julie since we were children.
6 I felt hot and tired because I (had been running/had run) in the park.
7 Jeff (was working/worked) on his geography project when I phoned him.
8 Beth is writing postcards. She (has written/has been writing) five so far.
9 My moped is broken, so I (walk/am walking) to school this week.
10 I'm sorry I'm late. (Have you waited/Have you been waiting) long?
11 What (were you doing/did you do) when I phoned you last night?
12 I (have downloaded/have been downloading) info about my favourite pop bands all morning.
13 Colin (passed/was passing) his driving test last year, on his eighteenth birthday.
14 Jill says her parents own a yacht, but I (am not believing/don't believe) her.
15 Rob isn't in. He (takes/is taking) the dog for a walk.

B **Complete the mini-dialogues. Choose from the tenses given in the simple or progressive form.**

present • present perfect • past

Tom: Where's Lisa? (16 she – still – work) … for her exams? I (17 not – see) … her for a month.
Ed: She (18 go) … to a concert. She (19 leave) … about half an hour ago.
Tom: I tried to phone you last night at about eight, but you weren't at home.
Ed: Oh, at eight o'clock I (20 sit) … in the cinema with Jeff and Rob. We (21 go) … to see *Men In Black 2*. It was great.
Tom: (22 you – see) … the new Stephen King horror film yet?
Ed: No, I (23 not – watch) … a horror film since *Alien 3*. I think they're stupid.

present perfect • past • past perfect

Ben: I (24 take) … an art course since January. It's on Tuesdays at seven. It's a lot of fun.
Ali: But you can't draw. You hated art in school.
Ben: You're right. I (25 never – draw) … a portrait in my life before I joined the art class. But, you see, last December I (26 meet) … a girl at a party. She (27 already – do) … the course for two months, so I decided to join too. Well, I (28 try) … to draw a portrait of our dog for five weeks now, and I (29 not – finish) … it yet. Poor Rover looks more like a donkey[1] – but I see Fiona every week. She's very good at art. So far she (30 do) … three portraits and some cool paintings. I think she likes me too. Yesterday evening she was hungry because she (31 not – have) … time to eat before the class. So afterwards we (32 go) … for a hamburger together.

1 donkey *Esel*

The tenses of the full verbs

? Correct yourself

A 1: *do you usually get up?* 2: *is working* 3: *was walking* 4: *often go* 5: *have known* 6: *had been running* 7: *was working* 8: *has written* 9: *am walking* 10: *Have you been waiting* 11: *were you doing* 12: *have been downloading* 13: *passed* 14: *don't believe* 15: *is taking*

B 16: *Is she still working* 17: *haven't seen* 18: *has gone* 19: *left* 20: *was sitting* 21: *went* 22: *Have you seen* 23: *haven't watched* 24: *have been taking* 25: *had never drawn* 26: *met* 27: *had already been doing* 28: *have been trying* 29: *haven't finished* 30: *has done* 31: *hadn't had* 32: *went*

Exercise finder

Sentences	CEG	Exercises
1, 4	▶ 75a, 78	▶ 6, 7, 11a, 12
2, 9	▶ 68, 77b, 78	▶ 3b, 10, 12
3, 7, 11, 20	▶ 89a/b, 90	▶26-28
5, 14	▶ 70	▶ 4, 5
6, 27	▶ 94	▶ 30
8, 30	▶ 83	▶ 18
10, 12, 24, 28	▶ 68, 82a, 83	▶ 3a, 16-18
13, 19, 21, 26, 32	▶ 86a, 87	▶ 19-25
15, 16	▶ 77a, 78	▶ 9, 11b, 12
17, 23	▶ 84	▶ 15
18, 22, 29	▶ 80a, 87	▶ 13, 14, 23-25
25, 31	▶ 92a	▶ 29

A **Choose the correct form from the brackets.**

1 I suppose the bus (comes/will come) late again.
2 Janet has got her boots on. She (is going to take/will take) the dog out.
3 Hi! I (will meet/am meeting) some friends in the pizza bar. Do you want to come?
4 The next bus to Winchester (is leaving/leaves) at 8.30, I think.
5 Look at the dark sky. It (is raining/is going to rain) soon.
6 What (are you going to be/will you be) when you grow up? – A racing driver, of course.
7 Are you going to the youth club? Just a moment, I (go/will go) with you.
8 Beth (will study/is going to study) biology at university.
9 How many pages (will you read/will you have read) by this evening?
10 What (will you be doing/will you do) next year at this time?

B **Now put in the correct tense/form of the verb given.**

simple present • *will*-future • *going to*-future • future progressive

Jeff: What time (11 your train – leave) … this afternoon? I (12 take) … you to the station on my motorbike if you like.
Carol: Thanks, but look at those black clouds. It (13 rain) … I don't want to get wet.
Jeff: OK. Well, I'm sure you (14 enjoy) … your weekend in London.
Carol: Yes, tomorrow afternoon at this time I (15 shop) … in Oxford Street. Great!

present progressive • *will*-future • future perfect

Penny: Hi, Serena. What (16 you – do) … tonight?
Serena: Nothing special. I expect I (17 stay) … at home and watch TV.
Penny: We (18 go) … to the cinema to see *Die Another Day* at eight. Why don't you come?
Serena: Well, I don't think there (19 be) … enough time after supper.
Penny: But you (20 finish) … eating by seven-thirty, surely. So just come.

C **Spot the mistakes (present/past/future time). There is one mistake in each sentence (pair).**

21 David didn't eat his lunch. Look, his plate's still full.
22 I lost my new sunglasses. I can't find them anywhere.
23 Look. It rains again.
24 We have been here since two hours.
25 At the moment everybody talks about the new *Nickelback* album.
26 Have you gone to the concert last night?
27 Do you go anywhere tomorrow afternoon?
28 I was very thirsty because I didn't have a drink since breakfast.
29 Ray lives in Stratford, but just now he spends a holiday in Wales with some friends.
30 We have met Phil in town a week ago.
31 At this time next week I will sit in the sun on the beach.
32 Beth knows David for five years.
33 By next year at this time I will save over two hundred pounds.
34 What have you done yesterday?
35 I couldn't buy anything because I forgot my money.

Correct yourself

A 1: *will come* 2: *is going to take* 3: *am meeting* 4: *leaves* 5: *is going to rain* 6: *are you going to be* 7: *will go* 8: *is going to study* 9: *will you have read* 10: *will you be doing*

B 11: *does your train leave* 12: *will take* 13: *is going to rain* 14: *will enjoy* 15: *will be shopping* 16: *are you doing* 17: *will stay* 18: *are going* 19: *will be* 20: *will have finished*

C 21: *David hasn't eaten his lunch …* 22: *I have lost my new sunglasses …* 23: *Look. It is raining again.* 24: *We have been here for two hours.* 25: *At the moment everybody is talking about …* 26: *Did you go to the concert last night?* 27: *Are you going anywhere tomorrow afternoon?* 28: *… because I hadn't had a drink since breakfast.* 29: *Ray lives in Stratford, but just now he is spending a holiday …* 30: *We met Phil in town a week ago.* 31: *At this time next week I will be sitting …* 32: *Beth has known David for five years.* 33: *By next year at this time I will have saved over two hundred pounds.* 34: *What did you do yesterday?* 35: *I couldn't buy anything because I had forgotten my money.*

Exercise finder

Sentences	CEG	Exercises
1, 14, 17, 19	▶ 96a	▶ 31, 35,40
2, 5, 13	▶ 98b	▶ 34
3, 16, 18, 27	▶ 99	▶ 12, 36, 40
4, 11	▶ 100	▶ 37
6, 8	▶ 98a	▶ 33, 35, 40
7, 12	▶ 96b	▶ 32, 35
9, 20, 33	▶ 104	▶ 39, 40
10, 15, 31	▶ 102a	▶ 38, 40
21, 22	▶ 80a, 87	▶ 13
23, 25	▶ 77a, 78	▶ 9, 11b, 12
24, 32	▶ 80b, 84	▶ 15
26, 30, 34	▶ 86a, 87	▶ 19-25
28, 35	▶ 92a	▶ 29
29	▶ 77b, 78	▶ 10, 11b, 12

1 *Spelling check* **3rd person singular simple present, *-ing* form**

▶ 64a/b, 65

a Make three lists. Write the 3rd person singular simple present of these verbs in the correct list.

buy ▪ carry ▪ ~~catch~~ ▪ come ▪ cry ▪ do ▪ enjoy ▪ fly ▪ go ▪ ~~hurry~~ ▪ miss ▪ mix ▪ say ▪ study ▪ teach ▪ try ▪ walk ▪ wash ▪ watch ▪ ~~work~~

Examples:

-s	-es	-ies
works	*catches*	*hurries*
...	...	...

b Now write the 3rd person singular simple present of the following verbs. How do they fit into the puzzle?

fly ▪ have ▪ go ▪ wish ▪ travel ▪ be

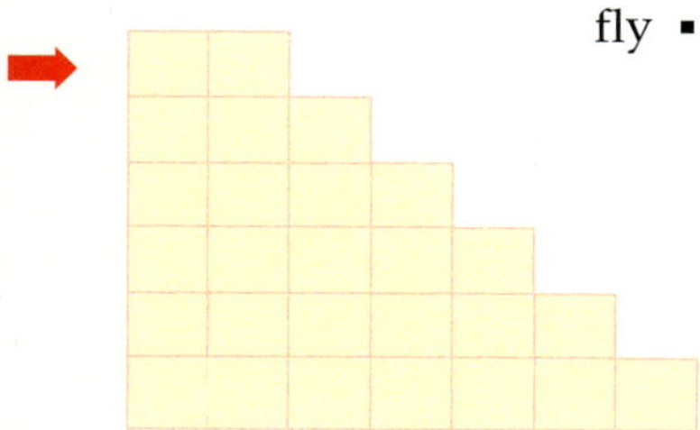

c Can you spot five spelling mistakes in the following list of *-ing* forms? Tick (✔) the right ones and correct the wrong ones. Use British spelling.

dancing	✔
planing	*planning*
prefering	
lying	
comming	
stopping	
offerring	
running	
controling	
swiming	
hoping	

d Now write the *-ing* forms of these verbs. How do they fit into the puzzle?

fit ▪ travel ▪ lie ▪ promise ▪ hurry ▪ rise

2 *Check your forms* **simple past form, past participle**

▶ 66, 79, 85

a Which ending makes the correct simple past form of these regular verbs? Write the number.

+ ed	**+ d**	**y → ied**	**double consonant + ed**
1	**2**	**3**	**4**

Examples: remember	*1*	carry	*3*
hurry	—	cook	—
watch	—	rob	—
dry	—	plan	—
wish	—	enjoy	—
chat	—	invite	—
phone	—	drop	—

b Write the simple past forms of these irregular verbs in the puzzle. Where do they fit? If you're not sure, count the letters.

bring ▪ catch ▪ grow ▪ mean ▪ meet

➡

c Simple past form or past participle? Which is which? Make two lists, like this:

~~eaten~~ ▪ ~~flew~~ ▪ seen ▪ stole ▪ swum ▪ wrote ▪ drunk ▪ broke ▪ was ▪ did ▪ driven ▪ forgot

Examples:

simple past	**past participle**
flew	
	eaten

d Now put the missing forms into the lists.

e Use six of the past participles from your list to complete what these people say.

Example: I have ***forgotten*** the address.

1 I have … all my homework.
2 Someone has … my bike.
3 My sister has … her arm.
4 I have … some letters.
5 We haven't … to Turkey.
6 Have you … *Jurassic Park 3*?

3 *Simple or progressive?* **aspect: simple form, progressive form**

▶ 68

a Can you match the statements to the pictures? Write down the right letter and number.

Example: *Tony **is playing** football with some friends.*

Example: *Tony **plays** football for the school team.*

1 Dan has been reading comics all morning.
2 Janet speaks German quite well.
3 Laura is working at the computer at the moment.
4 Dan has read three comics this morning.
5 Laura works for a software firm called ICM.
6 Janet is speaking German to her penfriend in Bremen.

b Would you use the simple or the progressive form to translate these sentences into English? Write '*s*' or '*p*'.

Examples: Nick ist Verkäufer. Er arbeitet in einem Sportgeschäft in der Walton Street. *s*
Diesen Sommer arbeitet Nick als Animateur in einer Ferienanlage auf Mallorca. *p*

1 Angela singt in einer Rockband.
2 Hör zu. Angela singt gerade ein neues Lied.
3 Diese Woche arbeitet Paul als Aushilfe in einer Autowerkstatt.
4 Paul arbeitet immer fleißig.
5 Sally hat heute drei Bewerbungen geschrieben.
6 Sally schreibt schon den ganzen Tag Bewerbungen.

4 *Quick and easy* state verbs ▶ 70

a Which verbs can we use in the progressive form? (✔) Which verbs do we not usually use in the progressive form (state verbs)? (✘)

listen	✔	prefer	☐	recognize	☐	learn	☐
own	✘	hurry	☐	need	☐	seem	☐
drive	☐	believe	☐	visit	☐	try	☐
know	☐	contain	☐	suppose	☐	want	☐

b Choose four state verbs from the list and use them to make four sentences in the simple present.

Example: own *Mark says his father* ***owns*** *a yacht and a house in Spain.*

5 *Meet Chris* activity verbs, state verbs ▶ 69, 70

a This is Chris with his girlfriend Nicki. He has written a letter to a new pen pal in Berlin. Chris lives in a small village, but he doesn't like village life. In his letter, he tells his pen pal about it. Which verb forms does Chris use in his letter? Simple or progressive? Choose the correct one.

Hello, Markus!

*Last time I told you about my school. Now I'll tell you about where I live – and about my girlfriend. I (**live**/am living) in a small village just outside Exeter. I (1 am knowing/know) most people in the village. They are friendly – sometimes too friendly. They (2 want/are wanting) to know everything. I (3 am not liking/don't like) village life much. Whenever I can, I (4 go/am going) to town with my girlfriend, Nicki. But she's not at home just now. She (5 does/is doing) a course in London. She (6 learns/is learning) to be a physiotherapist, so she (7 is working/works) in a big hospital for three months. She (8 is seeming/seems) to like it. I (9 love/am loving) London too. I (10 am preferring/prefer) city life to village life. People (11 don't watch/aren't watching) you all day. In the city your neighbour (12 isn't asking/doesn't ask) you questions every time he (13 sees/is seeing) you.*
Here's a photo of Nicki and me. We (14 are taking/take) my dog for a long walk. We usually (15 go/are going) in the woods with him. At least the neighbours (16 don't watch/aren't watching) us there.

I hope you'll tell me all about life in Berlin. How wonderful to live in a big city!

Best wishes, Chris

b Imagine you are Markus. Can you answer Chris's letter? Tell him about yourself, your friends, your school, city life, etc.

6 *Meet Mike* — simple present: actions/events that happen repeatedly, regularly ▶ 74, 75a

Read about Mike and put in the correct form of the missing verbs. Use the simple present and think about the spelling. How quickly can you get it all right?

buy ▪ chat ▪ do ▪ get up ▪ ~~go~~ ▪ know ▪ leave ▪ ~~live~~ ▪ read ▪ stop ▪ tell ▪ want ▪ ~~work~~

Examples: Mike ***lives*** in Luton and he ***goes*** to the comprehensive school there.
His parents both ***work***.

Mike's parents (1) … the house early, so he (2) … more or less what he (3) … He almost always (4) … too late. On the way to the bus stop he (5) … at the newsagent's[1]. He (6) … a comic every day and (7) … it standing up in the bus. Some of the regular passengers (8) … him. They sometimes (9) … about football and (10) … jokes.

arrive ▪ catch ▪ get ▪ give ▪ hurry ▪ look forward to ▪ miss ▪ pass ▪ plan ▪ say ▪ take ▪ try

Mike normally (11) … the 8.35 bus, but he sometimes (12) … it. The bus ride (13) … about twenty minutes. He (14) … to school but he usually (15) … late to the first lesson. The teachers (16) … angry, of course. They often (17) … him extra homework. Time (18) … slowly at school. Mike never (19) … hard to do well. He always (20) … the breaks when he and his friends (21) … their evening activities. He (22) … that's the best thing about school.

7 *When school is out …* — simple present with adverbs of frequency ▶ 74, 75a

a What do these Year 11 teenagers do after school? How often do they do it? Write sentences in the simple present, as in the examples.

	never	sometimes	often	usually	always
go straight home	~~Pam~~				Ed, Janet
look round the shops		~~Liz, Kate~~			
meet friends				Cathy	
hang around[2] in town			Ann, Lucy		
play football	the girls	Ben			
go for a hamburger		Dave	Chris, Ed		
phone some friends				Nicola	Sita, Beth

Examples: *Pam **never goes** straight home.*
*Liz and Kate **sometimes look** round the shops.*

Continue:
1 Ed and Janet …
2 Cathy …
3 Ann and Lucy …
4 The girls …
5 Ben …
6 Dave …
7 Chris and Ed …
8 Nicola …
9 Sita and Beth …

b What about you? What do you and your friends do after school? Write five sentences in the simple present, one each with *never*, *sometimes*, *often*, *usually*, *always*.

Examples: *I **never do** my homework immediately[3] after school. My best friend **usually comes** home with me.*

1 newsagent *Zeitungshändler/in* 2 hang around *herumhängen* 3 immediately *sofort*

8 Choose a pen pal **simple present: permanent states; positive/negative**

▶ 74, 75b

a Kim, Josie and Steve would like to write to you, but you don't have time for three pen pals. Look at the things they like and don't like, etc. Perhaps it will help you to choose. Write sentences in the simple present, as in the examples.

	Kim	Josie	Steve
What I like:			
punk hairstyles	✗	✓	✗
politics	✗	✓	✓

Examples: *Josie* ***likes*** *punk hairstyles.*
Kim and Steve ***don't like*** *punk hairstyles.*
Josie and Steve ***like*** *politics.*
Kim ***doesn't like*** *politics.*

	Kim	Josie	Steve
What I enjoy:			
1 school	✗	✗	✓
2 parties	✓	✗	✓
What I hate:			
3 snakes[1], spiders[2]	✗	✓	✓
4 homework	✓	✓	✗
What I find boring:			
5 shopping	✓	✗	✓
6 sightseeing holidays	✓	✓	✗

b Now you. What *do you like, enjoy, hate* and *find boring*? Use the ideas in a) or your own.

Example: *I* ***like*** *punk hairstyles.*
Or: *I* ***don't like*** *punk hairstyles.*

Continue.

c Who would you choose as a pen pal? Why? Give three reasons.

Example: *I would choose Steve as a pen pal because he* ***doesn't like*** *punk hairstyles, he* ***enjoys*** *parties and he* ***hates*** *snakes and spiders.*

1 snake *Schlange* 2 spider *Spinne*

9 *A barbecue* **present progr.: actions/events that are in progress; pos./neg.** ▶ 76, 77a

a It's five o'clock on Saturday afternoon. Teenagers at the Brentwood Youth Club are having a barbecue. Describe the picture in the present progressive. What is happening at the moment?

Use: carry ▪ dance ▪ eat ▪ enjoy ▪ grill ▪ lie ▪ play ▪ serve[1] ▪ ~~shine~~ ▪ ~~sit~~

Examples: *The sun **is shining**.*
*Jill and Marion **are sitting** under an umbrella.*

1 Loud music … from the loudspeakers.
2 Four teenagers …
3 Ali and Sam … on the grass.
4 Katie and Jenny … food.
5 Sanjay … chops[2] and sausages.
6 Dave … a big chop.
7 Sandra … bottles of cola to the table.
8 Everybody … the barbecue.

b It's six o'clock on the same afternoon. What is different now? Write six sentences in the present progressive negative form. The sentences in a) will help you.

Example: *The sun **isn't shining** now. It's raining.*

1 serve *servieren* 2 chop *Kotelett*

10 *Summer jobs* **present progressive: repeated actions that are temporary** ▶ 77b

a The summer holidays have started. Some *pupils* from Rose Hill Comprehensive *are* already *doing* holiday jobs. *Who is doing* what? Use the present progressive and the notes below.

Example: do farm work – Devon – for the whole of the holidays
*Bina **is doing** farm work in Devon for the whole of the holidays.*

do restoration work – old churches – for five weeks
serve petrol – local garage – until September
look after children – local kindergarten – for four weeks
clean stables – riding school – for three weeks
work on a dig[1] – Scotland – until the end of August
clean up old steam engines – Wales – for the whole of the holidays

b Work with a partner. Write a list of holiday jobs. Imagine *you* and *your friends are doing* these jobs. Write a short dialogue. Ask and answer questions using the present progressive. Here are some ideas.

work at/in a shop/restaurant	clean offices
serve[2] in a café	help out at a garage/supermarket/garden centre
deliver[3] pizzas	drive a taxi

Example: You: ***Are** you **doing** a job these holidays?*
Partner: *Yes, I am. I**'m working** at Burger Castle for six weeks.*
You: *What **are** your friends **doing**?*
Partner: *Ben**'s delivering** pizzas and Julia and Jürgen **are serving** in a café.*

1 dig *Ausgrabungsstätte* 2 serve *servieren* 3 deliver *liefern*

11 *Term time and holidays* **simple present, present progressive**

▶ 78

a This is David.  Look what *he* usually *does* in the week.

Monday	Wednesday	Friday	Saturday morning	Saturday evening	Sunday morning	Sunday evening

play football ▪ ~~do taekwondo~~ ▪ sleep until lunch time ▪ help his father ▪ go to the youth club ▪ do his homework ▪ practise the guitar

Example: *On Mondays he **does** taekwondo.*

Continue: 1 On Wednesdays he …
2 …

b Now it's the school holidays. What's different? What *is David doing* now?

Monday	Wednesday	Friday	Saturday morning	Saturday evening	Sunday morning	Sunday evening

sit in a café with friends ▪ shop in town ▪ enjoy an evening at the cinema ▪ dance at the disco ▪ play computer games ▪ cycle with friends ▪ ~~watch TV~~

Example: *It's Monday. David usually **does** taekwondo, but now he **is watching** TV.*

Continue: 1 It's Wednesday. David usually … , but now …
2 …

12 *Mini-dialogues* **simple present, present progressive** ▶ 78, 99

Look at the short conversations between Dan and his mother. Which forms do you think they use, simple present or present progressive? Complete the mini-dialogues with the correct form of the verb in brackets.

Dan: I ***am going*** (go) to my judo class now.
Mum: Take your raincoat. It ***is still raining*** (still – rain).
Dan: I ***know*** (know). It ***always rains*** (always – rain) on Tuesdays.

1 Mum: Where's Laura? (1 she – still – phone) … her boyfriend?
Dan: No, she (2 watch) … something on TV at the moment. Then she (3 go) … out.
Mum: Where (4 she – go) … ? (5 you – know) …?
Dan: To Sarah's. She (6 always – go) … to Sarah's on Mondays.

2 Dan: James (7 work) … at Smith's book store for the whole of the summer holidays.
Mum: Oh? He (8 usually – work) … at Rowntree's, doesn't he?
Dan: Yes, but not this year. They (9 not – pay) … him enough. I (10 meet) … him in town soon. We (11 do) … some shopping together. Max (12 come) … too. He (13 work) … at Piper's garage for six weeks, but he (14 not – work) … on Friday afternoons.

3 Mum: What time (15 you – come) … home tonight?
Dan: I can't say. We (16 practise) … for our karaoke competition at the youth club.
Mum: (17 you – bring) … your friends home with you?
Dan: Well, mmm … , what (18 you – make) … for supper?
Mum: Chinese tonight, chicken chop suey.
Dan: Oh, cool. You (19 know) … that when you (20 make) … chop suey, I (21 always – bring) … my friends with me. Well, I (22 go) … now. Bye!

13 *Consequences*[1] **present perf.: actions/events with consequences for the present** ▶ 80a

a Can you match the actions or happenings in A with the results or consequences in B?

Example: *I've hurt my foot.* → *I can't run.*

A	B
~~I've hurt my foot~~.	~~I can't run~~.
1 I've bought some new glasses.	a Now I can buy a car.
2 Someone has taken my rucksack.	b I shall get wet.
3 I haven't had lunch yet.	c I can see better now.
4 Simon hasn't eaten all the cake.	d She can't go to the youth club.
5 I've passed my driving test.	e I'm really hungry.
6 I've forgotten my umbrella.	f I can't find it anywhere.
7 The shops have closed.	g She's feeling miserable.
8 Jane hasn't done her homework.	h There's some left.
9 Sally has quarrelled[2] with her boyfriend.	i You should stay at home.
10 You've caught a cold.	j We can't buy any bread now.

1 consequence *Folge* 2 quarrel *(sich) streiten*

b Work with a partner. Write five sentences in the present perfect, as in A (five actions/happenings). Exchange sentences with your partner. Now write five suitable results/consequences (as in B) to match your partner's sentences.

Examples: You: *Dave **has lost** his Saturday job.* (action/happening)
Partner: *Now he has no money.* (result/consequence)

14 *Have you ever … ?* present perfect with phrases of time

▶ 79, 80a

a Which of these things *have you …*
… never done? … often done? … done once or twice? … not done yet?

1 eat Mexican food
2 do a bungee jump
3 speak English on the telephone
4 be on television
5 fail a test or exam
6 see a snake
7 win a prize
8 put up a tent
9 make lasagna
10 stay up all night
11 go to Italy

Use the phrase which is true for you.

Examples: *I **have** often **eaten** Mexican food.*
*I **have** never **done** a bungee jump.*
*I **haven't been** on television yet.*
*I **have failed** a test once or twice.*

b Now write four sentences about other people, for example a good friend or a member of your family.

Examples: *My sister **has** never **made** lasagna.*
*My grandmother **hasn't done** a bungee jump yet.*

c Work with a partner. Ask questions to find the following four things:

1 something you have both done
2 something neither of you has done
3 something only you have done
4 something only your partner has done

Ask questions and give short answers.

Examples: You: ***Have** you ever **been** to the USA?*
Partner: *Yes, I **have**.* Or: *No, I **haven't** (but I **have** always **wanted** to).*
You: ***Have** you ever **won** any money?*
Partner: …

15 For *or* since? **present perfect with *for* and *since***

80b, 84

a Where would you use *for*? Where *since*?

Example: *I **haven't seen** Tom **for** two weeks.*
*I **haven't seen** Tom **since** Christmas.*

Make a table, like this:

for	since
two weeks	*Christmas*

Put these phrases into the table:

last week ▪ a long time ▪ last Tuesday ▪ we left school ▪ several years ▪ my birthday ▪ weeks ▪ I visited him in hospital ▪ 1998 ▪ two months

b Add four more phrases to each list.

c Now complete what the people are saying with the present perfect and *for* or *since*.

Example:

… so I ***have had*** it ***for*** *five months.*

Example:

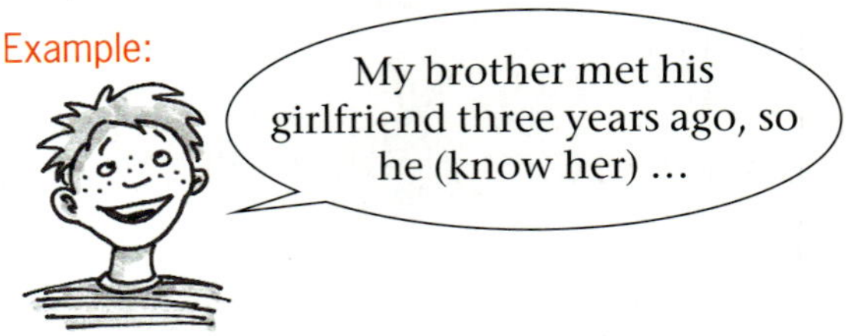

… so he ***has known*** her ***since*** *1999.*

1

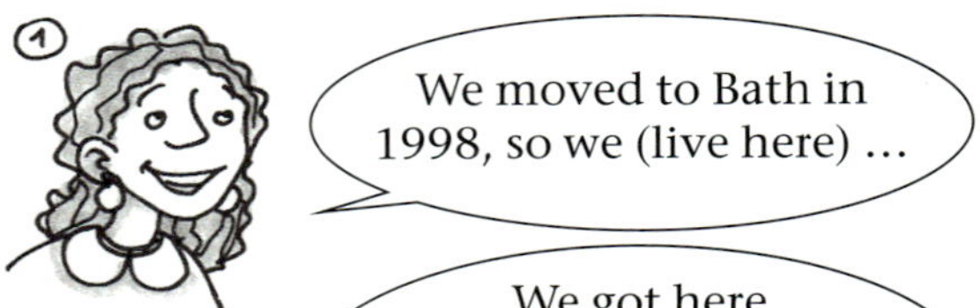

2

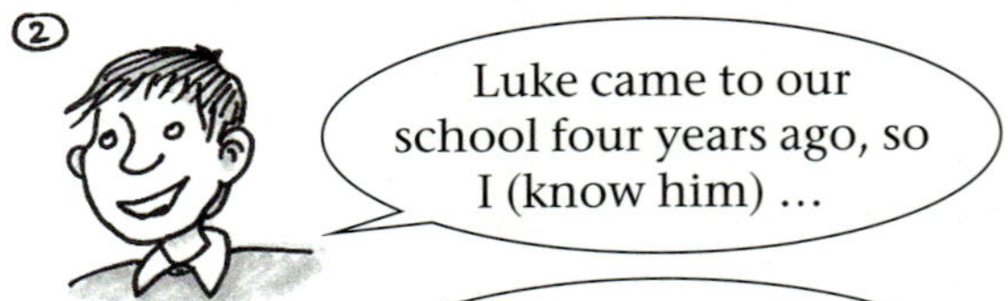

3

4

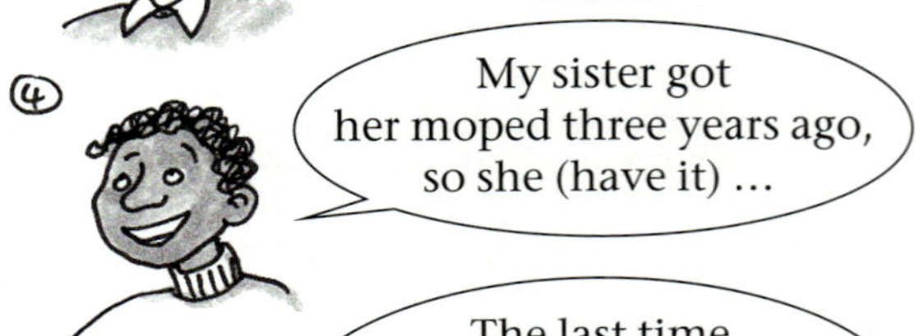

5

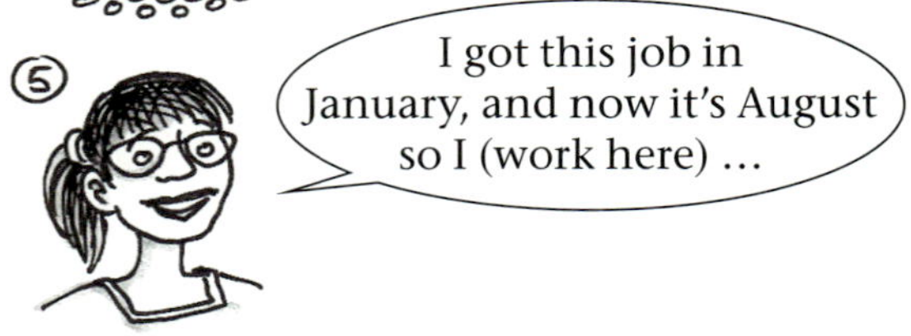

6

d Work with a partner. Ask him/her these questions with the verbs *know*, *live* and *be*. Answer with *for* or *since*. Then ask two more similar questions with *work* and *have*.

1 How long have you known your best friend?
2 How long have you been at this school?
3 How long have you lived here?
4 How long have you had your bike?

1 dentist *Zahnarzt/-ärztin*

16 *What have they been doing?* **present perfect progressive** ▶ 81, 82

a What *have the people* in the pictures *been doing*?
Answer the questions using these words:

oil – bike ▪ chop[1] – onions ▪ lie – sun ▪
~~run – park~~ ▪ walk – woods ▪
watch – horror movie ▪ work – computer

Example: Why is Jerry out of breath?
Because he ***has been running*** *in the park.*

1 Why does Martin look tired?
2 Why are Jane's eyes red and swollen?
3 Why have Pat and Ben got mud[2] on their boots?
4 Why are Gemma's face and arms red?
5 Why has Terry got oil on his hands?
6 Why do Pam and Rachel look nervous?

b Work with a partner. Ask three questions and give three answers. Use *tired, hot, dirty* and the present perfect progressive.

Example: You: *Your hands are dirty. What* ***have*** *you* ***been doing?***
Partner: *I****'ve been helping*** *my mother to clean out the cellar*[3].

1 chop *hacken* 2 mud *Schlamm* 3 cellar *Keller*

17 *Evening classes* **present perfect progressive with *for* and *since***

▶ 82, 84

a In England evening classes are very popular. The following people are all doing courses at their local adult education centre. Who is learning what? How long *has he/she been learning* it? Give answers in the present perfect progressive with *for* or *since*.

Pam	*Aromatherapy*	*January*
	Russian Здравствуй!	*2 months*
Jason	*Yoga* 	*3 months*
	Karate	*March*
Beth	*German*	*April*
	Web site design	*4 months*
Ben	*Multimedia*	*6 months*
	Russian	*2 months*
Anita	*Guitar* 	*February*
	German	*April*
Jerry	*E-commerce* 	*September*
Megan	*Jazzdance*	*April*
	Multimedia	*6 months*

Examples: Who's doing a course in aromatherapy?
*Pam. She***'s been doing** *it* **since** *January.*
Who's learning Russian?
*Pam and Ben. They***'ve been learning** *it* **for** *two months.*

1 Who's doing yoga?
2 Who's taking a course in German?
3 Who's learning e-commerce?
4 Who's doing a course in multimedia?
5 Who's learning karate?
6 Who's taking a course in web site design?
7 Who's learning the guitar?
8 Who's taking a class in jazzdance?

b Are you learning a language or doing a course? How long *have you been doing* it? Write two sentences.

Example: You: *I'm learning French. I* **have been learning** *it* **for** *three years.*
Partner: *I'm doing a course in IT*[1] *at school. I***'ve been doing** *it* **since** *last September.*

1 IT = Information Technology *Informationstechnologie*

18 *Describe the pictures* **present perfect, present perfect progressive**

▶ 83

Describe the pictures using the present perfect simple or progressive of the given verb.

write

Example: Sue is writing letters.
She … letters all morning.
She ***has been writing*** letters all morning.

Example: She … four so far.
She ***has written*** four so far.

1 **repair**

There's something wrong with Mike's motorbike. He … it for hours.

At last he … it.
Now everything's fine.

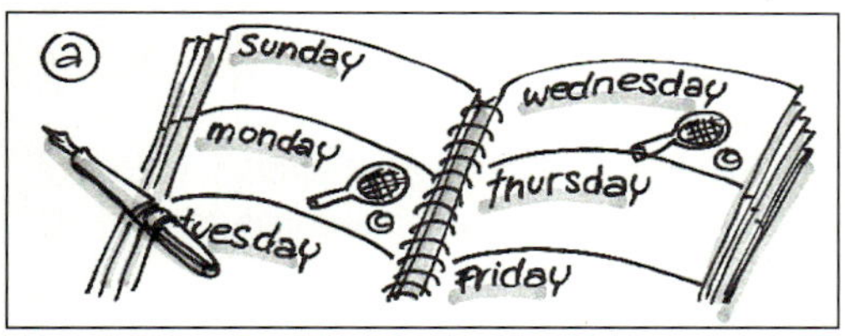

2 **play**

Jan and Kim … tennis twice this week.

This is the third time. They … tennis all afternoon.

3 **learn**

Jeff … German for four years.

He … almost all the irregular verbs.

4 **snow**

The children are happy.
It … every day this week.

It … since yesterday evening.

19 *What did you do, and when?* **simple past with phrases of time**

▶ 85, 86a

a Look at the phrases of time (*last year*, etc.) and write sentences which were true for you, your family and friends at those times. Write about everyday things, or use your imagination. Use the simple past in the positive (+) or negative (–) form, as in the examples.

Example: My parents … last year. (+)
My parents ***bought*** *a new car* last year.

Example: Last night I … (–)
Last night I ***didn't go*** *to bed until midnight.*

1 Last Saturday I … (+)
2 We all … two years ago. (+)
3 My best friend … yesterday. (–)
4 Last week I … (–)
5 My mother … yesterday afternoon. (+)
6 On my last birthday I … (+)
7 We … last Friday. (–)
8 In my last holidays I … (+)
9 A week ago a friend of mine … (+)
10 My parents … last night. (–)

b When was the last time *you did* the following things? Use the simple past and a time expression.

Example: clean your shoes
*I **cleaned** my shoes two days ago.*

1 brush your teeth
2 phone your best friend
3 buy something new
4 go to a party
5 listen to the news
6 help at home

20 *A weekend in London* **simple past: past actions/events; negative**

▶ 85, 86a

a Tim, John, Mel and Anna have just returned from a weekend trip to London. There wasn't enough time to see and do everything. What *didn't they do*? Complete the sentences with simple past negative forms.

Example: They went to Westminster Abbey, but *they **didn't go*** to St. Paul's Cathedral.
Tim: I saw Buckingham Palace, but *I **didn't see*** Hampton Court Palace.

1 Mel: I bought lots of postcards, but … many souvenirs.
2 John: We took a tour of the Houses of Parliament, but … a tour of Windsor Castle.
3 Tim: We went to the disco *Camden Palace*, but … to the *Underworld*.
4 Anna looked round Dali Universe, but … the Tate Gallery.
5 Tim: We got tickets for the musical *Fame*, but … tickets for *The Lion King*.
6 John: We ate burgers and pizzas. … in expensive restaurants.
7 Tim and John visited Rock Circus. … Madame Tussaud's.
8 Anna: We walked through Soho, but … through Chinatown.
9 Mel shopped in Oxford Street. … at Harrod's.
10 John saw Hyde Park, but … Regent's Park.

b Now translate these sentences into English. Use the simple past and the words in brackets.

1 Sie haben nicht im Ritz gewohnt. *(stay at)*
2 Tim kaufte keine Souvenirs. *(not … any)*
3 Leider *(unfortunately)* haben sie Prinz William nicht gesehen.
4 Anna besuchte den Tower nicht.
5 John und Mel gingen nicht in einen Pub.
6 Mel hat keine Stadtrundfahrt gemacht. *(do – bus tour)*

21 *The story of Fred* **simple past: past actions/events, stories**

▶ 86a/b

a The picture story shows what *happened* to Fred in just one week, about a year ago.

Tell the story of Fred in the simple past. Choose words from the list and add some words of your own.

skis ▪ ~~lose~~ ▪ £100.000 ▪ lottery ticket ▪ break ▪ buy ▪ Switzerland ▪ find ▪ eat ▪ fly ▪ Gino's ▪ win

Example: On Monday Fred ***lost*** *his job.*

1 On Tuesday he …
2 On Wednesday he …
3 On Thursday he …
4 On Friday he …
5 On Saturday he …
6 On Sunday he …

b Continue the story in the simple past. Use the words below and your imagination. Add a few details, for example adjectives, names, times and places. The beginning is done for you.

Example: in hospital – meet – nurse
In hospital in the Swiss Alps Fred ***met*** *a pretty young nurse called Heidi. His arm and his leg were broken, but he still* (1) …

(1) feel happy (2) fall in love (3) leave hospital (4) give – diamond ring (5) get married (6) go on honeymoon[1] – Bahamas (7) sun – shine – every day (8) spend – lottery winnings (9) at home – sell – skis (10) buy – fifty tickets for next lottery

1 honeymoon *Flitterwochen*

22 *Boyfriends* **simple past: questions, short answers**

▶ 85, 86a

a After school Amy and Beth are chatting about boyfriends. Amy wants to know about Beth's first date with Terry. What were Amy's questions? Use the question form of the simple past. Then complete Beth's short answers.

Examples: Amy: ***Did** you **meet** Terry in town?* — Beth: Yes, *I* ***did***.
Amy: ***Did** he **get** there on time?* — Beth: No, *he* ***didn't***. He got there early.

Amy:	Beth:
1 you – wear – new jeans?	No, … I wore my black trousers and a new top.
2 you – go – disco?	Yes, … To that new one near the Odeon.
3 you – like – it?	Yes, … It was great. The DJ is really cool.
4 you – see – anybody we know?	No, …
5 Terry – take – you – home – car?	Yes, …
6 he – ask you out – again?	No, … I asked him.

b Now it's Beth's turn to ask Amy questions. Look at Amy's answers. What were Beth's questions? Be careful, one question is negative. Use these question words:

where ▪ who ▪ what ▪ when ▪ how much ▪ why

Examples: Beth: ***Where did** you **go** yesterday afternoon?*
Amy: To town to do some shopping.
Beth: ***Who did** you **go** with?*
Amy: With Tim, my new boyfriend.

1 Beth: … buy?
Amy: A pullover and some boots.
2 Beth: … ?
Amy: The pullover only cost £20, but the boots were expensive – £75.
3 Beth: … in the evening?
Amy: To the cinema.
4 Beth: … see?
Amy: The new Will Smith film. It was great.
5 Beth: … get home?
Amy: Not too late. About eleven.
6 Beth: … your homework?
Amy: I didn't do it.
7 Beth: … do it? It was for today.
Amy: Because I was too tired.

A letter **present perfect, simple past**

▶ 87

a Here is a letter from Kate to her friend Liz. Can you complete it with the correct tense, present perfect or simple past?

Hi, Liz!

We **have been** *in Mallorca since last Saturday and we (1 have) ... a great time up to now.*

The weather (2 be) ... marvellous all the week. It (3 not - rain) ... so far and we (4 be) ... in the hotel pool or in the sea every day.

Last night we (5 go) ... to a super disco. My brother (6 meet) ... a nice Spanish girl. She (7 can) ... speak English, so he (8 not - have to) ... speak Spanish. They (9 dance) ... together all the evening. I think he (10 fall) ... in love! I (11 also - make) ... some nice friends here, but I (12 not - meet) ... anyone special so far - unfortunately. I (13 take) ... lots of photos to show you.

How (14 be) ... your trip to Greece? (15 you - have) ... a good time? (16 you - meet) ... anyone exciting?
What a pity that I (17 leave) ... home before you (18 get) ... back.

See you soon. Ciao!
Kate

b Imagine you are on holiday. Write a short postcard to a good friend back home.
You can use ideas from Kate's letter. Use the present perfect and the simple past.

24 *Visitors to Germany* **present perfect, simple past; questions** ▶ 87

You meet a group of British teenagers who are hitchhiking[1] through Germany. You start a conversation with them, but they don't speak much German.
How do you ask them the following questions in English? Present perfect or simple past?

Example: Wie lange seid ihr schon in Deutschland?
*How long **have** you **been** in Germany?*

Example: Wann seid ihr hier angekommen?
*When **did** you **arrive** here?*

1 Seid ihr auch in *(to)* anderen Ländern gewesen?
2 Seid ihr schon in Berlin gewesen?
3 Wann seid ihr dort gewesen?
4 Was habt ihr dort gesehen?
5 Hat es euch dort gefallen?
6 Welche Städte habt ihr auch noch besucht? *(Which other …)*
7 Seid ihr in Köln *(Cologne)* gewesen?
8 Habt ihr den berühmten Kölner Dom *(cathedral)* gesehen?
9 Wo seid ihr letztes Wochenende hingefahren?
10 Nach München? Habt ihr am letzten Sonnabend das Fußballspiel gesehen?

25 *Chat before school* **present perfect, simple past** ▶ 87

Some Year 11 pupils are chatting before school. Complete the mini-dialogues with the present perfect or the simple past.

1 Al: Where's your sister? She ***hasn't been*** (not – be) to school for over a week.
Tim: Oh, she ***has gone*** (go) to the States for a year. Last year she ***applied*** (apply) to do a high school year in the USA and she (1 get) … a place in Boston.
Al: (2 she – write) … a letter home yet?
Tim: No, she (3 not – have) … much time. She only (4 leave) … last week. But she (5 phone) … home as soon as she (6 arrive) … there, so we know she's all right.

2 Ann: (7 you – see) … Ashraf this morning?
Rob: No, but I (8 just – arrive)… Perhaps he (9 already – go) … to the physics lab.
Ann: No, I (10 already – look) … in the lab. He isn't there.
Rob: Well, then, he (11 not – arrive) … yet. Why the hurry to see him?
Ann: I (12 lend) … him five pounds last week and he (13 still – not – pay) … me back.

3 Jane: I (14 buy) … some really fantastic jeans. You'll love them.
Penny: Great. When (15 you – buy) … them?
Jane: Yesterday, in that new boutique in Winslow Road.
Penny: How much (16 they – cost) …?
Jane: Forty-five-ninety-nine. And I almost (17 buy) … some new trainers[2].
Penny: More trainers? You (18 not – wear) … the last ones you (19 buy)…
Jane: Of course I have. I (20 wear) … them twice last week and I (21 wear) … them three times this week so far.

1 hitchhike *per Anhalter fahren* 2 trainers *Turnschuhe*

26 *What were they doing?* past progressive ▶ 88, 89

a Last night at nine o'clock the electricity went off in Wilton Street. What *were* all *the people* in the street *doing* when it happened?
Look at the pictures and give answers in the past progressive.

Example: *At number 1 the Millers* ***were watching*** *television.*

At number 2 Mr Johnson ..., and Mrs Johnson ...
At number 3 ...

Continue.

b Now you. What *were you doing* at the following times? Use the past progressive.

1 at six o'clock yesterday evening
2 at seven o'clock this morning
3 at 11.30 last night
4 at two o'clock yesterday afternoon

27 *Accidents* **simple past, past progressive**

▶ 90

a The patients in the hospital waiting room have all had an accident. How *did the accident happen*? What *were they doing*? Join the sentence parts with *when* and use the simple past and the past progressive.

Example: Mrs Jones – fall – ladder / clean – windows
*Mrs Jones **fell off** the ladder when she **was cleaning** the windows.*

1 Mrs Baxter – burn – hand / take – cake – oven
2 Mr Granger – hurt – back / move – furniture
3 Billy – hurt – leg / play football
4 Mr Simpson – bump[1] – head / clean out – attic[2]
5 Mrs Walker – cut – finger / chop[3] – onions
6 Kate – fall off – bike / ride – to school

b Now you. When was the last time that you hurt yourself or had an accident? What happened? What *were you doing* when *it happened*? Write two sentences as in a) above, one sentence about yourself and one about your family or a friend.

Example: *A year ago I **broke** my arm when I **was skiing**.*
*Last Easter my parents **had** a car accident when they **were driving** to Berlin.*

28 *Jenny's story* **simple past, past progressive**

▶ 90

a Last night Jenny went to the cinema with a friend. Can you complete the story with the simple past or the past progressive in the correct form?

Examples: After the cinema Jenny ***caught*** the last bus. There ***were*** a few teenagers in the bus who ***were going*** home after the disco – and a man opposite her.

Jenny (1 notice) … that the man (2 watch) … her. When she (3 get off) … the bus, it (4 rain) … and the wind (5 blow) … the leaves from the trees. She (6 look) … behind nervously. The street (7 be) … empty apart from a man who (8 cycle) … in the other direction[4]. Jenny suddenly (9 feel) … frightened. She (10 still – think) … about the murdered girl in the film. Just as she (11 cross) … the road, she (12 hear) … footsteps behind her.
Someone (13 follow) … her. She (14 begin) … to run. Her heart (15 beat) … loudly. Not far now, almost home. Only two more streets. She (16 feel) … in her bag for her keys – but where were they? Thank goodness. Home at last, but no lights on. Everybody (17 sleep) … Then suddenly she (18 feel) … a hand on her arm. She (19 ring) … the door bell in panic. 'Hey, Miss. Your keys. You (20 drop) … them in the bus. Goodnight!'

1 bump *stoßen* 2 attic *Dachboden* 3 chop *hacken* 4 direction *Richtung*

b Have you ever felt frightened? Where were you? What *were you doing*? What *happened*? Write a short paragraph. If you can't think of a true story, work with a partner and make a story up.

Example: *I **was babysitting** for our neighbour. The children **were** asleep so I **was watching** TV. Suddenly someone **knocked** at the door. I …*

Or: Write a short paragraph about a bad dream that you once had. Where were you in your dream? Describe the scene. What *were you doing*? What *were others doing*? What suddenly *happened*? Use your imagination.

Example: *In my dream I **was running** through a long tunnel. It **was** cold and dark. Someone **was chasing** me. Suddenly I **heard** a scream.*

29 *A bad day …* past perfect

► 91, 92a

a Chris had a really bad day yesterday. Everything went wrong. Why did things go wrong? What *had happened* before?

Decide which action came first, then write one sentence with the past perfect and *because*. Hint[1]: write the numbers 1 and 2 over the sentences. Of course you use *because* and the past perfect for the action which came first. Study the examples.

Examples: [2] He got up late. [1] He didn't set his alarm clock.
*He **got up** late because he **hadn't set** his alarm clock.*

[1] He went out without breakfast. [2] He felt hungry.
*He **felt** hungry because he **had gone out** without breakfast.*

1 He missed the bus to school. He was late for the first lesson.
2 He forgot his wallet[2]. He couldn't buy anything to eat in the break.
3 He failed the French test. He didn't learn any grammar.
4 He couldn't play football in the sports lesson. He left his football boots at home.
5 He forgot to set the video recorder. He missed his favourite sports programme.
6 His girlfriend saw him flirting with another girl in the break. She was very angry.
7 He couldn't phone the other girl. He lost the phone number.
8 He didn't do his homework. He couldn't go out in the evening.

b Think of something annoying that happened to you last week. What happened and why? What *had you done* or what *hadn't you done*?

Example: *Last week I wanted to stay overnight at a friend's. My parents said no because I **hadn't done** any homework for three days.*

1 hint *Tipp, Hinweis* 2 wallet *Brieftasche*

30 *What had they been doing?* **past perfect progressive**

▶ 93, 94

a What *had the people* in the pictures *been doing*? Add a suitable sentence.

Jane

1 Ed

2 Mr Parker

3 Janet and Kim

4 Liz and Tom

5 Mrs Ashton

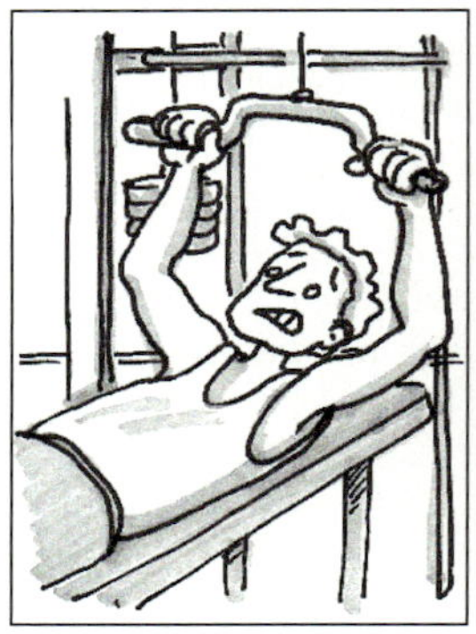

6 Pete

7 Gina

Example: In the evening Jane felt very tired.
She ***had been learning*** *for an exam all day.*

1 Ed felt annoyed because the film had started. He …
2 When Mr Parker went to bed, his back hurt. He …
3 At eight o'clock in the evening Janet and Kim were tired. They …
4 Liz and Tom felt hot and tired. They …
5 Mrs Ashton's clothes were wet. She …
6 When Pete got home from the fitness club, his muscles hurt. He …
7 Gina was glad when the lesson was over. She …

b When was the last time that …

1 you felt very tired? 2 you felt angry? 3 you were wet? 4 your feet hurt?

What *had you been doing*? Write four sentences with *because*.

Example: *I felt very tired last Saturday because I* ***had been training*** *with our football team all afternoon.*

31 *A class trip* ***will*-future: predictions, assumptions**

▶ 95, 96a

a Simon and Melanie are discussing the class trip to Athens. Simon has negative feelings about the trip. Melanie thinks *it will be* fun. Complete the sentences with *will* or *won't* and the words in brackets.

Examples: Simon: I (suppose – we – have to) go on study trips to old ruins every day.
I suppose we ***will have to*** go on study trips to old ruins every day.
Melanie: I (sure – the Greek ruins – bore) us. They are really quite beautiful.
I'm sure the Greek ruins ***won't bore*** us …

1 Simon: I (expect – hotel – be) small and not very nice.
2 Melanie: Well, (it – certainly – be) a five-star – perhaps a two-star, or a one-star …
3 Simon: I (hope – we – have to) get up at seven every morning.
4 Melanie: Well, that doesn't matter. I (sure – it – be) more fun than school.
5 Simon: I (hope – the teachers – bore) us with Greek history.
6 Melanie: I (suppose – Mr Jones – talk) about temples all day.
7 Simon: (Perhaps – there – be) much free time.
8 Melanie: Perhaps not, but I (sure – there – be) time for swimming and sunbathing.
9 Simon: I (suppose – whole trip – be) mega-boring.
10 Melanie: I (think – most of us – have) a good time – you too.

b What *will you* probably *do* in your next holidays? Write three sentences beginning with *I think*, *I expect* or *I suppose*.

Examples: *I expect I* ***will stay*** *at home.* *I suppose we'****ll go*** *somewhere where it's hot.*

c What *won't you do* in your next holidays? Write three sentences using *I/we won't …*

Examples: *I (certainly)* ***won't lie*** *in the sun all day.*
We (certainly) ***won't go*** *camping again.*

32 *A helping hand* ***will*-future: spontaneous decisions**

▶ 96b

You're a friendly, helpful person. What would you say to your family and friends in the following situations? Make suitable short sentences with *I'll* or *I won't* and the verb in brackets. You can begin with *OK …*, *All right …*, *Well …*, *Don't worry …*, etc. if suitable.

Examples: Dad: There's someone at the door. (see)
*OK. I'****ll see*** *who it is.*
Friend: I don't think Rob should know about our plan. (tell)
All right. I ***won't tell*** *him.*

1 Mum: There's someone on the phone for Dad. (tell)
2 Dad: I don't like that music. (play)
3 Friend: I've lost my red pen. (lend[1])
4 Mum: Be careful with those glasses. (break)
5 Sister: I can't do this maths homework. (help)
6 Friend: This present for Liz is a secret. (tell)
7 Mum: Those sandwiches are for later. (eat – now)
8 Sister: Take good care of my CDs. (lose)

1 lend *leihen*

33 *Future jobs* *going to*-future: intentions, plans

▶ 97, 98a

a These pupils have already got plans for their future. What do you think *they are going to do*? Choose from the answers in the box.

study medicine ✔
become an actress
open a fitness club
work in tourism
study space technology
become a mechanic[1]
study information technology
learn graphic design
work in the fashion industry
play professional tennis
work in a research laboratory

I want to be a doctor.

Angela

Example: *Angela* ***is going to study*** *medicine.*

I love cars and engines.

1 Pete

I've won a lot of tennis tournaments[2].

2 Zoe

Ted and I are both computer freaks.

3 Dave

I'm good at drawing and designing things.

4 Jane

I love acting, dancing and singing.

5 Jill

Simon and I both like doing experiments.

6 Luke

I'm interested in aerobics and fitness training.

7 Sally

Ann and I both love clothes and fashion.

8 Sue

I find spacecraft fascinating.

9 Will

I'm very interested in foreign travel.

10 Brian

b What *are you going to do* when you leave school? Write two sentences. What *are you not going to do* when you leave school? Write two sentences.

Examples: ***I'm going to travel*** *for a year. /* ***I'm going to do*** *an au pair year in England.*
I'm not going to go *to university. /* ***I'm not going to get*** *a job immediately*[3] *after school.*

1 mechanic *Mechaniker/in* 2 tournament *Turnier* 3 immediately *sofort*

34 *What's going to happen?* ***going to*-future: present signs for actions/events** ▶ 98b

a What *is going to happen* in the pictures?
Use: ~~fall off~~ ▪ break ▪ crash ▪ drop ▪ rain ▪ sink ▪ walk into

Example: Jack …
Jack ***is going to fall off*** *the ladder.*

1 Penny …

2 The ice …

3 Tony …

4 It …

5 The boat …

6 Tom …

b Look around you (e.g. in the classroom, out of the window). What *are people going to do*? Look at the weather. What *is going to happen*? Write three sentences.

Examples: *Brigitte* ***is going to write*** *on the board. The sun* ***is going to come out.***

35 *Money talk* ***will*-future, *going to*-future** ▶ 96, 98a

Some teenagers are talking about money. Find the correct form to complete the mini-dialogues.

1 Tony: I got some money for Christmas. Perhaps I (***will***/am going to) buy something for my computer, like a good graphics card.
Don: I (***am going to***/will) save my Christmas money for a new bike.

2 Pat: I (am going to/will) stay with a friend in Poole at Easter.
Anna: I've got an aunt in Poole. There are some great shops there.
Pat: Oh. Then perhaps I (will/am going to) buy something cool.

3 Joe: *(To the shop assistant)* I (will/am going to) take this poster, please. Oh, I haven't got enough money.
Ed: I (will/am going to) lend you some. Here are five pounds.
Joe: Thanks. I (am not going to/won't) forget to pay you back.

4 Jane: Pat (will/is going to) look for a Saturday job. She needs some money.
Emma: Good idea. Perhaps she (will/is going to) get something at Smith's where I work on Saturdays. I (am going to/will) ask my boss.

5 Chris: (Are you going to/Will you) buy a ticket for the open air rock festival?
Lisa: I'm afraid I (am not going to/won't) be able to go. No money.

36 *Are you doing anything tonight?* **present progressive: future arrangements** ▶ 99

a Jeff is bored. He phones lots of people, but *they are* all *doing* other things tonight. What do they answer? Use the present progressive.

Example: Liz: Sorry, Jeff. I – meet – friends – six o'clock
*I'm **meeting** some friends at six o'clock.*

1 Pete: Yes, I am. Tim – come – seven-thirty.
2 Laura: Sorry, Jeff. I – wash – hair – tonight.
3 Latif: Paul and I – play – computer games.
4 Jill: I – write – letters – tonight.
5 Steve: I – go – sports centre – Ed.
6 Pam: Ann and I – do – history project.
7 Kim: Mick – pick me up – seven.
8 Lucy: Sorry, Jeff. I – go – pizza – Dave.

b Now you. What *are you doing* at the following times? Give answers in the present progressive.

Example: Tonight?
*I **am staying** at home tonight.*

Continue: On Friday night? On Saturday afternoon? On Sunday?

37 *A study trip* **simple present: timetable future** ▶ 100

Ben's class is going on a study trip to the Lake District. Mr Gray, their teacher, is telling them about the programme.
What does he tell the class? Complete the sentences with a suitable verb in the simple present.
Here are Mr Gray's notes:

Monday, 1st:	*bus from school main gate*	*9.30 a.m.*	*Tuesday:*	*tour – Geological Museum*	*10 a.m.*
	stop on way – lunch	*12.30 p.m.*		*guided tour Wordsworth Museum*	*2 p.m.*
	arrive Grasmere	*5 p.m.*			
	4 nights youth hostel		*Thursday:*	*Ruskin Museum in Coniston*	*10 a.m.*
Wednesday:	*climb Helvellyn (950m)*				

Example: Mr Gray: *Our trip **starts** on Monday 1st.*

The bus (1) … from the main gate at 9.30. We (2) … for lunch at 12.30, and the bus (3) … in Grasmere at about five o'clock. We (4) … at the youth hostel for four nights. On Tuesday we (5) … the Geological Museum with its wonderful rocks and minerals. After that in the afternoon we (6) … a guided tour of the Wordsworth Museum. You know, of course, that Wordsworth was a famous poet[1]. On Wednesday we (7) … Helvellyn, the third highest mountain in the Lake District. On Thursday we (8) … the Ruskin Museum in Coniston. You know, of course, that Ruskin was another famous writer.

Ben to Nick: Oh no. This sounds like hard work …

1 poet *Dichter/in*

38 *At this time tomorrow …* future progressive

▶ 101, 102a

a The young people in the pictures are thinking about what *they will be doing* at a future time. Make sentences with the future progressive, as in the example.

Example: Debbie is doing a maths test. (fly – L.A.)
She's thinking: At this time tomorrow *I* ***won't be doing*** *a maths test. I'****ll be flying*** *to L.A.*

John is sitting in his office. (lie – beach)
He's thinking: At this time tomorrow I …

Sarah is studying for exams. (work – model)
She's thinking: At this time next year I …

Susie is doing homework. (ride – new motorbike)
She's thinking: At this time next week I …

Phil and his friend are watching a stupid film. (give – first concert)
Phil's thinking: At this time next week we …

b *Will you be doing* any of these things next week at this time? Write two sentences, one with *I'll be* and one with *I won't be*, as in the examples.

Examples: *I'****ll*** *(probably)* ***be doing*** *my homework.*
I (certainly) ***won't be dancing*** *at the disco.*

1 studying for a test
2 doing homework
3 sitting in school
4 dancing at the disco
5 having a party
6 watching TV

39 *Saving up* **future perfect** ▶ 103, 104

Luke and Kim are saving up. They spend most of their pocket money, but they both have Saturday jobs. Luke earns about £150 a month. He spends only £40, so he can save the rest. Kim earns about £135 a month and she spends about £50.
It's January. How much *will they have earned*, *spent* and *saved* at the following times in the future?

Example: after two months – Luke – earn
After two months Luke ***will have earned*** *£300.*

1 after two months – Kim – earn
2 after three months – Luke – save
3 after three months – Kim – spend
4 after six months – Luke – earn
5 after six months – Luke – spend
6 by the end of the year – Luke – save
7 by the end of the year – Kim – save

40 *Kate's birthday* **future time: mixed exercise** ▶ 96, 98a, 99, 102a, 104

a Kate and Janice are talking about Kate's birthday. Complete the dialogue in the following tenses:
will-future (4×), *going to*-future (3×), present progressive (3×), future progressive (2×), future perfect (2×)

Kate: I (be) … eighteen on May 1st.
I ***will be*** eighteen on May 1st.
Janice: (you – have) … a party? Who (you – invite) …?
Are *you* ***going to have*** a party? Who ***are*** *you* ***inviting?***
Kate: Well, it nearly always rains on my birthday, so I expect it (1 rain) … this year too. But yes, I (2 have) … a party.
Janice: Perhaps you (3 be) … lucky. Perhaps it (4 rain) … How many people (5 come) … to the party?
Kate: Well, I (6 invite) … all the class, and a few other friends. We (7 have) … a barbecue, and afterwards Tony's band (8 play) … for us. Just imagine. Two weeks today I (9 celebrate) … my first 'adult' party.
Janice: And six weeks today we (10 do) … our first 'adult' exams – A-levels. But by the end of July we (11 leave) … school. And by then we (12 get) … good jobs – I hope. By the way, do you know what your boyfriend (13 give) … you as a present?
Kate: Well, he wants it to be a surprise – but his sister has told me. A puppy[1]!
Janice: A puppy? But you've got exams soon.
Kate: I know. That's the problem. The puppy certainly (14 be) … a surprise – for my parents …

b Work with a partner. Write a dialogue about someone's birthday, presents, party, etc. Use future forms. You can use ideas from part a).

Example: You: *It* ***will be*** *my brother's birthday on the 28th.*
Partner: *Oh! How old* ***will*** *he* ***be? Is*** *he* ***going to have*** *a party?*
You: *He****'ll be*** *sixteen, so …*

1 puppy *Welpe*

The passive

A Complete the short dialogues with active or passive verb forms.

simple present (3 ×)

A: A lot of people (1 learn) … English as a foreign language.
B: Yes, English (2 understand) … all over the world.
A: In Switzerland four languages (3 speak) … officially, but not English.

simple past (2 ×) • past perfect (2 ×)

A: My CD player (4 repair) … yesterday. The man in the shop (5 repair) … it while I waited.
B: They had some DVD players on special offer last week. I wanted to buy one yesterday, but they (6 already – sell) … Pity, the shop (7 reduce) … the price by 30%.

present perfect (2 ×) • *will*-future (2 ×)

A: I'm going to the *Linkin Park* rock concert in May. I (8 buy) … a ticket.
B: So have I. More than 3000 tickets (9 sell) … so far. In fact, I think the concert (10 sell out) … very soon. They're a great band. Their new single (11 release[1]) … next month.

B Now put in the correct passive tense or form.

12 Do you know what time the postbox (usually – empty) …?
13 The mechanic says that our car radio can't (fix) … until next week.
14 Do you think our maths tests (give back) … in the next lesson?
15 Your football boots (not – clean) … for a few weeks. They are full of mud[2].
16 When Sue flew to Toronto, she (meet) … at the airport by her penfriend.
17 When I went to get my bike from the garage, I realized that it (steal) …

C The following sentences are active, but they can also be expressed in the passive. Try it. Where do you need *by* and where not? Think carefully.

18 You must leave your bags outside.
19 The Japanese design a lot of new computer games.
20 Annabel's parents gave her a computer.
21 An Englishwoman wrote the *Harry Potter* books.
22 They told me to sit down and wait.
23 People say that Julia Roberts is the best-paid actress in the world.
24 In the year 2000 they held the Olympic Games in Sydney.
25 A firm in Bristol has offered Martin a good job.
26 Someone has stolen Tim's moped.
27 You should invite Mike to your party. – 28 He always asks you to his.

D Spot the mistakes. There is one mistake in each sentence (pair).

29 Our new house is finished in June next year.
30 In our history lesson us was told something about American politics.
31 It was told that Mr Walker was going to be made headteacher, but it wasn't true.
32 *Romeo and Juliet* was written from Shakespeare. Everybody knows that.
33 Mobile phones may not been used during lessons.
34 A group of skiers have been killed through an avalanche[3] in the Alps.
35 To him was promised a better job and more money.

1 release *veröffentlichen* 2 mud *Schlamm* 3 avalanche *Lawine*

The passive

? Correct yourself

A 1: *learn* 2: *is understood* 3: *are spoken* 4: *was repaired* 5: *repaired* 6: *had already been sold.* 7: *had reduced* 8: *have bought* 9: *have been sold* 10: *will be sold out* 11: *will be released*

B 12: *is usually emptied?* 13: *be fixed* 14: *will be given back* 15: *haven't been cleaned* 16: *was met* 17: *had been stolen.*

C 18: *Your bags must be left outside.* 19: *… computer games are designed by the Japanese.* 20: *Annabel was given a computer by her parents.* 21: *The 'Harry Potter' books were written by an Englishwoman.* 22: *I was told to sit down and wait.* 23: *Julia Roberts is thought to be the … / It is thought that Julia Roberts is the…* 24: *… the Olympic Games were held in Sydney.* 25: *Martin has been offered a good job by a firm in Bristol.* 26: *Tim's moped has been stolen.* 27: *Mike should be invited to your party.* 28: *You are always asked to his.*

D 29: *Our new house will be finished …* 30: *… we were told something about …* 31: *It was said that Mr Walker …* 32: *… was written by Shakespeare.* 33: *… may not be used …* 34: *… have been killed by an avalanche…* 35: *He was promised …*

Exercise finder

Sentences	CEG	Exercises
1, 5, 7, 8	▶ 107	▶ 1
2, 3, 12, 28	▶ 108a	▶ 2, 11
4, 16, 24	▶ 108a	▶ 3, 11
6, 17	▶ 108a	▶ 5
9, 15, 26	▶ 108a	▶ 4, 11
10, 11, 14, 29	▶ 108a	▶ 6, 11
13, 18, 27, 33	▶ 108c	▶ 7, 11
19, 21, 32, 34	▶ 110	▶ 8
20, 22, 25, 30, 35	▶ 111, 112	▶ 9
23, 31	▶ 114	▶ 10, 11

1 *Quick puzzle: which state?* active, passive

▶ 107, 108

Read the clues and find out the name of the American state which is described.

Which verb forms are active? Which are passive? Make a decision and pick the corresponding letter in the table. Then put the letters in the right order to find the answer.

A lot of fruit and vegetables are grown here.
The climate[1] attracts a lot of tourists.
Long ago, Spanish missions were set up here.
One in ten Americans lives here.
The state has often been called 'earthquake country'.
The world's first theme park[2] was opened here in 1955.
The state belonged to Mexico until 1848.
A famous city was almost completely destroyed here in 1906.
Gold was found here in 1849.
The American high-tech industry grew up here.

passive	active
L	O
S	A
R	F
P	N
A	D
C	L
H	F
I	D
O	I
O	I

The name of the state is XXXXXXXXXX .

2 *What's done in school?* simple present passive

▶ 108a, 109

a A lot of people work hard to keep your school clean and tidy, warm and safe, and to make it as pleasant as possible. What kind of *work is done*, and how often do you think *it is done*? If you don't know, guess. In your answers use the simple present passive and the phrases *I think/probably* and *every day/year/twice a year*, etc. or *never*, etc.

Examples: toilets – clean
The toilets ***are cleaned*** *every day.*
heating – check
The heating ***is*** *probably* ***checked*** *once a month.*

1 classrooms – clean
2 windows – wash
3 classroom furniture – dust
4 waste bins[3] – empty
5 floors – polish
6 staff room – clean
7 school dustbins[4] – empty
8 school building – paint
9 grass – cut
10 fire alarm – test

b Now think about the kind of work that is done in a hotel every day. How many things can you think of? Write down at least five.

Example: *Beds* ***are made*** *every day.*

1 climate *Klima* 2 theme park *Themenpark* 3 waste bin *Abfalleimer* 4 dustbin *Mülltonne*

3 *Test yourself: where and when?* **simple past passive** ▶ 108a, 109

Here are some facts about past events. *What was done* where and when? Put the verb in the simple past passive and choose the correct time and place from the list on the right. If you're not sure, do the easy ones first, then guess.

	~~President John F. Kennedy~~	~~(kill)~~	in Hollywood from 1994-97
1	The Summer Olympics 2000	(hold)	in Liverpool in 1961
2	Coca Cola	(invent)	~~in Dallas in 1963~~
3	Queen Elizabeth II	(crown)	in Wimbledon in 1877
4	The film *Titanic*	(produce)	in Atlanta nearly 100 years ago
5	Madame Tussaud's wax museum	(open)	in New York in 1980
6	*The Beatles*	(discover)	in Sydney, Australia
7	John Lennon	(shoot)	in Westminster Abbey in 1953
8	The first lawn[1] tennis championships	(play)	in Baker Street, London, in 1835
9	The theme park[2] *Disneyland*	(set up)	in San Francisco in 1850
10	The first Levi jeans	(make)	in Anaheim, California, in 1955

Example: *President John F. Kennedy* ***was killed*** *in Dallas in 1963.*

4 *What's in the news?* **present perfect passive: newspaper headlines** ▶ 108a, 109a

Peter is reading the news headlines in the local paper. What does Peter say when he reads them out to his mother – in full sentences, of course? Use the present perfect passive, as in the example.

Example: Three hurt in gas explosion
Peter: *Three people* ***have been hurt*** *in a gas explosion.*

1 Man hit by falling tree in Woodland Road
2 New sports centre opened in Elm Street
3 Two youths arrested for drunk driving
4 Beech School chemistry lab destroyed by fire
5 Teenagers injured on motorway
6 Policeman fined[3] for speeding

1 lawn *Rasen* 2 theme park *Themenpark* 3 fine sb *jdm. eine Geldstrafe auferlegen*

5 *Before and after* **past perfect passive**

▶ 108a, 109

While her parents were away, Lucy invited her friends to a party. After the party there was a big mess in the living-room (picture 1). But when her parents returned on the next day, everything was back to normal (picture 2). Compare the pictures. *What had been done*, when Lucy's parents returned? Use the past perfect passive.

Example: the empty cans and bottles – throw away
The empty cans and bottles ***had been thrown away****.*

When Lucy's parents got back …

1 the carpet – clean
2 the glasses and plates – wash up
3 the big lamp – move
4 the furniture – put back
5 the CDs – take away
6 the candles – throw away
7 the waste bin[1] – empty
8 the table – polish
9 the plants – water
10 But, oh dear, one thing had been forgotten. Look carefully. What had not been done?

6 *Wedding preparations* ***will*-future passive**

▶ 108a

Julie is getting married in a few weeks' time. There is a lot to arrange. Here are some things on Julie's list that still have to be done. What *will be done* when?

	~~write invitations~~	–	~~next weekend~~
1	send off invitations	–	Monday
2	book band	–	Tuesday
3	pick up wedding dress	–	18th
4	order flowers	–	20th
5	book taxis	–	21st
6	order cake	–	next week

Example: *The invitations* ***will be written*** *next weekend.*

Continue: …

1 waste bin *Abfalleimer*

7 *School dos and don'ts* **modal auxiliary + passive infinitive** ▶ 108c, 115

a Write notices about dos and don'ts in school, using a modal auxiliary + passive infinitive, as in the examples.

Examples: Pupils must return all library books by July 1st.
All library books ***must be returned*** *by July 1st.*

Pupils may not use mobile phones during school hours.
Mobile phones ***may not be used*** *during school hours.*

1 Pupils should put litter[1] in bins.
2 Pupils should not leave food and drinks cans in classrooms.
3 Pupils must not leave bicycles in front of the school gates.
4 Pupils may use walkmans in the breaks only.
5 Pupils must take sports equipment back to the gym after use.
6 Pupils may not take mobile phones to an exam.
7 Pupils should keep the toilets and showers clean at all times.
8 Pupils must not hang wet clothing on radiators[2].

b What other rules do you have at your school? Write down three. Use an auxiliary + passive infinitive, as in a).

Example: *Expensive jewellery and watches* ***should not be taken*** *to school.*

8 *Writing a report* **passive sentences with *by*** ▶ 109, 110

Imagine you are an exchange pupil at Parkway Comprehensive School in Chester. The school has just held its annual[3] Open Day[4]. You have been asked to write up a short report of the events for the local newspaper. Use passive verb forms in the simple past + *by*, as in the example.

Example: Hundreds of visitors attended[5] the annual Open Day at Parkway Comprehensive School.
The annual Open Day at Parkway Comprehensive School ***was attended by*** *hundreds of visitors.*

1 First, the head teacher, Mrs F. D. Fox, welcomed parents and visitors.
2 Then the school choir sang the school song.
3 Afterwards, the head teacher gave a speech on the successes of the past year.
4 Mr J. Rolls from the Education Department awarded[6] prizes and certificates.
5 Mrs Fox then thanked Mr Rolls for the support and cooperation of the Education Department.
6 Two sixth-form pupils then announced the programme of events and activities.
7 Pupils showed parents and visitors round the school.
8 Pupils and teachers sold food and soft drinks.

1 litter *Abfall* 2 radiator *Heizkörper* 3 annual *alljährlich* 4 Open Day *Tag der offenen Tür* 5 attend *teilnehmen*
6 award *verleihen*

9 *An exciting day* person as the subject; verbs with two objects ▶ 109, 111, 112

Melanie is very excited. She has been for audition[1] to a casting agency. She is telling Emma about her day. Rewrite what Melanie says using the passive. Begin with the underlined word, but remember that it will be the subject of the passive sentence (e.g. *me* → *I*, *us* → *we*).

Example: Melanie: First, they gave me a script – and a fantastic-looking partner called Leo.
*First, **I was given** a script – and a fantastic-looking partner called Leo.*

1 Then they asked us to study the script.
2 They advised us to read it aloud.
3 I was nervous, so they told me to relax.
4 They gave us some stage instructions[2].
5 They told me not to look into the camera.
6 They asked Leo to speak a bit louder. He was so scared that his knees were shaking.
7 Well, after it was all over they thanked everybody for taking part.
8 They paid all the candidates their expenses[3] for the day.
9 Before I left, they showed me into the casting agent's office.
10 Then, just imagine! He offered me a small part in a new soap opera.
11 And he promised me the chance of a bigger part in their next project.
Emma: Wow! And what about Leo? Melanie: Oh, they …

Finish the story yourself. Write what Melanie says about Leo, using a verb such as *give*, *show*, *promise*, *tell*, *offer*, etc. Then rewrite Melanie's sentence in the passive.

10 *It is said …* verbs of speaking and thinking ▶ 114

a Here are some facts and opinions about Britain and the British. First, rewrite the sentences using the passive structure *It is said that/It is thought that …*, etc. Use the verb underlined.

Example: In Britain, people think that school uniform is a good idea.
*In Britain, **it is thought that** school uniform is a good idea.*

Continue: 1 People believe that Prince William is the most popular Royal.
2 They say that the British are a nation of tea-drinkers.
3 People think that the British are bad at learning foreign languages.
4 They expect that Britain will introduce the euro soon.
5 In Britain, people think that the Prime Minister has improved education.
6 They say that British people are great animal lovers.

b Now rewrite the sentences in a) using the structure subject + passive + *to*-infinitive, as in the example:

Example: In Britain, people think that school uniform is a good idea.
*In Britain, **school uniform is thought to be** a good idea.*

c Work with a partner. Think of three things that are often said about Germany and the Germans, beginning with *It is said/thought that …* or *The Germans are said to …* Think of stereotypes for other countries too.

Example: ***It is thought that** the Germans make good cars.*
*The Germans **are thought to make** good cars.*

1 audition *Vorsprechen* 2 stage instruction *Regieanweisung* 3 expenses *Spesen*

11 *The Tower of London* **passive: mixed exercise** ▶ 108, 109, 114-117

Here's part of a brochure about the Tower of London. Have you ever been there? Complete the text with the correct passive tenses and forms.

Examples: For over 900 years England's capital ***has been dominated***[1] by the Tower of London.
It ***is thought to be*** London's most famous landmark[2].

The Tower of London is not one single tower, but several towers.

The White Tower (1 start) … in 1078 by William the Conqueror and (2 complete) … twenty years later. It was 30m high, at the time the tallest building in London.

Since the Tower was built, many important events in British history (3 witness[3]) … there. A long time ago it (4 use) … for many different purposes[4], for example as a fortress[5] and as a royal palace. But mostly it was a place to (5 fear) …, a terrible prison and a place of execution[6].

It (6 say) … that in the Bloody Tower in 1483 two boy princes (7 murder) … by their uncle Richard, who wanted to (8 crown) … king himself in their place. Two of Henry VIII's six wives (9 behead[7]) … there. The Bloody Tower (10 say) … to (11 haunt[8]) … by Anne Boleyn, who was one of the wives. Thomas More (12 execute) … there in 1521, after (13 imprison) … in the Tower for many years. Sir Walter Raleigh (14 also – keep) … prisoner there.

Today the Tower (15 use) … as a museum. In the Martin Tower cruel instruments of torture[9] can (16 view) … This tower (17 not recommend) … for people with weak nerves!

But there are more pleasant things to see, such as the Jewel House. Some of Britain's greatest treasures (18 keep) … there, for example the Cullinan I, the largest cut diamond in the world. If you have any questions, they (19 answer) … by the Jewel House Wardens. They will tell you fascinating and mysterious stories that (20 tell) … again and again through the years from generation to generation.

Tours of the Tower can (21 take) … all day. Tickets may (22 buy) … at the Tower or at underground stations. The Tower can (23 reach) … by underground, train, Docklands Light Railway, bus or riverboat.

The Tower (24 visit) … by millions of tourists every year, and in future it (25 visit) … by millions more. Will you be one of them?

1 dominate *dominieren* 2 landmark *Wahrzeichen* 3 witness *bezeugen, miterleben* 4 purpose *Zweck* 5 fortress *Festung* 6 execution *Hinrichtung* 7 behead *enthaupten* 8 haunt *spuken* 9 torture *Folter*

The infinitive and the gerund

A Complete the sentences with *to* where necessary.

1 If you're going to town today, I'd like ... go with you.
2 If you want, we can go to the disco. But I would rather ... stay at home.
3 Japanese is too difficult for me ... learn.
4 My dad made me ... stay at home last night to finish my history essay.
5 I had better ... hurry. My friends are waiting for me.

B Write the English equivalent of the German sentence part, using an infinitive structure.

6 At parties Tony is always *(der Erste, der kommt, und der Letzte, der geht)* ...
7 Can you tell us how *(wir zum neuen Einkaufszentrum kommen)* ...?
8 Mr Hill's explanation was *(für die Klasse zu schwer zu verstehen)* ...
9 We saw *(wie Ben das Fenster mit seinem Ball zerbrach)* ...
10 Tim went to the post office *(um Briefmarken zu kaufen)* ...

C Infinitive or gerund? Choose the correct form.

My boyfriend suggested (11 go/to go/going) to see the new *Star Wars* film. I don't enjoy (12 wait/to wait/waiting) in long cinema queues, and we knew it would be a long wait, but I felt like (13 have/to have/having) an evening out. I wanted (14 buy/to buy/buying) my own ticket, but my boyfriend wouldn't let me (15 pay/to pay/paying). But he gets less pocket money than me, so I made him (16 take/to take/taking) the money. Instead of (17 go/to go/going) to see the film, we could have waited for the video. But (18 watch/to watch/watching) the film at the cinema with popcorn and ice cream is more fun.

D Translate the German sentence parts using an infinitive or a gerund.

19 My penfriend in Canada would like *(dass ich sie im Juli besuche)* ...
20 If a test is too difficult, Leo is always *(der Erste, der sich beschwert)* ...
21 Sarah ran across the road *(ohne zu schauen)* ...
22 Does your teacher allow you *(ein Wörterbuch zu verwenden)* ... during an English test?
23 We went to the concert early *(um gute Plätze vorne zu bekommen)* ...
24 Can you tell us *(welchen Weg wir nehmen müssen)* ...?
25 *(Du solltest besser)* ... report the accident to the police.
26 I am used to *(früh aufzustehen)* ...
27 I remember *(wie ich das erste Mal geflogen bin)* ... I was so excited.

E Spot the mistakes. There is one mistake in each sentence (pair).

28 I'm not very interested to collect things.
29 I saw Jill slipping on the ice.
30 Did you remember making a dentist's[1] appointment[2] for next week? Or did you forget?
31 Mr Fox doesn't want that his daughter leaves school.
32 To collect posters is one of my hobbies.
33 Our teacher warned us to not waste time.
34 We're looking forward to see you on Saturday.

1 dentist *Zahnarzt/-ärztin* 2 appointment *Termin*

The infinitive and the gerund

? Correct yourself

A 1: *to* 2: – 3: *to* 4: – 5: –

B 6: *the first to come and the last to go.* 7: *to get to the new shopping centre?* 8: *too difficult for the class to understand.* 9: *Ben break the window with his ball.* 10: *to buy stamps.*

C 11: *going* 12: *waiting* 13: *having* 14: *to buy* 15: *pay* 16: *take* 17: *going* 18: *watching*

D 19: *me to visit her in July.* 20: *the first to complain.* 21: *without looking.* 22: *to use a dictionary* 23: *to get good seats at the front.* 24: *which way to take?* 25: *You had better* 26: *getting up early.* 27: *flying (for) the first time.*

E 28: *I'm not very interested in collecting things.* 29: *I saw Jill slip on the ice.* 30: *Did you remember to make a dentist's appointment for next week?* 31: *Mr Fox doesn't want his daughter to leave school.* 32: *Collecting posters is one of my hobbies.* 33: *Our teacher warned us not to waste time.* 34: *We're looking forward to seeing you on Saturday.*

Exercise finder

Sentences	CEG	Exercises
1, 14	▶ 122	▶ 12, 13, 21
2, 5, 25	▶ 132	▶ 9, 12, 13, 21, 22
3, 8	▶ 127b	▶ 6
4, 15, 16	▶ 133	▶ 10, 12, 13
6, 20	▶ 125	▶ 4
7, 24	▶ 128	▶ 7, 13
9, 29	▶ 134	▶ 11
10, 23	▶ 129	▶ 8
11, 12	▶ 139a	▶ 15, 21, 22
13, 34	▶ 143	▶ 18, 21
17, 21	▶ 144	▶ 19
18, 32	▶ 138	▶ 14
19, 31	▶ 123b	▶ 2, 3, 13
22, 33	▶ 123a	▶ 1, 12
26, 28	▶ 141	▶ 17
27, 30	▶ 139c	▶ 16

1 *What are your teachers like?* **verb + object + *to*-infinitive** ▶ 123a

a Mark asks Tom what his teachers are like. Tom tells Mark what *they allow/ask the pupils to do*, etc. Complete the sentences with an object + (not) *to*-infinitive of the correct verb from the list.

~~work~~ ▪ ~~waste~~ ▪ be ▪ bring ▪ copy ▪ do ▪ eat ▪ listen to ▪ stick ▪ talk

Examples: Our English teacher sometimes allows … in groups. That's cool, not so boring.
Our English teacher sometimes allows *us **to work*** in groups.
She often warns … time – but we do.
She often warns *us **not to waste*** time – but we do.

Our French teacher often asks (1) … quiet, because we're pretty noisy. But she's nice. Once a week she allows (2) … French pop songs. She brings CDs for us. And if the homework's difficult, she helps (3) … it in the lesson. She also asks (4) … letters from our French pen pals to the lessons. That's cool too.
The maths teacher is strict. Nobody likes him. He doesn't allow (5) … to each other at all. Every day he warns (6 not) … other pupils' homework – but we do, of course. Our form teacher[1] is OK. He allows (7) … funny posters and pictures on the walls. He asks (8 not) … and drink in the lessons, but if we do he doesn't get very angry.

b Now you. What are your teachers like? Do *they allow you to do* any of these things during lessons? Write three sentences in the positive and negative form. Use the following notes:

walk around the classroom	do your homework	listen to walkmans
work in groups	read comics	use calculators[3]
chew gum[2]	talk to your neighbours	use your mobiles

2 *He wants her to meet him* **verb + object + *to*-infinitive** ▶ 123b

a Last week Julie met a boy at the disco. Since then he has texted her on her mobile phone[4] every day. What does *he want her to do*?

Example: Will you go to a party with me on Friday?
He wants her …
He wants her ***to go** to a party with him on Friday.*

1 Will you go to the cinema with me tomorrow?
He would like her …
2 Can you meet me after school?
He wants …
3 Am waiting for your phone call.
He is expecting …
4 Will you please give me an answer?
He wants …
5 Don't miss the party on Friday!
He doesn't want …
6 You can meet my friends.
He would like …

b Write down three things that *you would like your friends to do* this week or next week.

Example: *I **would like** X **to go** to town with me tomorrow.*

1 form teacher *Klassenlehrer* 2 chew gum *Kaugummi kauen* 3 calculator *Taschenrechner* 4 text sb on their mobile phone *jdm. eine SMS schicken*

3 *A message on the answer phone* **verb + object + *to*-infinitive**

▶ 123b

a When Luke and Katie come home from school, they find a message from their mother on the answer phone.

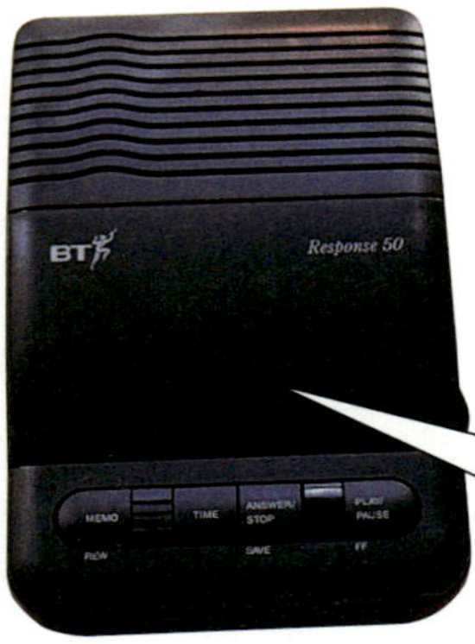

Hi, this is mum.

Example: Katie, could you go to the supermarket, please? Don't forget the shopping list. It's on the table.

And Luke, (1) phone Mr Briggs, please. (2) Give Mrs Hill the parcel that's in the hall. And (3) take the bottles to the bottle bank, will you? Then (4) don't forget the dentist's[1] at five. Katie, could you (5) turn the oven on at six? (6) Put the meat pie[2] in at 6.15, then (7) peel[3] the potatoes, will you? And both of you, (8) take Spike for a walk. OK? See you later. Bye!

What does *she want them to do*? Use the verb in brackets ( ) + object + *to*-infinitive.

Examples: Katie, could you go to the supermarket, please? (want)
*She **wants Katie to go** to the supermarket.*
Don't forget the shopping list. (tell)
*She **tells Katie/her not to forget** the shopping list.*

1 (want)
2 (tell)
3 (would like)
4 (tell)
5 (would like)
6 (tell)
7 (want)
8 (would like)

b What do members of your family want you to do this week? Write three sentences.

Example: *My dad **wants me to find** out some Internet addresses for him.*

4 *Who's the first?* ***the first, the last,* etc. + *to*-infinitive**

▶ 125

Who's *the first* or *last*, etc. *to do* these things in your family? Use the words in the table and a *to*-infinitive to make nine true sentences. If you wish, add *always, usually, never,* etc.

		get up
I		*have a shower*
My mother	*first*	*make breakfast*
My father	*second*	*leave home*
My sister	*next*	*come home*
My brother	*last*	*watch TV*
My parents	*only one(s)*	*do homework*
Our dog/cat		*go to bed*
		sleep all day

Examples: *My mother is always **the first to get up**.*
*Our cat is **the only one to sleep** all day.*

1 dentist *Zahnarzt/-ärztin* 2 pie *Pastete* 3 peel *schälen*

5 *There's nothing to do* **noun + *to*-infinitive** ▶ 126

Sharon is at home on her own – and she's bored. Most of her friends are on holiday and her parents are away for the weekend. Complete the sentences with the *to*-infinitive of the correct verb from the list:

do (2x) ▪ eat ▪ go ▪ ~~go with~~ ▪ listen to ▪ read ▪ chat to ▪ watch

Example: Sharon would like to go to a disco, but she's got nobody …
… ***to go with***.

1 She can't think of anywhere … on her own.
2 She's got nothing … , so she's just lying on her bed.
3 She hasn't got any new CDs …
4 She hasn't got any new magazines …
5 There isn't anybody … on the phone.
6 Perhaps there's something … on TV.
7 Perhaps there's something … in the fridge.
8 It's so boring. In fact, she wishes she had some homework …

6 *Moving* ***for*** **+ pronoun + *to*-infinitive** ▶ 127b

a The Webbs are moving. Everybody is trying to do something, but it isn't always easy. Comment on the pictures. Use *for* + pronoun (object form) + *to*-infinitive and the words given.

Examples: Mr W. can't move the piano. (heavy)
The piano is too heavy ***for him to move****.*

Mr W. can't move the piano. (It's impossible …)
It's impossible ***for him to move*** *the piano.*

1 Sarah can't lift the box. (big)
2 Mr Webb can't carry the carpet. (heavy)
3 The men can't push the sofa through the door. (It's impossible …)
4 The men can't move the cupboard. (It's impossible …)
5 Ben can't reach the picture. (high)
6 Mrs Webb can't lift the TV set. (heavy)

b Say what is sometimes *hard* or *easy for you to do*. Write three sentences. Use these ideas or your own:

finish something on time ▪ get up early ▪ learn something ▪ be honest to friends

Example: *Sometimes it's difficult* ***for me to give in*** *my homework on time.*

7 *I don't know how to do it* question word + *to*-infinitive

▶ 128

a Ed wants to use his brother's computer to play a game. His brother isn't at home and he doesn't know *how to install* programs. He asks his friend Tom to help him. Complete the dialogue with a suitable question word + *to*.

Tom: I think you should ask someone else.
Ed: But I don't know ***who to*** ask.
Tom: At least we know (1) … turn it on.
Ed: Yes, but I wonder (2) … do after that.
Tom: Well, I don't think the mouse is connected. We must find out (3) … connect the mouse first. I'm not sure (4) … put this cable. Let's phone someone.
Ed: But I don't know (5) … phone.
Tom: I'd like to know (6) … put this disc. Which drive does it go in? There must be a handbook that tells you (7) … do.
Ed: I suppose there is. But I don't know (8) … look. I'm going to put the disc in here. We'll see what happens.
Tom: Oh, the computer's making a funny noise. Do you know (9) … switch it off[1]? Wait until your brother comes home. He'll show you (10) … install your game.
Ed: No, he won't. He hasn't let me use his computer since I erased[2] all his files.

b You have a friend who doesn't know anything about computers, but he/she would like to learn. Name six things that you could show him/her. Use a question word + *to*-infinitive.

Examples: *I could show him/her* ***how to copy*** *a file.*
I could show him/her ***where to put*** *the discs.*

8 *Why* *to*-infinitive to indicate the purpose of an action

▶ 129

a Why would you go to these places? Write sentences with *to* + infinitive.

Example: a driving school
I would go to a driving school ***to learn*** *to drive/to take/ask about driving lessons.*

1 a fitness studio
2 a travel agency
3 a riding school
4 an Internet café
5 a music store

b Why do you think people do these things? Write sentences with *to* + infinitive.

Example: write letters to problem pages
I think people write letters to problem pages ***to share*** *their problems with others/****to get*** *advice from experts.*

1 go on chat shows
2 learn English
3 join sports clubs
4 use the Internet
5 take part in TV game shows or quiz shows

---

1 switch off *ausschalten* 2 erase *löschen*

9 *I'd rather go somewhere hot* **fixed phrases + infinitive without *to*** ▶ 132

a The Ashtons are discussing holiday plans. Complete their conversation with the following phrases:

had better ▪ would rather ▪ rather than ▪ let's ▪ why not?

Father: Well, where shall we go this year? Any suggestions?
Jenny: Please, not Scotland again. ***Let's*** go somewhere hot, like Spain or Turkey.
Tim: Or (1) … go somewhere exciting, like Australia or Florida.
Mother: No, it's too far – and much too expensive. I (2) … go to the mountains. (3) … tour Austria or Switzerland?
Jenny: No, I don't want to tour Austria. Mountains are boring. And I don't want to sit in the car all day.
Mother: Well, somewhere quiet and relaxing would be nice, like Cornwall.
Tim: Oh, no. That's even worse. I (4) … stay at home than go there again.
Jenny: Well, (5) … do something more adventurous for a change? We've seen enough of Cornwall and Scotland. I (6) … go camping in Italy. At least that's fun.
Father: Well, we (7) … decide where to go soon, or we won't get any flights.
Jenny: I agree. We'll make compromises[1] (8) … stay at home. So, (9) … go to a Robinson holiday club with lots of discos and sports …
Tim: … and food and fun and girls. Cool. Great compromise, Jenny!
Father: Mmmm. Well, (10) … argue now, we'll go to a travel agency and get some brochures and prices.
Jenny: Good, then we can argue again tomorrow.

b Where *would you rather go*? What *would you rather do*?

Example: climb a mountain – lie on a beach
*I **would rather lie** on a beach than **climb** a mountain.*

1 go sightseeing – get a suntan
2 go ponytrekking – stay at home
3 sleep in a tent – stay at a big hotel
4 do a tennis course – learn waterskiing
5 do a bus tour – travel alone

1 compromise *Kompromiss*

10 *A welcome visit* **let/make + object + infinitive without *to***

▶ 133

Joanne is going to visit her aunt Trish and uncle Simon in Wales. She likes her aunt and uncle, because they aren't as strict as her parents. Joanne is telling her friend about them. Complete what she says with *let* or *make*, positive or negative forms.

Examples: Aunt Trish ***lets*** me do what I want. She ***doesn't make*** me get up early if I don't want to.

Uncle Simon (1) ... me stay out until midnight and he (2) ... me surf on his computer for as long as I want.
Aunt Trish (3) ... me clean my room and she (4) ... me bring friends home whenever I want.
They (5) ... me go to church on Sundays, and they (6) ... me watch videos. They're really cool.
My parents are much stricter. My mum always (7) ... me do my homework straight after lunch. Dad (8) ... me stay at home at the weekend if I haven't done all my homework.
They (9) ... me watch late-night movies on TV. They think they're bad for me.
Mum (10) ... me clean my shoes every day. Stupid, they're never really dirty.
They (11) ... me go to discos and parties very often either. They think I'm too young.
I suppose they will (12) ... me do these things when I'm older.

11 *Rachel's story* **verbs of perception + object + infinitive without *to***

▶ 134

a In the disco Rachel is telling her friend Diane about something she saw when she was shopping. The music's very loud, so Rachel has to say everything twice.

Examples: Rachel: A blond girl came into the shop. I noticed her.
Diane: Sorry? Can you say that again?
Rachel: *I **noticed a blond girl come** into the shop.*
Rachel: She asked the assistant something. I heard her.
Diane: What? What did you say?
Rachel: *I **heard her ask** the assistant something.*

Now continue. Make one sentence out of two. Use an object + infinitive without *to*.

Rachel:

1 A dark girl came in five minutes later. I noticed her.
2 The blond girl asked the assistant another question. I heard her.
3 The dark girl went to the perfumes. I saw her.
4 She picked up a large bottle of Calvin Klein. I noticed.
5 She put it in the inside pocket of her jacket. I saw her.
6 She said to the blond girl 'I've got it. Let's go.' I heard her.
7 They walked past the cash desk[1]. I saw them.
8 They left the shop with the stolen perfume. I watched them.
9 They got into a car across the road. I saw them.
10 It drove off immediately[2]. I saw it.

b Rachel *saw the girls steal* something, and she said nothing. Have you ever *seen anyone do* anything dishonest? Have you ever heard anyone tell a lie? Describe when and what you saw or heard. Write two or three sentences.

Example: *I once **heard a boy** at our youth club **lie** to a policeman. He said he was 18, but I know he's only 16.*

12 *A whizz-kid* *to*-inf., inf. without *to*: mixed exercise

► 122-124, 129, 132-133

David Benson is a computer 'whizz-kid'. He has won a scholarship[3] to study IT[4] at the Massachusetts Institute of Technology (MIT) in the USA – at just seventeen. David talked to the editor of his school magazine. This is his story. Put in *to* where it is necessary.

Examples: 'Computers are exciting. I would rather ***sit*** at my computer than ***watch*** a video.
Today school-leavers are expected ***to know*** a lot about computers, so it's best ***to start*** early.'

I wanted (1) … have a computer when I was about eight, but my parents couldn't afford (2) … buy me one, and they didn't want me (3) … damage my eyes. My friend had a computer, so he let me (4) … use his. My teacher also allowed me (5) … use the school computers, and he advised my parents (6) … buy one for me.

When I was eleven, my parents finally decided (7) … buy me a computer rather than (8) … disappoint me again on my birthday. At first they let me (9) … use it only for an hour in the evening. At nine o'clock they made me (10) … turn it off and go to bed. My uncle taught me (11) … program when I was twelve. He let me (12) … borrow all his books. He was great.

Well, that's how it started, and now I've won a scholarship in the States (13) … study IT. My parents don't really want me (14) … go so far away. But they seem (15) … realize that it's what I want (16) … do. My uncle says it's a wonderful opportunity, so why not (17) … take it? My mum just said I had better (18) … phone home every week. Of course, I have promised (19) … keep regular contact. On the one hand I would rather (20) … stay here with my friends and family, but on the other hand it would be stupid (21) … miss the chance. But I'll be back.'

1 cash desk *Kasse* 2 immediately *sofort* 3 scholarship *Stipendium*
4 IT = Information Technology *Informationstechnologie*

13 *Future plans* *to*-inf., inf. without *to*: mixed exercise ▶ 122-124, 128-130, 132-133

a A teenage magazine asked 16- to 18-year-olds about their future plans: what do *you want to do* when you leave school? Here are some answers. Complete what the teenagers say with *to* where necessary.

Alan: I want … go abroad first. I would rather … see the world than … start work immediately.

Example: I want ***to go*** abroad first. I would rather ***see*** the world than ***start*** work immediately.

1 **Penny**: I have always wanted … be a doctor, so I hope … study medicine. I'd like … stay in England rather than … go abroad.

2 **Luke**: My uncle owns a travel agency. He has offered … give me a good job there. So I am planning … learn the tourist business. Next year I'm going to a college in Hull … do a course.

3 **Mike**: I would rather … leave school next year than … do A-levels. I'd like … leave home too, but I don't know what … do or where … go. My sister says it's better not … leave school without a qualification.

4 **Peggy**: I have a Saturday job at a garage. I think it would be nice … have my own garage one day, so I hope … train there as a mechanic. My dad wants me … go to college, but I don't want …

5 **James**: I expect … pass my A-levels. I've got a university place … study journalism in London. I don't like London, but the chance is too good … miss. So why not … take it?

6 **Sarah**: I'm tired of school, but my parents won't let me … leave at 16. They say I had better … think about my future, but they can't make me … do exams. I'd like … take singing lessons … become a professional singer for our band.

b Now you. What do *you want to do* when you leave school? Write a short paragraph using some of the following verbs and phrases. Remember to use a *to*-infinitive where it is necessary.

allow ▪ decide ▪ hope ▪ let ▪ plan ▪ want ▪ would like ▪ would rather ▪ had better

14 *Rick's hobbies* **gerund as subject** ▶ 138

a All these things belong to Rick. What do they tell you about his hobbies and interests? Use gerunds and think carefully about the spelling.

Examples: *I think Rick's hobbies and interests are **camping**, **making** model planes, …*

Continue.

b Which of Rick's activities do you think is fun, interesting, stupid or boring?

Examples: *I think **camping** is fun. I think **making** model planes is boring.*

c What are your favourite hobbies/free time activities? Write down five things.

Example: *My favourite free time activities are **swimming**, …*

15 *Meet Claire* gerund as object

▶ 139a

a Claire Honeywell is a well-known fashion model. She talked to the magazine *Young Fashion* about her career.
Complete her story with gerunds. Read each paragraph first, then choose the correct verb from the list.

Examples: ~~model~~ ▪ ~~enter~~

It all began about five years ago. I was just sixteen. A friend suggested ***entering*** a photo competition – just for fun. I won the first prize, a course in modelling. Someone on the jury asked if I had considered[1] ***modelling*** as a career.

make ▪ meet ▪ travel ▪ try

I said I wouldn't mind (1) … it – just for fun. After the course I got my first job with a small London fashion house. The work involved (2) … , to Paris and Rome mainly. I enjoyed (3) … new people and (4) … international contacts. Then I did some TV commercials[2], and by this time I found that my job had changed my life.

be ▪ catch ▪ cut ▪ eat ▪ get up ▪ go ▪ smoke

I had given up (5) … I had stopped (6) … to late-night parties. I never risk (7) … a cold now, and I always avoid (8) … things that make me fat.
Disadvantages? Well, I dislike (9) … early and I miss (10) … with my old friends. And I can't always decide things myself now. For example, I think my hair needs (11) …, but my agent says no. So my hair stays long.

ask ▪ do ▪ model ▪ wear

It's hard work, but I admit that I enjoy (12) … expensive clothes all the time. My friends keep (13) … me when I'm going to get a normal job, but I shall carry on (14) … for as long as possible. I really haven't considered (15) … anything else. For me it's a perfect job.

b What things would you enjoy if you had a job like Claire's? What things wouldn't you enjoy? Write five sentences altogether. Use gerunds in your answers.

Examples: *I would **enjoy being** famous.*
*I wouldn't **enjoy getting up** early.*

c Now use gerunds and name something that …

1 you miss. 2 you never risk[3]. 3 you have given up. 4 you avoid.

Example: *I **miss watching** my favourite TV soap. It isn't on now.*

1 consider *in Betracht ziehen* 2 commercial *Werbespot* 3 risk *riskieren*

16 *I don't remember doing it* verbs with different meanings: gerund or *to*-inf. ▶ 139c

a Trish and Angela are riding to town on Trish's moped. Can you complete their dialogue with the correct form, a gerund or *to*-infinitive? Think carefully about the meaning.

Trish: I must remember (***to post***/posting) this birthday card for Diane. Do you remember (to see/***seeing***) a postbox anywhere around here?
Angela: No, I don't. Shall we stop (1 to ask/asking) someone?
Trish: No, I'll post the card in town. Have you got your mobile phone?
Angela: Yes. Why? Where's yours? Did you forget (2 to bring/bringing) it with you?
Trish: No, I can remember (3 to put/putting) it in my pocket. But it isn't there now.
Angela: Well, try (4 to feel/feeling) in your other pockets. You had better stop (5 to look/looking). Is it in your jacket? Is it in your trouser pocket?
Trish: Stop (6 to ask/asking) silly questions. No, it isn't. Perhaps it's still at home. I meant (7 to put/putting) it in my pocket, but just then the telephone rang. Oh dear. That call was for my mother and I forgot (8 to tell/telling) her about it.
Angela: Well, if you've lost your mobile, it will mean (9 to buy/buying) a new one.
Trish: My parents will go wild. I can remember (10 to tell/telling) them two years ago that I had lost my watch. My dad went on (11 to talk/talking) about it for months.
Angela: Well, at least you'll remember (12 to put/putting) it in a safe place next time.
Trish: Mmm. Well, let's go back home and look for it.

b What do you sometimes *forget to do*? Write three sentences.

Example: *I sometimes **forget to feed** our cat.*

17 *Judy, her family and friends* adjective + preposition + gerund ▶ 141

What does Judy say about herself, her family and friends? Use a gerund and make one sentence out of two.

Examples: My dad repairs everything that breaks or goes wrong. He's good at it.
*He is **good at repairing** things that break or go wrong.*
My sister didn't pass her driving test. She's disappointed about it.
*She is **disappointed about not passing** her driving test.*

1 My brother tells stupid jokes. He's famous for it.
2 My sister is going out with a cool sixth-former on Friday. She's excited about it.
3 My friend Di enters karaoke competitions. She's crazy about it.
4 I didn't send my cousin a birthday card last week. I'm sorry about it.
5 My friend Liz is the best disco-dancer in the class. She's proud of it.
6 I can't dance very well at all. I'm pretty bad at it.
7 My friend Pete is moving to London soon. He's glad about it.
8 My friend Josie is learning how to program. She's really interested in it.
9 My mum cooks a lot of foreign food. She's good at it.
10 I might not pass some of my GCSEs. I'm a bit worried about it.
11 Our school team didn't win the football match. We were disappointed about it.
12 My dad works late quite a lot. He's used to it.
13 My brother gets up early for his Saturday job. He's tired of it.
14 I didn't get an invitation to Sue's party. I'm a bit angry about it.

18 *Make sentences* **verb + preposition + gerund**

▶ 143

a Use the table to make ten sentences which are (more or less) true for you and your friends. Choose the correct preposition after the verb and use a gerund after the preposition. Lots of sentences are possible, but try to use each verb once.

		verb +	preposition	
			about	*work too hard*
		believe		*go on holiday*
		complain	*in*	*make a mistake*
	don't	*look forward*		*have a good time*
I	*doesn't*	*dream*	*on*	*have too much homework*
	can't	*worry*		*not pass exams*
My best friend		*feel*	*to*	*become rich and famous*
	sometimes	*concentrate*		*go out*
My friends	*always*	*apologize*	*for*	*leave school*
	never	*talk*		*do (my) homework*
		think	*like*	*not have enough money*

Examples: *I **believe in having** a good time.*
*My friends always **complain about not having** enough money.*

b Now answer these questions using a gerund after the verb + preposition.

1 What do you always look forward to doing?
2 What do you sometimes worry about doing (or not doing)?
3 What do you and your best friend often talk about doing?
4 What do you sometimes feel like doing after school?
5 What are you thinking about doing in your next holidays?

Example: *I always **look forward to going out** with my friends at the weekend.*

19 *Ben* **preposition + gerund**

▶ 144

a The bubbles show you what Ben is thinking or saying. Write one sentence about him with the preposition given and a gerund. The first part of the sentence is done for you.

Examples: Ben's going to take the bus …
instead of walking.

Ben passed the maths test …
***without copying** from Sam.*

Ben thinks he can earn money ...

He wants to go skating after school ...

He's still going to the party ...

Ben can't get better marks ...

Ben's mum gave him five pounds ...

He's going to watch a video ...

b How do you think you could earn extra pocket money? Write three sentences using *by* + gerund.

20 *Exam tips* **adjective/noun/fixed phrase + gerund**

▶ 145-147

Before a test your English teacher might give you some good advice. Make one sentence with a gerund.

Examples: Don't learn texts by heart. It's no good.
It's ***no good learning*** *texts by heart*[1].
Check your spelling carefully. It's worth it.
It's ***worth checking*** *your spelling carefully.*

1 Start early with your revision. It's worth it.
2 Don't learn everything the night before. It's hopeless.
3 Don't stay up late to learn. It's no use.
4 Don't learn grammar rules by heart. It's a waste of time.
5 You may make a few careless mistakes[2]. You can't help it.
6 Don't write more than necessary. There's no point.
7 Don't copy from your neighbour. It's no good.
8 Remember - I don't like marking bad tests. It's no fun.

1 learn sth by heart *etwas auswendig lernen* 2 careless mistake *Flüchtigkeitsfehler*

21 *No, thank you* gerund or infinitive ▶ 122, 124, 131, 132, 139a/b, 143, 145-147

Jason likes Sharon, a girl in his class. He is talking to her in the break.
Choose the correct form of the verb in brackets, either an infinitive (with or without *to*) or a gerund.

Examples: Jason would like ***to ask*** Sharon out, but she doesn't seem interested in ***going out*** with him.

Jason: Would you like (1 drive) … into town with me on my new motorbike?
Sharon: No, thanks, I dislike (2 drive) … in so much traffic.
Jason: Well, let's (3 go) … for a drive in the country.
Sharon: No, thanks. I'm not a nature freak.
Jason: Well, we could always (4 go) … for a walk somewhere.
Sharon: Oh, no. I don't enjoy (5 walk) … much.
Jason: Mmmm. Well, in that case I suggest (6 go) … to see a film tonight.
Sharon: No. There's nothing on that's worth (7 see)…
Jason: Well, how about (8 go) … for a meal, to that new Indian on Thames Street, perhaps? And don't worry about (9 pay) …
Sharon: Jason, I really don't feel like (10 go out) … today. I'm looking forward to (11 stay) … at home tonight. Really, I'm too tired (12 go) … anywhere.
Jason: It isn't much fun (13 ask) … you out. I can't help (14 think) … that you just don't want (15 go out) … with me. I'll ask your sister instead.

22 *A day trip* gerund or infinitive ▶ 124, 126, 132, 139a, 145, 147

Teenagers are discussing where to go for the youth club's day trip. They all have different suggestions.
Complete the sentences with a suitable verb as gerund or infinitive (with or without *to*).

Examples: Sandra thinks they should go to the coast for the day.
Sandra: Why don't we …?
Why don't we ***go*** *to the coast for the day?*
Pam thinks that Brighton beach would be a good idea.
Pam: How about …?
How about ***going*** *to Brighton beach?*

1 Nick thinks spending a quiet day by a lake would be better.
Nick: It would be better …
2 Gil says they shouldn't do that if it's too cold.
Gil: There's no point …
3 Jane suggests going for a ride on the London Eye[1]. She thinks it would be good fun doing that in a group.
Jane: Let's … It would be a cool thing …
4 Matt would like to go shopping in London, then see a musical in the evening.
Matt: What about …? And in the evening it would be worth …
5 Sophie has never been to Windsor Castle. She thinks it would be a good idea.
Sophie: Wouldn't it be a good idea …?
6 David thinks a day in Oxford would be interesting.
David: I suggest …
7 Fran says they should wait and see what the weather is like.
Fran: It's best …

1 London Eye *Riesenrad im Zentrum Londons*

The participle

A Present participle or past participle? Put in *having* or *when* where necessary.

1 Can you introduce me to the girl (wear) … the red pullover?
2 We're having the TV (repair) … just now, so the evenings are really boring.
3 I've just finished reading a horror story. It was really (frighten) …
4 Joe hurt his leg (do) … judo.
5 We ate at a very nice hotel (situate[1]) … on a lake.
6 I felt terrified[2] when I saw the snake (move) … in my direction[3].
7 We decided not to buy the video, (see) … the film at the cinema.
8 When I opened the door, I could hear my sister (practise) … the violin.
9 Why don't you have your hair (dye[4]) … blond? It would suit you.
10 I saw my ex-girlfriend with a man (get) … into my sportscar.
11 The school-bag (find) … at the bus stop belongs to Dave Turner.
12 Ali ran down the road (sing) … his favourite pop song.
13 (sleep) … in a tent for three weeks, it was wonderful to be at home in my bed again.
14 Serena cut her finger (chop[5]) … tomatoes for the spaghetti sauce.
15 Who's the boy (dance) … with Janet?

B Change or shorten the underlined sentence parts without changing the meaning. Use participle constructions.

16 Marie broke her right leg when she was skiing in Switzerland.
17 Jerry walked through the supermarket and chatted on his mobile.
18 When we heard the news that our team had won, we all cheered.
19 The woman who is wearing the big sunglasses is the camp leader.
20 Because we didn't have enough money with us, we couldn't go for a meal.
21 After I had arrived at school, I realized that I had forgotten my project.
22 Justin burnt his hand while he was lighting the camp fire.
23 After the phone call Nina ran out of the house and she felt very excited.
24 Since we had been to Spain the year before, we decided to go to Italy.
25 The silver that was stolen from the Ashtons' house has all been found.

C Spot the mistakes. There is one mistake in each sentence (pair).

26 Why don't you let your hair cut? It would suit you short.
27 When I rode past the football ground on my bike, I saw our team play football.
28 There was nothing good on TV, so I felt boring.
29 I saw a huge, brown dog waiting for the bus.
30 I'm not very interesting in football.
31 We smelt smoke come from the house next door, so we phoned the fire brigade.
32 Mrs Jones had cleaned her windows. But the window-cleaner wasn't cheap.

1 situate *legen* 2 feel terrified *schrecklich Angst haben* 3 direction *Richtung* 4 dye *färben* 5 chop *klein hacken*

The participle

? Correct yourself

A 1: *wearing* 2: *repaired* 3: *frightening.* 4: *doing* 5: *situated* 6: *moving* 7: *having seen* 8: *practising* 9: *dyed* 10: *when getting* 11: *found* 12: *singing* 13: *Having slept* 14: *chopping* 15: *dancing*

B 16: *Marie broke her right leg skiing in Switzerland.* 17: *Jerry walked through the supermarket chatting on his mobile.* 18: *Hearing the news that our team had won, we all cheered.* 19: *The woman wearing the big sunglasses is the camp leader.* 20: *Not having enough money with us, we couldn't go for a meal.* 21: *Having arrived at school, I realized that I had forgotten my project.* 22: *Justin burnt his hand lighting the camp fire.* 23: *After the phone call Nina ran out of the house feeling very excited.* 24: *Having been to Spain the year before, we decided to go to Italy.* 25: *The silver stolen from the Ashtons' house has all been found.*

C 26: *Why don't you have your hair cut?* 27: *… , I saw our team playing football.* 28: *… , so I felt bored.* 29: *I saw a huge, brown dog when/while waiting for the bus.* 30: *I'm not very interested in football.* 31: *We smelt smoke coming from the house next door, …* 32: *Mrs Jones had her windows cleaned.*

Exercise finder

Sentences	CEG	Exercises
1, 5, 11, 15, 19, 25	▶ 153c	▶ 2, 11
2, 9, 26, 32	▶ 156	▶ 4
3, 28, 30	▶ 153a	▶ 1
4, 14, 16, 18, 21, 22	▶ 158	▶ 5, 7, 10, 11
6, 8, 27, 31	▶ 154a	▶ 3
7, 13, 20, 24	▶ 159	▶ 6, 7, 11
10, 29	▶ 161a	▶ 9, 10
12, 17, 23	▶ 160	▶ 8, 10, 11

1 *Reading habits* **participles used with a noun**

▶ 151a, 153a/b

a Some participles are often mixed up. Find matching pairs. Which is correct?

1 *langweilig*	a interesting
2 *interessant*	b surprising
3 *gelangweilt*	c interested
4 *überrascht*	d surprised
5 *faszinierend*	e boring
6 *überraschend*	f bored
7 *fasziniert*	g fascinating
8 *interessiert*	h fascinated

b Ann and Dan are talking about what kind of books they like to read. Complete the text with the present participle or past participle of the verb given.

Ann: What do you usually read?

Dan: Mainly comics and magazines, and school books, of course. We're reading some ***amusing*** French short stories at the moment, but our teacher is the only one who is ***amused.*** Poor Mr Lenox. We all sit there with a (1 bore) … look on our faces.

Ann: Well, I've always got my nose in a book.

Dan: Yes, but girls read more than boys anyway, especially romantic stuff with a (2 bore) … happy ending.

Ann: That's not true. I'm (3 interest) … in most things, even history. I like stories with (4 interest) … characters and a (5 surprise) … twist[1] at the end.

Dan: The last book I read was a Stephen King horror thriller. I used to read it in bed. It was so (6 frighten) … in parts that I was too (7 frighten) … to switch off[2] the light.

Ann: I like adventures with (8 excite) … storylines. Detective novels can be good too, but sometimes the story is (9 confuse)… At least, I am often (10 confuse) …

Dan: I know what you mean. I once read a spy[3] story. I was really (11 excite) … all the way through, but then the story had a (12 disappoint) … ending.

Ann: I like travel books. I'm just reading about a girl who made a (13 fascinate) … journey on foot through the jungle in Peru. She had some quite (14 amaze) … experiences.

Dan: With killer-snakes and scorpions and man-(15 eat) … tigers? Wow! Better than Stephen King. Can I borrow it?

Ann: Sure. You won't be (16 disappoint) …

c Write a short paragraph about a film that you have seen. Write about the characters, the story, the atmosphere, the special effects, the ending, etc. (*interesting, exciting, terrifying, shocking, fascinating, amazing*, etc.). Write about how you felt during the film (*interested, excited, shocked, fascinated, frightened, amazed, surprised*, etc.).

Example: *Last Sunday I saw an **interesting** film about …*

1 twist *Wendung* 2 switch off *ausmachen* 3 spy *Spion*

2 *A party* participles instead of relative clauses

▶ 153c/d

A friend takes you to a party. Some of the people there look interesting and you would like to know who they are. Ask your friend. Describe the people using a present participle: *Who is/Who are the girl(s)/ boy(s)* + present participle …

Examples: *Who's the **girl wearing** the grey sweater and the grey jeans?*
*Who are the **boys playing** cards?*

3 *On the way home* verbs of perception + object + present participle

▶ 154a

It was a warm day and Tony was on his way home from school. He saw, heard, smelt, noticed things because people had their windows open. What did he *see*, *hear*, *smell*, *notice*, etc. *happening*? Use the words under the pictures with a present participle.

sing – shower

someone's toast – burn

Examples: *He **heard** someone **singing** in the shower. He **smelt** someone's toast **burning**.*

someone's parrot – talk

someone's dinner – burn

boy – play – violin

notice – man – shave

boy – kiss – girlfriend

man – woman – quarrel

man – have – bath

listen to – girl – practise – karaoke

4 *Don the punk* ***have something done*** ▶ 156

a This is Don. He loves music and he wants to play in a punk band, so he has changed his image.

Use the verbs in the list to make sentences with *have sth done*. What *has* Don *had done*?

pierce (2×) ▪ tattoo ▪ fit ▪ dye[1] ▪ cut

Example: *He* ***has had*** *his right ear* ***pierced****.*

1 … hair … short.
2 … hair … blond.
3 … nose …
4 … arms …
5 … contact lenses …

b Have you had a piercing or a tattoo? Do you know anyone who has? *Have you* or your friends *had* contact lenses *fitted* or your hair *dyed*? Write a short paragraph.

Example: *Three years ago I* ***had*** *my hair* ***dyed*** *blond, but it didn't really suit me.*
I don't know anyone who ***has had*** *contact lenses* ***fitted****.*

1 dye *färben*

5 *The Grand Canyon* **participles expressing time**

▶ 158

Jane and two friends visited Grand Canyon National Park in the holidays. Back home, Jane wrote an essay for school about the visit. She improved the style of her essay by using participle constructions. How did she change the following sentences? Replace the underlined sentence part with a participle construction (a present participle or *having* + past participle).

Examples: After we had spent a few days in Las Vegas, we drove to the Grand Canyon in Arizona.
Having spent *a few days in Las Vegas, we drove to the Grand Canyon in Arizona.*
When Tony and Gina saw the Canyon, they were speechless.
Seeing *the Canyon, Tony and Gina were speechless.*

1 As we drove along the South Rim[1], we stopped at all the viewpoints to take photographs.
2 While Tony was taking a photo, he dropped his camera case over the edge – it probably fell about one and a half kilometres, so we didn't look for it.
3 When we hiked[2] down into the Canyon, we realized how gigantic it is.
4 On the first evening we saw the IMAX film *Grand Canyon – The Hidden Secrets*. After we had seen the film, we all wanted to do a helicopter flight over the Canyon too.
5 However, after Tony had asked the price of helicopter tours, he suggested a mule[3] trip instead.
6 Unfortunately, when she was getting on the mule, Gina dropped her binoculars[4].
7 After we had been in the saddle for a few hours, we could feel every muscle.
8 While we watched the sunset[5] over the Canyon, we saw some squirrels[6].
9 The highlight of our stay was a whitewater rafting trip down the Colorado River. It was great fun, but after we had rafted down the Colorado for three days, we felt really tired.
10 After we had camped in the Canyon for a week, we were looking forward to a comfortable bed.

1 rim *Rand* 2 hike *wandern* 3 mule *Maultier* 4 binoculars [bɪˈnɒkjʊləz] *Fernglas* 5 sunset *Sonnenuntergang*
6 squirrel *Eichhörnchen*

6 *Learning to drive* **participles expressing reason** ▶ 159

People taking driving lessons make mistakes. Read the text about Tom's first driving lessons, the mistakes he made and the reason why they happened. Change the sentence parts that say why (i. e. the sub-clauses of reason) into participle constructions. Use a present participle or *having* + past participle.

Examples: As he was a beginner, Tom was nervous when he got into the car the first time.
Being *a beginner, Tom was nervous when he got into the car the first time.*
Because he had not looked in the mirror, he almost bumped into[1] a van.
Not having looked *in the mirror, he almost bumped into a van.*

(1) In his first lesson, because he felt nervous, Tom drove too slowly at first. (2) As he had not learnt the Highway Code[2], he did not know what some traffic signs meant. (3) Once, he turned into a one-way street, because he hadn't seen the sign. (4) In his second lesson, since he was driving too fast, he missed a right turn. (5) As he had gone to bed late, he couldn't concentrate[3] on what the instructor[4] said. (6) In his third lesson, because he had not noticed a red light, he didn't stop. (7) As he wasn't used to the gears[5], he made the car jump a few times. (8) In his fourth lesson, because he had left the handbrake[6] on, he couldn't get the car to move off. But after over forty driving lessons, he passed his test.

7 *Bad luck* **participles expressing time/reason: mixed exercise** ▶ 158, 159

The sentences tell you when or why something happened to the pupils in Year 11. None of them had a very good day. Find the sentence parts that go together, then join them using a present participle or *having* + past participle.

Examples: When he was walking to school, → Tom slipped on some ice.
Because she had forgotten her project, → Sandra got a detention[7].
As he hadn't learnt any grammar, → Sean failed the French test.

Walking *to school, Tom slipped on some ice.*
Having forgotten *her project, Sandra got a detention.*
Not having learnt *any grammar, Sean failed the French test.*

1 When he was getting out of the shower,	Leo couldn't give it in.
2 Because she had forgotten her purse,	Vanessa got lost.
3 Since he hadn't finished his project,	David swallowed[8] a fishbone.
4 Since she didn't know the way to the job centre,	Ed threw down his tennis racket[9].
5 While he was eating his school lunch,	Vince slipped on the soap.
6 Because he had lost the number,	Gina had to borrow some money.
7 After he had played badly for two hours,	Marc injured his shoulder[10].
8 When he was lifting weights,	Jerry couldn't phone Claire.
9 Because she was tired,	Greg couldn't play football.
10 As he hadn't taken his boots to school,	Ann fell asleep in the maths lesson.

1 bump into *auffahren auf* 2 Highway Code *Straßenverkehrsordnung* 3 concentrate *sich konzentrieren*
4 instructor *(Fahr-)Lehrer/in* 5 gear *Gang (bei einer Gangschaltung)* 6 handbrake *Handbremse*
7 detention *Nachsitzen* 8 swallow *(hinunter)schlucken* 9 tennis racket *Tennisschläger* 10 shoulder *Schulter*

8 *What were they doing?* **participles expressing accompanying circumstances** ▶ 160

Jane saw some of her friends by chance[1] while she was out. Where were they and what were they doing? Join the sentences using a present participle or a past participle.

Examples: Jeff was walking down Market Street. He was chatting to a girl.
*Jeff was walking down Market Street, **chatting** to a girl.*
Marion was driving down Mill Road. She was accompanied[2] by her new boyfriend.
*Marion was driving down Mill Road, **accompanied** by her new boyfriend.*

1 Dave was just leaving the house. He was talking on his mobile.
2 Phil was jogging in the park. He was listening to his walkman.
3 Jan was putting bottles in the bottle bank. She was being helped by her brother.
4 Vanessa was walking to the station. She was carrying a heavy bag.
5 Steve was driving down East Street. He was playing loud music.
6 Lou was crossing a busy road. He was helping an old lady with her shopping.
7 Lisa and Beth were chatting in a café. They were having an ice-cream.
8 Paul and Ed were fighting on the street. They were being cheered on by their friends.

9 *Describe the pictures* **participle constructions introduced by conjunctions** ▶ 161a

Put in *when* or *while* where necessary. There is little difference, so both can be correct. But generally we use *when* for a short action, *while* for a longer action.

Examples: Tim bumped into[3] an old lady *leaving* the restaurant.

Tim bumped into an old lady ***when leaving*** the restaurant.

1 by chance *zufällig* 2 accompany *begleiten* 3 bump into *stoßen gegen*

1 Tom met his maths teacher … coming out of the post office.
2 Julie noticed her boyfriend … protesting outside the factory gates.
3 Mr Forbes bumped into a cyclist … running to catch a bus.
4 Marie saw the neighbour's dog … taking her poodle for a walk.
5 Mark took a photo of his brother … standing on his head on the beach.
6 Liz saw an old friend … reporting the theft[1] of her car to the police.

10 *Fly the Eye* **participles: mixed exercise** ▶ 155, 158, 160, 161, 163

The London Eye is the world's biggest revolving wheel. Read about it and complete the text. Use a present participle, a past participle, or *having* + past participle of the verb given.

Examples: The London Eye stands on the Thames, ***overlooking*** Big Ben and the Houses of Parliament. ***Designed*** to hold 25 passengers each, the 32 high tech capsules offer spectacular views over the city.

(1 take) … 30 minutes, the flight gives guests an unforgettable[2] experience. Generally (2 speak) …, from the top you can see for ten to fifteen miles, but on a really clear day, you can see for 25 miles (40 kilometres), as far as Windsor Castle and Heathrow Airport. (3 see) … the London Eye for the first time, visitors are amazed[3] at its size and attractive design. While (4 admire[4]) … the view from a height of 150 metres, you can even enjoy a champagne picnic, a sushi picnic, a buffet of sandwiches or full brunch – for only an extra £300* per capsule (for 20 guests).

(5 take) … seven years to build, the London Eye was completed for the new Millennium, at first (6 be) … called the Millennium Eye. Though (7 design) … by British architects and engineers, strictly (8 speak) …, the London Eye is really a European project. (9 measure[5]) … 135 metres in diameter[6] and (10 weigh[7]) …1,900 tonnes, it could not be built in one place. So different parts were built in different countries – the capsules in France, the main steel structure in the Netherlands, the cables in Italy. It was an expensive project.

(11 talk) … of prices, a ticket costs £5.50 for under-sixteens and £11 if you are older. After (12 buy) … your ticket, you will have to wait in the queue for about half an hour before (13 board) … People usually stand (14 stare) … up at the huge wheel, (15 look forward) … to their flight. If (16 give) … the chance to fly The Eye, you should take it.

1 theft *Diebstahl* 2 unforgettable *unvergesslich* 3 amazed *erstaunt* 4 admire *bewundern* 5 measure *messen* 6 diameter *Durchmesser* 7 weigh *wiegen* * £300 = ca. 450€

11 *The creator of Sherlock Holmes* **part.: mixed exercise** ▶ 153c/d, 158, 159, 160

Everybody has heard of the detective Sherlock Holmes, but what do you know about the man who created him?
First, read the facts about the author of the Sherlock Holmes stories, Arthur Conan Doyle, then write an article from the facts by adding the extra information given.
Improve the style by using participle constructions. For example, use a participle construction to make one sentence instead of two, and change the underlined structures into participle constructions.
Study the examples first.

Examples:

Arthur Conan Doyle was one of ten children. ←	*He was born in Edinburgh in 1859.*
His father disciplined all the children. ←	*His father was a civil servant*[1]*.*

***Born** in Edinburgh in 1859, Arthur Conan Doyle was one of ten children.*
***Being** a civil servant, his father disciplined all the children.*

1 At school Arthur did not like being told what to do. ← He was often punished.	*He was known for being untidy and rebellious*[2]*.*
2 He became editor[3] of the school magazine. ←	*He was interested in writing.*
3 He left school at sixteen. ←	*He had passed his university entrance exam.*
4 Before university he spent a year at a school in Austria. ←	*He improved his German.*
5 He had to take jobs. ← That is when he wrote his first stories. He became a doctor at the age of 26.	*He did not have much money for university.*
6 He decided to try writing. ← He wrote all kinds of books and short stories, with some success.	*He was not very successful as a doctor.*
7 He gave up medicine at 32. ←	*He found that he could make more money with books.*
8 His first collection of stories, which was called *The Adventures of Sherlock Holmes*, made him famous.	
9 Doyle wrote five collections of Sherlock Holmes mysteries. He officially killed him off in 1894. ←	*Doyle had become tired of his hero.*
10 But Doyle's readers complained. ← At the request of the government and his readers, Doyle brought Holmes back to life.	*They refused to believe that Holmes was dead.*
11 He wrote a story which involved Holmes in a secret mission for the government during war time.	
12 Doyle died of a heart attack in 1930. ←	*He had become one of the world's best paid authors.*

1 civil servant *Beamter/-in* 2 rebellious *rebellisch, aufsässig* 3 editor *Redakteur/in*

The noun

A Complete the sentences with nouns from the list in the plural.

aircraft • child • grown-up • life • lorry • tomato

1 I've made a salad – just cheese, lettuce, eggs and ...
2 ... of all ages like to play computer games.
3 There was a train crash last week. Three passengers lost their ...
4 Angela doesn't always do what ... say. She's almost adult herself.
5 If you live near an airport, you get used to the noise of ...
6 There was a lot of traffic on the M1, especially ...

B Choose the correct word(s) from the brackets.

7 On Saturdays, Megan usually goes to (her aunt/her aunt's).
8 The class (was/were) really nervous just before the exam results were read out.
9 (A strawberry jam[1]/A jar of strawberry jam), please, and four bananas.
10 I've found the scissors. (It was/They were) in the bedroom.
11 There has been an accident. We're waiting until the police (come/comes).
12 I've got (some/a) useful information for you.
13 Unfortunately we had to leave, although the band (was/were) still playing.

C Translate the German sentence parts into English.

14 My sister gave me (*einen neuen Schlafanzug*) ... for my birthday.
15 (*Ist Kleidung billiger*) ... in England than in Germany?
16 My parents are going to buy (*neue Möbel*) ... for my room.
17 Our maths teacher always makes us do (*viele Hausaufgaben*) ...
18 You can't wear your black jeans yet. (*Sie ist*) ... still in the washing-machine.
19 Did (*die Informationen*) ... that you got at the job centre help you?
20 Whose idea was it? (*Die Idee deines Freundes*) ...?
21 Dad doesn't feel well. He's gone (*zum Arzt*) ...

D Spot the mistakes. There is one mistake in each sentence (pair).

22 There was a lot of damages done by the storm last night.
23 I've packed two shorts and five T-shirts.
24 Sarah gave me a useful advice this morning.
25 Which floor are childrens' books on, please?
26 Do you like my new jacket's colour?
27 Do you know where my sunglasses is?
28 I usually have a cup cocoa for breakfast.
29 Have you seen the newspaper of yesterday anywhere?
30 Pepper is the dog of my uncle.
31 I can't find my shorts. Where is it?
32 It was my parent's idea. I don't want to go on a language course.
33 I have bought an orange juice. Are you thirsty?
34 I've spent the pocket money of a month in just a week.
35 We need a new soap in the bathroom.

---

1 strawberry jam *Erdbeermarmelade*

The noun

? Correct yourself

A 1: *tomatoes.* 2: *Children* 3: *lives.* 4: *grown-ups* 5: *aircraft.* 6: *lorries.*

B 7: *her aunt's.* 8: *was/were* 9: *A jar of strawberry jam,* 10: *They were* 11: *come.* 12: *some* 13: *was/were*

C 14: *a new pair of pyjamas/some new pyjamas* 15: *Are clothes cheaper* 16: *(some) new furniture* 17: *a lot of homework.* 18: *They are* 19: *the information* 20: *Your friend's/ boyfriend's idea?* 21: *to the doctor's.*

D 22: *There was a lot of damage done by the storm last night.* 23: *I've packed two pairs of shorts and five T-shirts.* 24: *Sarah gave me a useful piece of/bit of advice/some useful advice this morning.* 25: *Which floor are children's books on, please?* 26: *Do you like the colour of my new jacket?* 27: *Do you know where my sunglasses are?* 28: *I usually have a cup of cocoa for breakfast.* 29: *Have you seen yesterday's newspaper anywhere?* 30: *Pepper is my uncle's dog.* 31: *… Where are they?* 32: *It was my parents' idea …* 33: *I have bought a carton of/some orange juice …* 34: *I've spent a month's pocket money in just a week.* 35: *We need a piece of/some new soap in the bathroom.*

Exercise finder

Sentences	CEG	Exercises
1–6	▶ 171, 172	▶ 1
7, 21, 25, 30, 32	▶ 179a–c	▶ 10
8, 11, 13	▶ 176	▶ 4
9, 28	▶ 177b, 180c	▶ 6
10, 14, 18, 23	▶ 175a	▶ 2, 3
12, 16, 17, 19, 22, 24	▶ 177c	▶ 7, 8, 9
15, 27, 31	▶ 175	▶ 3
20, 26	▶ 179, 180	▶ 10, 11
29, 34	▶ 179e	▶ 11
33, 35	▶ 177a/b	▶ 5, 6

1 *Puzzles with plurals* regular/irregular plurals ▶ 171, 172

How do the plurals of these words fit into the puzzles?

a foot ▪ knife ▪ man ▪ party ▪ potato ▪ tooth

b child ▪ crossroads ▪ disco ▪ grown-up ▪ mouse ▪ roof ▪ watch

a ➡

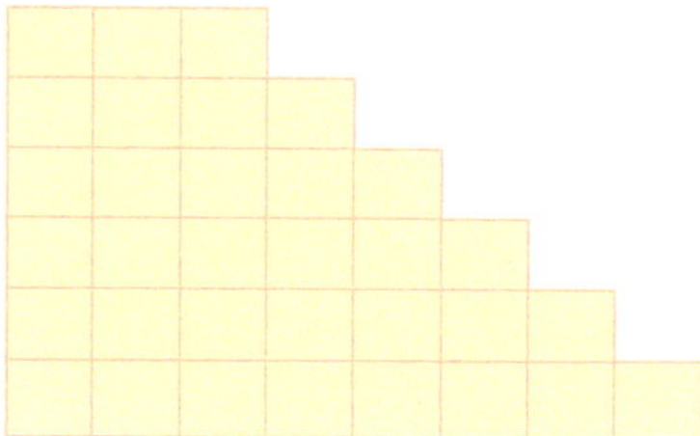

b ➡

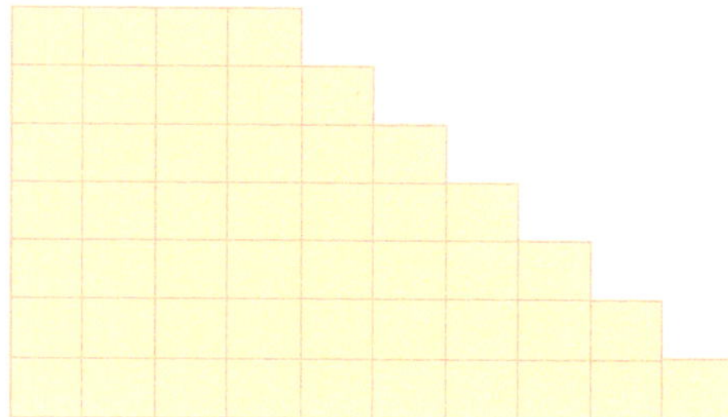

c Write three sentences using plural forms from a) and b). Use as many of the 13 plurals as you can. Your sentences should make sense, but they needn't be serious. Use your imagination.

Example: *I don't like* ***men*** *with big* ***feet****.*

2 *Clothes* nouns that are used only in the plural: pair nouns ▶ 175a

a Sarah is a student. She can't wash her clothes in her student's room, so she takes them to the launderette[1] or to the dry cleaner's. She has made a list of things to take. She has marked them with c (cleaner's) and l (launderette). Which things is she going to take where?

Begin with *a/an* or *a pair of*:

Examples: What is she taking to the cleaner's?
She's taking ***a pair of*** *black* ***trousers****,* ***a*** *red* ***sweater****, ...*

Continue.

b Now begin with *a/an* or *some*:

Examples: What is she taking to the launderette?
She's taking ***some shorts****,* ***an*** *orange* ***T-shirt****, ...*

Continue.

c Write a list of clothes you would like to buy soon. Use some 'pair nouns' (*trousers, jeans, shorts*, etc.) with *a pair of* or *some*.

Example: *I'd like to buy* ***a pair of*** *dark blue* ***trousers****, a sweater and* ***some*** *black* ***jeans****. I need* ***a pair of shorts*** *for my holidays as well.*

black trousers	c
red sweater	c
white jeans	c
trouser suit	c
shorts	l
blue trousers	c
orange T-shirt	l
pyjamas	l
white blouse	l
anorak	c
overalls	c
Bermuda shorts	l
red jacket	c
leggings	l

1 launderette *Waschsalon*

3 *Packing* **nouns that are used only in the plural**

▶ 175a/b

Jenny is going to Canada to visit a pen pal. She's packing her suitcase and her friend Marion is helping her. Complete their conversation with the correct words from the brackets.

Marion: Are you taking (this/***these***) sunglasses?
Jenny: No, I'm taking my new (one/***pair***). (It looks/***They look***) really good.
Marion: And do you need (1 this/these) headphones[1] for the plane?
Jenny: No, they always give you (2 some/one). Where (3 is/are) my soap?
Marion: And what about (4 these/this) dress?
Jenny: No, I'll take my new (5 pair/one). I need three (6 –/pairs of) tights[2]. And where (7 is/are) my shorts? I think I've already packed (8 them/it/one). I'll take a second (9 one/pair) too. It might be hot.
Marion: Well, you could always buy another (10 pair of/–) shorts or (11 some/a) jeans there. Clothes (12 is/are) cheaper in Canada and the USA.
Jenny: You're right, and earnings (13 is/are) generally higher than here. I'm taking three (14 –/pairs of) jeans. Do you like my new T-shirts? I must cut the price labels off. Where (15 is/are) the scissors?
Marion: I can't see (16 it/one/them). Oh, here (17 it is/they are).
Jenny: OK. Finished. Now all my belongings (18 is/are) in this one suitcase, so I hope my luggage[3] (19 don't/doesn't) get lost. I can't wait to see Canada. My penfriend lives in Banff in the Rockies, so the surroundings[4] (20 is/are) really beautiful. Oh, my pyjamas. I almost forgot (21 it/one/them).

4 *Richard's school* **collective nouns**

▶ 176a/b

a Read about Richard and his activities. Put in the missing noun and the correct singular or plural verb form of *be*, *have* or of the verb in brackets. What is more suitable? A singular or a plural verb form? If you think both are possible, write both. Hint: sometimes the pronouns used will help you.

band ▪ choir ▪ class ▪ ~~family~~ ▪ group ▪ police ▪ ~~staff~~ ▪ team

Examples: Richard's … (live) … in York.
Richard's ***family live/lives*** in York.
Richard goes to a comprehensive school. The teaching … … quite young.
Richard likes most of them. The teaching ***staff are*** quite young.

Richard's (1) … (2) … 9B. He has a lot of friends and a nice form teacher. Richard's a good singer, so he's a member of the school (3) …, which (4 meet) … every Wednesday. He's also good at football and he plays for the school. The (5) … (6) … bad losers, so they try hard to win all their matches against other schools. Richard has just joined the drama (7) … which (8 perform) … a play every year. That's a lot of fun too. In his free time Richard plays the guitar. His (9) … (10) … just given their first concert at the local youth club. They were great. The kids loved them. Unfortunately, Richard's bike has been stolen. In fact, a lot of bikes have been stolen from school. The (11) … (12) … warned pupils to keep expensive bikes locked or to leave them at home.

b Three of the following nouns always have a plural verb form. Which are they? If you're not sure, look up the words in a dictionary. Can you write a short story using all these words? Use your imagination.

cattle ▪ crowd ▪ government ▪ people ▪ police ▪ press ▪ public

1 headphones *Kopfhörer* 2 tights *Strumpfhose* 3 luggage *Gepäck* 4 surroundings *Umgebung*

5 *What has Emma bought?* **uncountable nouns** ▶ 177a

Emma has been shopping. What has she bought? Use *a* or *some*.

Examples: *She has bought* ***a CD, some apples, some nail polish …***

Continue.

6 *At the corner shop* **uncountable nouns** ▶ 177b, 180c

a Heike is staying with her penfriend Vicky in Scotland. Vicky's mother asks Heike to go shopping to the corner shop. She gives her a shopping list. How does Heike ask for the articles on the list? Use *a … of*, *two … of*, etc.:

bar ▪ bottle ▪ box ▪ can ▪ carton ▪ grammes ▪ jar ▪ kilo ▪ litre ▪ packet ▪ tube[2]

Examples: ***A kilo of potatoes****, please.*
Two packets of cheese *and* ***onion crisps****.*

potatoes – 1 kilo ✔
cheese and onion crisps – 2 ✔
chocolate biscuits
milk chocolate (large)
After Nine mints
strawberry jam
orange juice (large)
toothpaste – Everclean
fruit yoghurt – 6
vegetable soup – 2
tomato ketchup
sugar – kilo bag
cheese – 400 g
milk – 1 lt

b What do you buy in a *box*, a *can* and a *bottle*? Write down as many different things as you can think of.

Examples: ***a box of matches, a can of cola, a bottle of beer****, …*

1 battery *Batterie* 2 tube *Tube*

7 *Poor Amy* **uncountable nouns** ▶ 177c

a Which of the following words are uncountable? Think carefully.

advice ▪ damage ▪ cupboard ▪ furniture ▪ homework ▪ information ▪ ~~ironing~~[1] ▪ job ▪ luggage ▪ shopping ▪ ~~suitcase~~

Now do the exercise about Amy. Several people want her help. What do they want? Choose the missing word from the list above and use it with *a/an* or *some* to complete what the people are saying.

Examples: Mother: There's ***some ironing*** to do, Amy. Will you do the shirts?
Mother: And I've got ***a suitcase*** to pack. Have you got time to help me?

1 *Friend: I've got a problem, Amy. I need*		*Can you meet me to talk?*
2 *Sister: I'm going to Glasgow. I need*		*on train times. Can you phone the station?*
3 *Brother: Amy, I've got*		*that is really difficult. Can you do it for me?*
4 *Mother: Can you go to the supermarket? There's*		*to do for the weekend.*
5 *Father: Last night the wind caused*	*a/an ...* *some ...*	*to the trees. Can you help me in the garden, Amy?*
6 *Brother: Can you help me to clean out*		*in my room, Amy? It's full of rubbish.*
And can you help me to move		*around? I'd like my bed in a different place.*
7 *Friend: I'm going to the station. I've got*		*to carry. Only three big travelbags and two small ones. Can you help me, Amy?*
8 *Sister: I've got*		*for you, Amy. Can you take these things to the cleaner's for me?*

b Amy's mother and brother want help with three more things. What do they say? Write three sentences, as in part a). Use the notes below or your own ideas.

1 Mother: washing[2]
2 Brother: move – equipment – garage
3 Mother: housework – clean windows

8 *Quick check* **uncountable nouns** ▶ 177, 178

Countable or uncountable? The boy next door asked you to check his English homework. Unfortunately, only three sentences are correct. Can you spot the mistakes and correct them?

1 Tim has got blue eyes and black hairs.
2 I've got a good news for you.
3 Sarah gave me two informations.
4 There's a lot of cake left.
5 There isn't any bread, so we can't make sandwiches.
6 We haven't got many homeworks today.
7 We'd like two teas and a coffee, please.
8 They played a cool music at the disco.
9 That's a useful advice.
10 Walking up the hill was a hard work.

1 ironing *Bügeln* 2 washing *Wäsche*

9 *A crossword puzzle* **uncountable nouns** ▶ 177a/c/d

a Which nouns are uncountable? Read the clues and fit the correct words into the crossword. Write your answers across (→).

damage ▪ fire ▪ excuse ▪ holiday ▪ homework ▪ laws ▪ news ▪ painter ▪ plastic ▪ problem ▪ progress ▪ schoolday ▪ station ▪ traffic ▪ waitress ▪ weather ▪ work

1 There's some every day. It can be good or bad.
2 An accident can cause this.
3 There's a lot of this in town.
4 A material.
5 You probably get too much of this.
6 You are making this in English.
7 You usually get money for this.

Correct answers give you the grey word. It is _ _ _ _ _ _ _.

b Use the eight words of the crossword to write eight sentences. Remember that the words are uncountable. Write four sentences with *some* and four with *a bit of* or *a piece of*. Choose the most suitable phrase.

10 *Cathy's family and friends* **the possessive form** ▶ 179a-c

a Cathy Wilson is 16. She has a younger brother called James. The Wilsons live in Banbury Road, next to the Smiths. They also have two children, Sally and Tom. James and Tom are best friends. The boys are both in the school football team. They have a good football coach called Frank Miller. The Smiths have a big Labrador called Candy. She barks a lot, but everybody loves her. Mrs Wilson has a sister called Mary. The children like her because she's good fun. Sally and Tom have a favourite uncle called William. He always tells them new jokes. William has a son called Rick.

Who's who? Answer the questions with a possessive form (-'s or -s'). Sometimes there are two or more answers, so give them all as in the example.

Example: James? *He is **Cathy's brother**. He is **the Wilsons' son**. He is **Tom's best friend**.*

1 Tom?
2 The Smiths?
3 Cathy?
4 Frank Miller?
5 Candy?
6 Mary?
7 William?
8 Rick?

b Where can you leave out the word *house(s)* or *shop*?

1 The Wilsons are often invited to the neighbours' house for tea or supper.
2 The Smiths' house is quite big. It has a huge garden too.
3 Cathy and James are often invited to their friends' houses.
4 On Sundays they often go to their aunt's house.
5 Cathy sometimes goes to her friend Ann's house after school.
6 There are some shops in Banbury Road. There's a butcher's shop and a baker's shop and a newsagent's shop on the corner.
7 Uncle William's house is quite old. It has lots of small windows and ivy[1] on the walls.
8 There's a computer shop near his house too.

11 *A visit to the cinema* **the possessive form, the *of*-phrase** ▶ **179a/b/e, 180a/b/d**

a Complete Dan's conversation with his mother. Use a possessive form (*-'s/-s'*) or *of*.

Dan: I'm going to the cinema tonight, Mum.
Mother: In the ***middle of the week*** (week – middle)? Whose idea was that?
Dan: Actually it was the ***teacher's idea*** (teacher – idea). Mr Jones, our English teacher, said we should watch film versions of literature, and *The Lord of the Rings* is literature. We ought to know the (1 works – famous English-speaking authors) ... such as Tolkien. So actually, going to the cinema is more work than pleasure.
Mother: Mmm. Really. Well, I think you should stay at home. Your (2 last term – report) ... was pretty bad. You ought to do some extra maths tonight.
Dan: I've already done (3 today – maths homework) ... Where's (4 yesterday – newspaper) ...? I can't remember the (5 name – cinema) ... I think it's the one at the (6 end – High Street) ..., that's the Odeon. It's a (7 twenty minutes – walk) ..., so I had better go now. I don't want to miss the (8 beginning – film) ... Andy and Sue are waiting for me.
Mother: Who's that?
Dan: Andy is the (9 captain – our school football team) ... and Sue is (10 Andy – sister) ...

b Now translate the German phrases into English.

1 Dan goes to the cinema about once a month, but usually *(am Ende der Woche)*.
2 The last time he went was *(am Geburtstag seiner Cousine Meg)*. It was his present for her.
3 They saw a film called (*'Das Geheimnis des 13. Stocks'* (floor)).
4 Meg is already 18, so they were allowed to drive in *(dem Auto ihres Vaters)*.
5 Afterwards Meg invited Dan to a new pizzeria. He wanted to go there again later, but he couldn't remember either *(den Namen der Pizzeria)* or *(den Namen der Straße)*.

1 ivy *Efeu*

The article

A **Put in *the* where it is necessary.**

1 ... life in big cities is exciting, but it's expensive and dangerous too.
2 What do you know about ... history of China?
3 My brother hates ... school. He wants to leave and get a job.
4 How long did your sister have to stay in ... hospital?
5 ... school I go to is quite old.
6 I don't usually eat much for ... breakfast.
7 Walk straight on past ... hospital, then you'll see the park on the right.
8 My sister plays ... piano, but I'm not very musical.
9 Shall we go to London in ... August?
10 What are you doing on ... Saturday evening?

B **Complete the mini-dialogue with *a*, *the* or nothing.**

John: I'm in (11) ... hurry. I'm going to (12) ... cinema with Katie.
Beth: I'm going to listen to (13) ... radio – *Top of the Pops*. Then I'm going to (14) ... bed early. I've got an English test tomorrow. I've got (15) ... headache too.

C **Translate the German parts in brackets into English.**

16 My dad used to smoke a packet of cigarettes *(am Tag)* ...
17 My brother would like to work abroad *(als Ingenieur)* ...
18 *(Die meisten Einwanderer)* ... in Britain are Asians.
19 I was thirsty so I bought some coke. I drank *(die halbe Flasche)* ... in the shop.
20 We're going to Berlin *(am letzten Freitag im Juli)* ...
21 I go to the dentist's[1] *(zweimal im Jahr)* ...
22 I think *(du hast Fieber)* ... Perhaps you should stay at home today.
23 *(Die Schüler in meiner Klasse)* ... are all interested in sport.
24 My sister always goes jogging *(vor dem Frühstück)* ... I think she's crazy.
25 *(Die Kirche)* ... in Beech Road is more modern than ours.
26 I went to my friend's to do homework, but we watched TV *(die ganze Zeit)* ...
27 *(Meine Schwester mag die Schule nicht)* ... but she enjoys seeing her friends every day.

D **Spot the mistakes. There is one mistake in each sentence (pair).**

28 It's my birthday on the Tuesday.
29 My dad has to work late two nights the week.
30 After school my brother wants to go to the university.
31 My father is systems analyst.
32 I don't eat much. My brother eats the double amount.
33 Your sister plays guitar, doesn't she?
34 Computers are great, but I don't think they will ever replace the teachers.

1 dentist *Zahnarzt/-ärztin*

The article

? Correct yourself

A 1: – 2: *the* 3: – 4: – 5: *The* 6: – 7: *the* 8: *the* 9: – 10: –

B 11: *a* 12: *the* 13: *the* 14: – 15: *a*

C 16: *a day.* 17: *as an engineer.* 18: *Most (of the) immigrants* 19: *half the bottle* 20: *on the last Friday in July.* 21: *twice a year.* 22: *you have (got) a temperature.* 23: *The pupils in my class* 24: *before breakfast.* 25: *The church* 26: *all the time.* 27: *My sister doesn't like school,*

D 28: *It's my birthday on Tuesday.* 29: *My dad has to work late two nights a week.* 30: *After school my brother wants to go to university.* 31: *My father is a systems analyst.* 32: *I don't eat much. My brother eats double the amount.* 33: *Your sister plays the guitar, doesn't she?* 34: *Computers are great, but I don't think they will ever replace teachers.*

Exercise finder

Sentences	CEG	Exercises
1, 2, 23, 34	▶ 183	▶ 1
3, 4, 5, 7, 25, 27, 30	▶ 184	▶ 2
6, 9, 10, 20, 24, 28	▶ 186	▶ 3
8, 11, 12, 13, 14, 15, 22, 33	▶ 188, 195	▶ 7
16, 21, 29	▶ 192	▶ 6
17, 31	▶ 190	▶ 5
18, 19, 26, 32	▶ 187	▶ 4

1 *Mini-dialogues* ***the*** **with abstract/material nouns, nouns in the plural**

▶ 183

a Complete the mini-dialogues between Jane and her brother. Use the word in brackets, with or without *the*, as in the examples.

1 Max: I'm thirsty. Where's ***the cola*** I bought yesterday?
Jane: ***Cola*** isn't good for you. And it makes you even thirstier. Why don't you drink (1 milk) … instead? You can take (2 milk) … that's in the fridge. I'll buy some more later. It's healthier than (3 cola) … There are lots of vitamins in (4 milk) … Remember that (5 health) … is important.
Max: Shut up, Jane! You sound just like mum.

2 Max: (6 pizza) … was great, Jane. I didn't know you could make (7 pizza) … so well. It was just right, not too thick, not too thin. (8 pizza) … is usually awful when you buy it frozen from a supermarket. And (9 pasta) … you made yesterday was cool too. I knew that it wasn't (10 pasta) … from a supermarket.
Jane: You're right. It was from the corner shop.

3 Max: History homework again. I hate (11 history) …
Jane: I like it, especially (12 history) … of England – you know, Henry the Eighth and his six wives, etc.
Max: I know that two of his wives were beheaded.
Jane: Well, (13 life) … in England wasn't easy at that time, not even (14 life) … of a queen. (15 people) … didn't know what democracy was. Perhaps we think Henry was terrible, but for (16 people) … of England at that time he was their king.

b Partner exercise. Take turns to choose a noun from the ones in brackets in a). Your partner or you must make a sentence using the noun twice, first in a general sense, then in a specific sense, as in the example.

Example: You: Pizza.
Partner: *I usually like **pizza**, but **the pizza** from the restaurant near us is awful.*

2 *Tony's e-mail* ***the*** **with *church, school,* etc.**

▶ 184, 188

Here's an e-mail from Tony to his German e-pal Florian in Hanover. Put in *the* where necessary.

Hi, Florian!

You wanted to know something about my school and where I live. So here goes!
The school that I go to is big and impersonal. I don't like it very much, but I don't like (1) … school anyway. Our town is really quite big. We've got a university and even a prison. I often go there – I mean to (2) … town, not to (3) … prison. By the way, (4) … prison is not far from our school. I would quite like to go to (5) … college or even to (6) … university if I pass my A-levels. It would be cool to be a student. It's only a bus ride from (7) … university to the football ground, where I could spend most of my time. I love football. Close to (8) … university is (9) … hospital where I had my leg in plaster for a few weeks last year. I broke it doing judo. Being in (10) … hospital wasn't too bad. At least I didn't have to go to (11) … school or to (12) … church. (13) … church we go to is quite a long walk away. I'm always bored, but at least I can see my friends after (14) … church because they live in that area. There are a lot of cinemas in town. My friends and I go to (15) … cinema almost every week. We like science fiction and action films. Well, it's time to go to (16) … bed. I often do homework or write e-mails before going to (17) … bed – that's why it sometimes gets very late.

Bye! Tony

3 *A visitor from England* ***the*** **with phrases of time**

▶ 186

a A cousin from England comes to visit you. He doesn't speak German. How would you ask him the following? Be careful with the time phrases. Do you need *the* or not?

Examples: Was möchtest du zum Frühstück?
What would you like for ***breakfast?***
Was machst du normalerweise am Wochenende?
What do you usually do at ***the weekend?***

1 Was möchtest du zu Mittag essen?
2 Welche Sportarten treibst *(do)* du im Sommer?
3 Sollen wir am Freitagabend ins Kino gehen?
4 Möchtest du mit mir am Nachmittag ein paar *(a few)* Freunde besuchen?
5 Möchtest du am Samstag ein Fußballspiel sehen?
6 Hast du *(Is your ...)* im August Geburtstag?

b Your cousin tells you the following things about himself. Put in *the* where necessary.

1 I don't eat much at ... lunchtime.
2 I eat quite a lot in ... evening.
3 I don't get up very early in ... mornings.
4 I go to bed late at ... night.
5 My birthday's in ... July, not in ... August.
6 Do you remember ... Sunday before the accident?
7 On ... Saturday evenings I usually go to the disco.
8 I'd like to go to the cinema on ... Friday – if it's an action film.
9 In ... summer I go swimming and rollerblading.

4 *Correct the mistakes* ***all, both, double, half,*** **etc. +** ***the***

▶ 187

A friend needs some help with his/her English homework. Some of the sentences are correct. Which ones? Can you correct his/her mistakes?

Examples: The most pupils in my class are sixteen.
Most of the *pupils ...*
My T-shirt was really cheap. I got it for the half price.
... for ***half the*** *price.*

1 We didn't do any homework. We played computer games the most time.
2 The film was boring. I was asleep the half time.
3 I can't ride my bike. The both tyres are flat.
4 I learnt vocabulary most of the time, not grammar.
5 Most of the people I know are nice.
6 I eat a lot, but Sam eats the twice amount.
7 Who's eaten all the chocolate?
8 My brother watches videos and plays computer games the all time.
9 There's a sale on at Dillon's. You can buy books for the half price.
10 Sandra's ice-cream was the double size of mine.

5 What are their jobs? ***a/an*** **before jobs**

▶ 190

Here's a list of jobs. Read the information and decide who does what. Answer with *a/an*, as in the example.

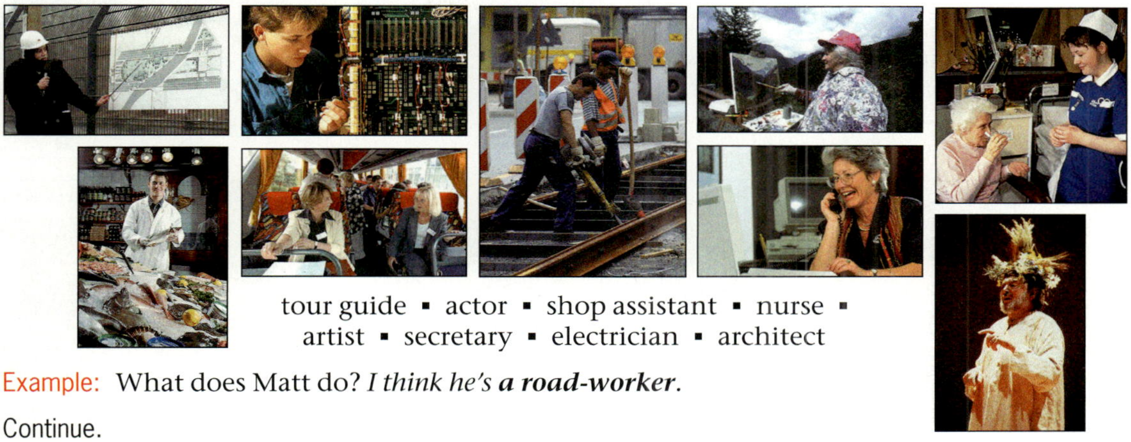

tour guide ▪ actor ▪ shop assistant ▪ nurse ▪ artist ▪ secretary ▪ electrician ▪ architect

Example: What does Matt do? *I think he's **a road-worker**.*

Continue.

	Matt	Sharon	Jane	Laura	Emma	Tim	Jerry	Nick	Lucy
works in an office		✔			✔				
works outside	✔	✔		✔					
is creative		✔				✔			✔
works with others	✔	✔	✔	✔	✔	✔	✔		
uses a computer		✔			✔				
sells things							✔		✔
works at night			✔			✔			
uses language				✔	✔				
visits customers		✔						✔	
is well-known						✔			✔
repairs things	✔							✔	

6 How often? How much? How fast? ***a/an*** **meaning *per***

▶ 192

Look at the signs and complete the sentences with phrases with *a/an*, as in the example.

Example: The restaurant is open *six days **a** week.*

1 Bed and breakfast costs only …
2 The speed limit here is …
3 Today's price for tomatoes is …
4 At the market red roses cost only (bunch[1]) …
5 The museum is open …
6 You can buy the champagne on offer for …

1 bunch *Strauß*

7 Meet the Martins   fixed phrases with and without *the* / with *a/an*

▶ 188, 195

a What are the Martins doing? Complete the sentences with the missing words and put in *a/an* or *the* where necessary.

Examples: Mr Martin is making ***breakfast***.
Mrs Martin is listening *to* ***the radio***.

1 Billy is having … Now he's having cornflakes … breakfast.

2 Jenny is … bed. She has … headache and …

3 Mr Martin is going … work. He usually goes … bus, but today he's … hurry, so he's going …

4 Billy is on his way … Now he's … class. … rule the first lesson is maths, but today it's French instead.

5 Now Jenny's feeling better. She would like to go … cinema, but she can't. Perhaps there's something good … instead.

6 Billy is very musical. After … school he usually plays … piano, but today he's playing … guitar … change.

b First, make questions with *a/an*, *the* or – . Ask a partner these questions and write down his/her answers.

What time do you usually go to		bed ?
When do you usually have		shower?
1 What do you watch on		TV?
2 Do you sometimes listen to		radio?
3 What do you have for	a/an	breakfast?
4 What time do you go to	–	school?
5 Do you go to school by	the	bus?
6 How often do you go to		cinema?
7 Do you sometimes do your homework in		bed?
8 What do you sometimes do after		school?
9 How often do you go to		town?
10 What time do you have		dinner?

Examples: *What time do you usually go to* ***bed?***
When do you usually have ***a shower?***

The adjective and the adverb

A **Use the correct form of the adjectives (comparative or superlative). Add words where necessary.**

1 That was the (difficult) … piece of maths homework that we've ever had. It took me an hour.
2 Diane is the (young) … of the four girls, and she's also the (good-looking) …
3 Selima is lazy in school, but her brother is even (lazy) …
4 Jason's mark in physics was bad, but mine was even (bad) …
5 If you need (far) … information, just phone this number.
6 Austria is nice for a holiday, but Spain is usually (hot) … Austria in summer.
7 Come on. We have to get off at the (near) … stop.
8 Which building is the (famous) … in the world? Is it the White House?
9 Who can tell the (silly) … jokes? You or your sister?

B **Complete the dialogue with the correct form of the words in brackets. Add words where necessary.**

A: Our school is collecting money for (10 disabled) … this week. We're having a disco and a concert on Friday. You'll come, won't you?
B: Sure. There's (11 disabled) … in our street. He's a good friend of my dad's. I hope your concert will be (12 successful) … than our last one. We collected money for (13 homeless) … The (14 unfortunate) … was, not many people came. Nobody knew about it.
A: Well, please tell everybody. Our band's playing. We're much (15 good) … than we were last year.

C **Translate the German sentence parts in brackets into English.**

16 Have you lost weight? You're *(dünner als)* … you were the last time I saw you.
17 These cakes are *(nicht so gut wie)* … the cakes from the baker's.
18 *(Das Gute)* … about school in Germany is that you have some free afternoons.
19 My car is smaller than yours, so it's *(weniger bequem* [comfortable]*)* …
20 Do you think *(die Reichen)* … pay enough taxes?
21 My computer is *(nicht so schnell wie)* … yours.

D **Spot the mistakes. There is one mistake in each sentence (pair).**

22 We saw a blind crossing the street alone.
23 Thank you. I haven't got any farther questions.
24 I'm eighteen, but my brother is elder.
25 The best about Charlie is that he plays fantastic football.
26 Shall we go to the chemist's[1] or to the butcher's first? Which is the next?
27 It would be more easy to start again from the beginning.
28 I think question number five was the difficultest.
29 I think Sarah is a bit taller as me.
30 Have you heard the last news about Arnie? He's going to make *Terminator 4*.

1 chemist *Apotheker/in*

? Correct yourself

A 1: *most difficult* 2: *youngest, best-looking/most good-looking.* 3: *lazier.* 4: *worse.* 5: *further* 6: *hotter than* 7: *next* 8: *most famous* 9: *silliest*

B 10: *the disabled* 11: *a disabled man/person* 12: *more successful* 13: *the homeless* 14: *unfortunate thing* 15: *better*

C 16: *thinner than* 17: *not as good as* 18: *The good thing* 19: *less comfortable* 20: *the rich* 21: *not as fast as*

D 22: *… a blind person/man/girl/…* 23: *… further questions.* 24: *… is older.* 25: *The best thing about Charlie …* 26: *… Which is the nearest?* 27: *It would be easier to start …* 28: *… the most difficult.* 29: *… taller than me.* 30: *… the latest news …*

Exercise finder

Sentences	CEG	Exercises
1, 3, 8, 9, 28	▶ 197 a/b	▶ 1, 2
2, 4, 12, 15, 27	▶ 197, 198	▶ 1
5, 7, 23, 24, 26, 30	▶ 199, 196d	▶ 3
6, 16, 17, 19, 21, 29	▶ 200	▶ 4
10, 11, 13, 20, 22	▶ 202 a/b	▶ 5a
14, 18, 25	▶ 202d	▶ 5b

A Change the words in brackets where necessary. Sometimes you have to add words.

1 The waiter didn't understand my Italian, but he smiled (polite) …
2 What's wrong with Layla? I think she's feeling (sad) … about something.
3 Mr Kahn always speaks to his pupils (friendly) …
4 If you want to get the seven o'clock bus, you'll have to get up (early) …
5 The little dog looked (sad) … at the children when they went out and left him behind.
6 Tim jumped as (high) … as he could, but he couldn't reach the apples.
7 Did your interview go (good) …?
8 It was a great concert. The best thing was, we got in (free) …
9 Ann lost the first set, but she was (extreme) … confident in the second. She won the match.
10 It's no use doing keep-fit exercises once a week. You have to do them (daily) …

B Which form is correct? Adjective or adverb?

A: I'm very (11 worried) … about my exams. I always get so (12 nervous) …
B: But you've worked very (13 hard) … I think you take things too (14 serious) … Just do as (15 good) … as you can. You've always been (16 pretty) … clever. Don't worry.
A: Well, I'm OK with languages, history and geography, but I can't remember maths and physics formulas very (17 easy) …
B: Well, learn them (18 thorough[1]) …, and in the exam try to feel (19 relaxed) … Don't panic.

C Translate the German words in brackets into English.

20 *(Fahr schneller.)* … We're late.
21 If you're always tired, you should go to bed *(früher)* …
22 My dad's flying (*morgen nach Madrid*) … for a few days.
23 Dave *(arbeitet kaum)* … He'll never pass his exams.
24 Pat, I forgot your birthday last week. *(Es tut mir schrecklich leid.)* …
25 My new jeans don't fit me. I'll have to *(weniger essen)* …
26 Your spaghetti sauce *(schmeckt fantastisch)* …
27 Your spoken English isn't very good. *(Du solltest regelmäßiger üben.)* …
28 We're meeting the others *(um sechs Uhr vor dem Kino)* …
29 Our band couldn't give the concert last night. *(Unser Sänger war leider krank.)* …

D Spot the mistakes. There is one mistake in each sentence (pair).

30 It rains never in Death Valley in California – well, very little.
31 Stop behaving sillily!
32 Ben works terrible hard, but his marks aren't very good.
33 Joe is great on the guitar. He plays fantastic.
34 It started to rain heavily. I had luckily an umbrella with me.
35 I go always to my best friend on Tuesdays.

1 thorough *gründlich*

Correct yourself

A 1: *politely* 2: *sad* 3: *in a friendly way/manner.* 4: *early.* 5: *sadly* 6: *high* 7: *well?* 8: *free.* 9: *extremely* 10: *daily.*

B 11: *worried* 12: *nervous.* 13: *hard.* 14: *seriously.* 15: *well* 16: *pretty* 17: *easily.* 18: *thoroughly,* 19: *relaxed.*

C 20: *Drive faster.* 21: *earlier.* 22: *to Madrid tomorrow* 23: *hardly works.* 24: *I am terribly sorry.* 25: *eat less.* 26: *… tastes fantastic.* 27: *You should/ought to practise more regularly.* 28: *… in front of the cinema at six o'clock.* 29: *Unfortunately, our singer was ill.*

D 30: *It never rains in Death Valley …* 31: *Stop behaving in a silly manner/way!* 32: *Ben works terribly hard, …* 33: *… He plays fantastically.* 34: *… Luckily, I had …* 35: *I always go …*

Exercise finder

Sentences	CEG	Exercises
1, 14, 17, 18	▶ 206	▶ 6, 7, 14, 15
2, 5, 12, 19, 26	▶ 209a	▶ 10
3, 31, 33	▶ 206b	▶ 6b
4, 10	▶ 207	▶ 8
6, 8, 16	▶ 208	▶ 9
7, 15	▶ 203b, 206b	▶ 6a, 14, 15
9, 11, 24, 32	▶ 203, 206	▶ 14
13, 23	▶ 207, 208	▶ 8, 9
20, 21, 25, 27	▶ 211, 212	▶ 11
22, 28, 29, 30, 34, 35	▶ 214, 215a/b/d	▶ 12, 13

1 *My best friend* **regular/irregular comparison**

▶ 197, 198

a How are you different from your best friend? Compare yourself with him/her. Write eight short sentences using these adjectives in the comparative forms:

~~young/old~~ ▪ fat/thin ▪ tall/small ▪ fair[1]/dark ▪ good at …/bad at … ▪ musical ▪ tidy athletic ▪ practical ▪ fit ▪ easy-going

Example: *She/He is (a bit)* ***younger***. Or: *I'm (a bit)* ***older***.

b Now compare yourself with your family – mother, father, sister, brother. Choose six adjectives from a) and use them in their superlative forms. Write six sentences.

Examples: *My father is* ***the oldest***. *My big brother is* ***the most athletic***.

2 *Eating in London* **regular/irregular comparison**

▶ 197, 198

Florian, a German student in London, is asking Vicky about the best places to eat. Complete their conversation with the superlative forms of the adjectives given.

Florian: Where are the (nice) … places to eat in London?
… ***nicest*** …

Vicky: There are lots of nice places. The (expensive) … restaurants are in the West End.
… ***most expensive*** …

That's where some of the (1 old) … and (2 traditional) … restaurants are too.

Florian: Well, actually I meant the (3 cheap) …

Vicky: Mmm. Well, the fast food chains. They're cheap, and they're also the (4 quick) … But try the chain cafés too. *Bon Appetit* has the (5 big) … sandwiches and salads. There's one on Carnaby Street and one next to Bond Street tube station. And *Café Russe* is the (6 cool) … for atmosphere, I think. Now, let's see. If you like Japanese, try *Sushi House*. And you get the (7 good) … coffee in London at *Starbucks*. For Italian food try *Pizza Palace*. They're on every street corner. If you like Chinese, you'll find some of the (8 inexpensive) … places in Chinatown. You can get a buffet lunch for just £3 to £4. Or try Bangla Town for the (9 hot[2]) … curries you've ever had in your life, real Bangladeshi style. You'll get some of the (10 tasty[3]) … food in London there. Some of the (11 trendy) … cafés and restaurants are in St James Street, and …

Florian: Hey, slow down. That's all fine, but where can I find the (12 typical) … *English* food?

Vicky: English food? Oh! Well, you can try the fish and chip shops. It's certainly not the (13 bad) … food – and it is *very* English.

1 fair *hier: hell, blond* 2 hot *hier: scharf* 3 tasty *schmackhaft*

3 *Mini-dialogues* **adjectives with two forms of comparison**

▶ 199, 196d

This is Amanda. In her conversations with different people she uses adjectives which have two comparative forms. The meanings of the two forms are different. Which form does Amanda use? Sometimes both forms are correct. Where?

Examples: Amanda: I'd like some information on pupil exchange programmes with the USA.
Teacher: Well, here's a brochure. If you need (farther/***further***) details you can phone this number. Tell me what they say in the (***next***/nearest) lesson. OK?

1 Amanda: Where's the (1 nearest/next) chemist's[1], please?
Woman: There's one just round the corner. If they're closed, the (2 nearest/next) one is in Lime Street.
Amanda: Where's that? Is it far?
Woman: Well, it's a bit (3 further/farther) than the station.

2 Amanda: Have you heard the (4 last/latest) news?
Jackie: What about?
Amanda: About the *Orion Boys*. They said in a TV interview that their (5 last/latest) album is also their (6 latest/last). That's terrible.

3 Amanda: Which bus stop is the (7 nearest/next) to the library, please?
Woman: East Street, I think. We're almost there. It's the (8 nearest/next) stop.

4 Jackie: I phoned about that job advert in the paper. The woman said you just need basic office skills, computer, etc. You get (9 further/farther) training on the job.
Amanda: Great. It sounds better than the (10 latest/last) job you phoned about.
Jackie: You're right. And that was much (11 farther/further) to travel every day.

5 Amanda: You've got an (12 older/elder) brother called Tim, haven't you?
Jackie: Yes, but his name is Mike. My brother Tim isn't (13 older/elder) than me. He's just fourteen.

4 *Compare the cars* **sentences with comparisons**

▶ 200a-c

John has just bought a new car. Mike has bought a car too, but it isn't new. Can you compare their cars? Complete the text with the missing words and the adjective given in its correct form. Make comparisons with the structures *not as ... as*, *-er/more ... than* or *less ... than*.

Examples: John's car is (big) ... Mike's and (comfortable) ... It wasn't (cheap) ... Mike's, but it's (noisy) ... his.
John's car is ***bigger than*** Mike's and ***more comfortable***. It wasn't ***as cheap as*** Mike's, but it's ***less noisy than*** his.

1 chemist *Apotheker/in*

Mike's car was not (1 expensive) … John's, but of course John's car is (2 luxurious) … Mike's. John's engine is (3 powerful) … Mike's too.
And what about Mike's car? It isn't (4 comfortable) … John's and it's (5 stylish[1]) … his, but it's (6 easy to park) … John's big car. Big cars use a lot of petrol[2], so Mike's car is (7 cheap to run) … John's. So John's car is (8 economical) … Mike's but it's (9 reliable) … his. John's car doesn't break down.
Of course, Mike's old car is (10 environment-friendly) … John's new one. It's (11 noisy) … John's and not (12 modern) … John's. But Mike loves his little car and he's very proud of it.

5 *Add a word* **adjectives used as a noun**

▶ 202a/b/d

a Where must you add a word? Add *person(s)/people, girl(s)/boy(s)* or *man (men)/woman (women)* where you think it is necessary, as in the examples.

Examples: I think the government should do more for the disabled … ✔
There was a blind … sitting next to me on the bus. He had a lovely dog with him. ✗
There was a blind ***man/boy*** …

1 There's a deaf[3] … in our road. She's 16 like me. We're really good friends.
2 I read in the paper that the police have found a dead … in the woods. She was quite young.
3 In America they have a lot of schools for the gifted[4] … I think we should have more of these schools in Europe.
4 We are giving a concert at the youth club. The money will help to buy a mini-bus for disabled …
5 Do you watch the soap opera *The Bold[5] … and the Beautiful …*?
6 In London every Christmas several homeless … are invited for Christmas dinner to a big hotel. I think that's great, don't you?
7 Several young … at our youth club say they never watch the news on TV.
8 There was a young … standing at the bus stop who looked just like my big sister's ex-boyfriend.
9 There are two new … in my class, two brothers. I think they're from Jamaica.
10 Does the government in your country do enough for the poor …?

b Now translate the German phrases and complete the sentences with your own ideas, as in the example.

Example: *(Das Gute)* about school is that …
The good thing *about school is that you have long holidays.*

1 *(Das Schlechte)* about school is that …
2 *(Das Beste)* about our last holiday was …
3 *(Das Schlimmste)* about our last holiday was …
4 *(Das Verrückte)* about my best friend is that …
5 *(Das Komische)* about the end of the film was that …

1 stylish *elegant* 2 petrol *Benzin* 3 deaf *taub* 4 gifted *begabt* 5 bold *mutig, kühn*

6 *Check your forms* **forms; formation of adverbs from adjectives**

▶ 205, 206

a Can you fit the adverb forms from these adjectives into the puzzle?

basic ▪ cheerful ▪ happy ▪ public ▪ simple ▪ true

b Which forms are adjectives, adverbs, or 'adjectives and adverbs'? Make three lists. Think carefully.

~~adventurous~~ ▪ ~~angrily~~ ▪ ~~daily~~ ▪ dull ▪ early ▪ fantastic ▪ fast ▪ friendly ▪ hard ▪ late ▪ nicely ▪ politely ▪ reliable ▪ shyly ▪ silly ▪ stupidly

	adjectives	adverbs	adjectives and adverbs
Examples:	***adventurous***	***angrily***	***daily***

7 *A first date* **formation of adverbs from adjectives**

▶ 206

Jill has got a date with a boy called Sean. But things go wrong. Complete the sentences with adverb forms of the adjectives given. Read the story through before you start.

angry ▪ careful ▪ careless ▪ loud ▪ nervous ▪ patient[1] ▪ polite ▪ ~~quick~~ ▪ slow

Example: Jill is going on her first date with Sean. She's late, so she's getting ready as ***quickly*** as she can.

Later, at the restaurant:

1 Sean hasn't arrived yet. Jill's a bit nervous. Has he decided not to come? Jill looks at her watch …
2 Jill thinks her watch may be wrong. She … asks a woman the time.
3 Half an hour later Jill is still waiting … in front of the restaurant. She feels sure that Sean will come.
4 Poor Sean is stuck in a traffic jam[2]. The traffic is moving very …
5 Sean sounds his horn[3] … but it doesn't help.
6 He waves[4] his fist[5] … but that doesn't help either.
7 Now the traffic is moving again, but Sean is very late, so he doesn't drive very …
8 There at last! But he parks his car … and bumps into[6] the car behind him. Oh, no! That will be expensive. And Jill has gone home anyway.

1 patient *geduldig* 2 traffic jam *(Verkehrs-)Stau* 3 horn *Hupe* 4 wave *winken, hier: drohen* 5 fist *Faust* 6 bump into *stoßen*

8 *A phone call* **adverbs with the form of adjectives** ▶ 207

a David phones a friend in Scotland and tells him the news, but the line is bad so he has to repeat the main things. Use adverbs in the new sentences. Think carefully. Some adverbs have the same forms as adjectives. What does David say? Can you complete the sentences?

Examples: Our football team won against another school. It was an easy win for us.
Our football team *won **easily***.
I'm going on a bike trip with a friend next Sunday. We're making an early start.
We're starting ***early***.

1 Someone kicked me in the stomach at school. It was terrible. My stomach hurt ...
2 The boy who kicked me is a bully. I'm a fast runner, but not fast enough. I ran ... but ...
3 I had to go to the doctor's. Luckily, it wasn't a long wait. Luckily, I didn't have to ...
4 We've got a maths test next week. I've practised a lot. It was hard work. I have worked ...
5 I got the right answers in my French test yesterday. I got the answers ...
6 There's been a lot of heavy rain today. I got wet. It has ...
7 I'm going to the cinema tonight. I have to go now because I'm a bit late.
I have to go now or I shall get there ...
8 By the way, there's a new daily comedy programme on TV. It's great.
There's a new comedy programme on TV. It is shown ... at 6.30.

b Use your imagination. Make up a short story using the following adverbs. You can change the order.

hard ▪ late ▪ early ▪ wrong ▪ right ▪ fast

Example: *On Monday evening I had to work **hard** for a school test, so I went to bed **late** ...*

9 *At the zoo* **adverbs with two forms** ▶ 208

Max and Tom decide to go to the zoo. Complete their conversation with the correct adverb form.

Max: Oh, no. I haven't got enough money for a ticket. Can't we get in (***free***/freely) somehow?
Tom: Well, how?
Max: What about the wall?
Tom: No, it's too high. I can't climb it. And I certainly can't jump that (1 high/highly).
Max: You can climb it if you try (2 hard/hardly) enough. Come on. I'll help you. Put your fingers and your toes[1] in the holes and pull yourself up. No, you're doing it (3 wrong/wrongly). Look. Like this.
Tom: Am I doing it (4 right/rightly) now?
Max: Sure, you've (5 near/nearly) reached the top.
Tom: Great! I can (6 hard/hardly) believe that I've done it. That was (7 fair/fairly) high.
Max: Now, where shall we go first?
Tom: To the reptiles. I want to see the Australian tiger snakes, they're (8 high/highly) poisonous[2]. It's a pity that some of the animals can't wander around[3] (9 free/freely).
Max: But not the snakes! Let's go to the gorillas and the monkeys. I like them (10 most/mostly).
Tom: It will be full there. People (11 most/mostly) take their kids to see the monkeys.
Max: Look, there's the reptile house with your snakes. That's (12 pretty/prettily) full too.
Tom: OK, then let's go to the monkeys first.

1 toe *Zehe* 2 poisonous *giftig* 3 wander around *herumlaufen*

10 *Describe the pictures* **adjectives after certain verbs** ▶ 209a

Choose a verb and an adjective to describe the pictures. Sometimes two verbs are suitable.

feel ▪ get ▪ look ▪ seem ▪ smell ▪ sound ▪ taste	awful ▪ bitter ▪ dark ▪ delicious ▪ comfortable ▪ friendly ▪ interested ▪ ~~miserable~~ ▪ untidy

Example: Laura has had some bad news. She …
… ***looks/feels miserable***.

1 I'll take these trainers. They …. really …

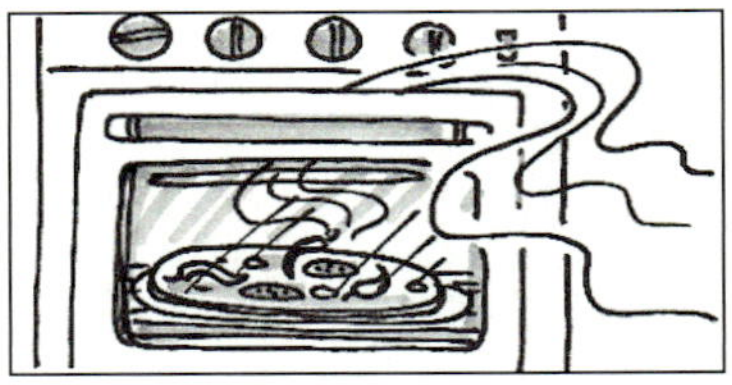

2 The pizza is almost done. It … …

3 Ann is practising the violin. It … …

4 He doesn't … …

5 Ben's medicine … …

6 Sarah's room … …

7 The pupils don't … …

8 Jason has put on the lights because it … … early in winter.

11 *I'll do things better* **regular/irregular comparison** ▶ 210-212

a It's January 1st, so Sally has made some New Year's resolutions[1]. She has decided to do things *better*. What exactly is she going to do? Complete the sentences with adverbs in the comparative form.

Examples: She doesn't behave well at home. — *She's going to behave **better** at home.*
She doesn't take school seriously enough. — *She's going to take school **more seriously**.*

1 She doesn't behave well in class.
2 She doesn't do her homework regularly.
3 She doesn't try hard in tests.
4 She never goes to bed early.
5 She never comes home punctually[2].
6 She doesn't write neatly.
7 She doesn't work fast enough in class.
8 She doesn't listen to the teachers much.
9 She doesn't concentrate[3] well in class.
10 She doesn't help much at home.

1 resolution *Vorsatz* 2 punctual *pünktlich* 3 concentrate *sich konzentrieren*

b What things could you do *better* at home and at school? Write three sentences using an adverb in the comparative form.

Examples: *I could do my homework **more carefully**.*
*I could stay at home **more** in the evenings.*
*I could chat **less** in class.*

12 *At the disco* position of adverbs

▶ 214, 215

Read about the disco visit and put the adverbs into their correct positions. Sometimes more than one position is correct.

Examples: Janet and Michelle go to the *Insomnia* (on Saturdays – usually).
(On Saturdays) Janet and Michelle ***usually*** go to the *Insomnia* ***(on Saturdays)***.
They went again (yesterday – in fact).
In fact, they went again ***yesterday***.

1 Janet and Michelle enjoyed their disco evening (really – this week).
2 They meet interesting people (in the *Insomnia* – often).
3 There are lots of students (at the weekend – there – usually).
4 They met two nice boys (rather[1] – in fact).
5 The music had stopped for a few minutes, when two boys came up and asked them if there was a phone anywhere (just – politely).
6 The disco wasn't very full, so they didn't have to shout (loudly – luckily).
7 They were chatting about everything and nothing (excitedly – soon).
8 They danced too (several times – of course).
9 They all decided to meet (the next day – in the shopping mall).
10 They will meet again (next week – at the disco – perhaps).

13 *Correct the mistakes* position of adverbs

▶ 214, 215

A friend has made some mistakes in her homework. Some of the adverbs are in the wrong position. The teacher told her to do the homework again. Unfortunately, she doesn't know what is wrong, so she asks you to help her. Can you find the mistakes and correct them? Not all the sentences are wrong. Look carefully.

Examples: Tony had almost an accident on his way to school. ✘
Tony ***almost*** *had* an accident …
We went to the cinema last night. ✔

1 My brother goes never to bed before midnight.
2 Tony speaks quite well German.
3 Sandra closed quietly the door and went upstairs.
4 I'll see you at six o'clock there.
5 We're going to Turkey next summer.
6 I never have been to Dublin.
7 Jane locked carefully the door and put the key in her bag.
8 We have decided already not to go to the party.
9 Hannah is still doing her homework.
10 I must really go now.
11 I'll meet you at the station at 5.30.
12 I clean my room always on Saturday mornings.

1 rather *hier: ziemlich*

14 *Oh dear!* **adjective or adverb: mixed exercise**

▶ 196, 203, 206

a Last week Sheila took her driving test – and failed. Here are some of the reasons. Choose the correct form of the words in brackets, adjective or adverb.

Examples: Sheila is usually quite a ***careful*** driver, but she was too ***nervous*** on the day of the test. She drove ***nervously*** from the very start.

Sheila is sometimes (1 lazy) … in school and she doesn't like learning, but for her driving test she learnt the theory part very (2 thorough[1]) … She did very (3 good) … in the written test. She answered all the questions (4 correct) … On the day of the (5 practical[2]) … test she got up (6 early) … She was (7 tired) … because she hadn't slept very (8 good) … all night. She had a (9 sore) … throat and her head ached (10 terrible) …
(11 Unfortunate) …, she was (12 extreme) … nervous when she got into the car. The examiner was not very (13 friendly) … – which didn't help much. She drove (14 bad) …, sometimes too (15 fast) … and sometimes too (16 slow) … The roads were very (17 busy) … She sounded the horn[3] by accident and a policeman looked at her (18 angry) … She knew that she had failed her test. Poor Sheila. Better luck next time …

b Write a short paragraph about a similar situation when you were *nervous* and did things *badly*, perhaps a test or an interview. Use six or more adjectives and adverbs.

15 *Marie's family* **adjective or adverb: mixed exercise**

▶ 203, 206, 209

Marie's mother is away for two weeks, so Marie is looking after her father and brother. She is telling her friend Claire about it. Complete the dialogue. Use the words given in either the adjective or the adverb form.

hungry/good
Marie: When dad got home yesterday he felt ***hungry***, so I made him a hamburger and a plate of chips. I'm afraid I didn't cook it very ***well*** – I burnt the hamburger and the chips were hard – but he said it tasted ***good***. I've never seen anyone eat so ***hungrily***. I think he was just being kind.

1 nice/angry
Claire: Your dad sounds … My dad would have got …
Marie: He doesn't always speak … to me. When he's in a bad mood he shouts … at me.

2 intelligent/stupid
Marie: Here's a photo of my brother Mike.
Claire: Oh, he looks very …
Marie: Well, he is. He's studying physics. But he seems a bit … sometimes. He doesn't always drive his car very … But even … people behave … sometimes, I suppose.

3 excited/serious
Marie: His girlfriend left him last week. I was surprised. It seemed … But he wasn't sad for long. Last night he sounded rather … about a girl he had just met in a disco. He talked … about her for ten minutes. He seems to be … in love again – until the next time.

4 good/bad
Claire: Something smells … Are you baking?
Marie: Oh! The cake for dad. I hope it doesn't turn out … like the first one.
Claire: I'm sure it will turn out … and taste … Don't worry.
Marie: Well, it doesn't smell too …, does it? And even if it is burnt, dad will eat it.

1 thorough *gründlich* 2 practical *praktisch* 3 horn *Hupe*

Quantifiers

A **Complete the sentences with the correct words from the list.**

a little • any • anybody • anything • anywhere • both • either • everybody • none • some

1 … of the girls play tennis – but Sarah plays better than Gina.
2 We've got plenty of crackers but only … cheese.
3 There's … milk in the fridge, but no butter.
4 The class gave several different answers, but … of them was correct.
5 You can take … bus. They all go to the town centre.
6 … cheered excitedly when Ballack scored the first goal.
7 Dave and Jeff have asked Ann to go to the disco with them, but she doesn't like … of them.
8 What Joe did is nothing special. … could do it. It isn't difficult.
9 I haven't had … to eat since early this morning.
10 I can't find my pen … Where can it be?

B **Translate the German words in brackets into English.**

11 There are *(viele)* … apples in the kitchen. We ought to eat them.
12 *(Keiner von uns)* … wants to leave school without passing our exams.
13 *(Alle Haustiere)* … need time and attention. If you haven't got time, don't get a pet.
14 On the computer course there are two groups. – And how many pupils are there *(in jeder Gruppe)* …?
15 Mr Jones teaches music, but *(keiner seiner zwei Söhne)* … is particularly[1] musical.
16 Can I have *(etwas Suppe)* …, please?
17 Do you take sugar in your coffee? – Yes, please. Just *(ein wenig)* …
18 I'm late. My boyfriend could arrive at *(jeden Moment)* … and I'm not ready.
19 All these stupid exams! I haven't had *(keine Freizeit)* … for two whole weeks.
20 I've got *(einige/ein paar)* … *Westlife* CDs. Would you like to borrow them?

C **Spot the mistakes. There is one mistake in each sentence (pair).**

21 How much peaches[2] did you buy?
22 Which of these two T-shirts do you like? – None of them. I want a red one.
23 All the shops are full. There are so much people in town today.
24 Nobody of us has seen Megan since she left school.
25 All pupils in my class are going on an exchange to France.
26 We've got sugar and flour[3], but we haven't got some eggs.
27 Sorry we're late. There was much traffic on the road today.
28 The Wilsons have got four girls, and every of them has her own room.
29 Have you seen any of those two girls before? – No, I don't know them.
30 There are only a little vegetables left. But there are plenty of potatoes.
31 The both boys are musical. One plays the keyboard and the other plays the drums.
32 Can we have some more cola, please? – Sorry, there's no left.

1 particular *besonders* 2 peach *Pfirsich* 3 flour *Mehl*

Quantifiers

? Correct yourself

A 1: *Both* 2: *a little* 3: *some* 4: *none* 5: *any* 6: *Everybody* 7: *either* 8: *Anybody* 9: *anything* 10: *anywhere.*

B 11: *a lot of/lots of* 12: *None of us* 13: *All pets* 14: *in each group?* 15: *neither of his two sons* 16: *some soup,* 17: *a little.* 18: *any moment* 19: *any free time* 20: *some/a few*

C 21: *How many peaches did you buy?* 22: *… Neither of them.* 23: *… There are so many people in town today.* 24: *None of us has seen Megan since she left school.* 25: *All the pupils in my class are going on an exchange to France.* 26: *… but we haven't got any eggs.* 27: *… There was a lot of/lots of traffic on the road today.* 28: *The Wilsons have got four girls, and each of them has her own room.* 29: *Have you seen either of those two girls before? – …* 30: *There are only a few vegetables left …* 31: *Both boys/Both (of) the boys are musical …* 32: *… – Sorry, there's none left.*

Exercise finder

Sentences	CEG	Exercises
1, 4, 7, 12, 15, 22, 24, 29, 31, 32	▶ 222, 223c	▶ 6
2, 11, 17, 20, 21, 23, 27, 30	▶ 219 a–e	▶ 3
3, 16, 19, 26	▶ 218	▶ 1, 2
5, 14, 18, 28	▶ 220	▶ 4
6, 8, 9, 10	▶ 224	▶ 7
13, 25	▶ 221	▶ 5, 6

1 *We need some butter* **some, any**

218a-d

a Meg and Louise are going to make some cakes and biscuits as a surprise for their brother's birthday. First, they write down what they have got and what they will need for the recipes[1].

What will they have to buy? What won't they need to buy? Use *some* and *any*.

Examples: *They will have to buy* ***some butter*** *and* ***some eggs****. They won't need to buy* ***any apples****.*

Continue.

We've got:	*We need altogether:*
250 g butter	*350 g butter*
no eggs	*8 eggs*
6 apples	*4 apples*
flour - half a bag	*1 kg flour (full bag)*
milk – a full carton	*half a carton*
no fresh cream	*a carton*
margarine – a full carton	*200 g*
1 lemon	*4 lemons*
sugar - kilo bag	*300 g*
chocolate - not much	*1 bar dark chocolate*
a few walnuts	*walnuts for decoration*

b Meg and Louise have finished their baking. Complete their conversation with *some* or *any*.

Louise: The apple cake looks good. Have we got (1) … icing sugar[2] for the top?
Meg: There should be (2) … in the cupboard.
Louise: I can't see (3) …
Meg: Perhaps there isn't (4) … after all. Well, then I'll buy (5) …
Louise: No, don't bother. I'm thirsty. Have we got (6) … cola?
Meg: There isn't (7) … cola, but there's (8) … orange juice. Would you like (9) …?
Louise: Yes, sure. Have we got (10) … candles for the birthday cake?
Meg: Oh, no, we forgot them. And I haven't got (11) … pocket money left. Have you got (12) …?
Louise: Not enough for twelve candles.
Meg: Well, how about just one for the middle?

2 *A walking tour* **some, any**

218a-c

Imagine that you are going on a walking tour in the hills with two friends. It's summer. The trip will last about four days. Apart from necessary things like a tent, compass, mobile phone, sleeping bags, etc., what else should you take with you? Remember, you have to carry everything on your back.

Examples: *I think we should take* ***some money****. I don't think we should take* ***any cameras****.*

1 recipe *Rezept* 2 icing sugar *Puderzucker*

3 *After the party* ***a lot of, much, many, a little, a few***

► 219a-e

a Angela's party guests have all gone home. Look at the food buffet. What's left?

Use *a lot of, not much* or *only a little*, and *not many* or *only a few*.

Examples: *There's* ***a lot of cake****. There isn't* ***much cheese****. / There's only* ***a little cheese****.*
There aren't ***many sandwiches****. / There are only* ***a few sandwiches****.*

b Anna asks Stacey about the party. Complete the conversation with *a lot of, much, many, a little, a few*.

Anna: How was Angela's party?
Stacey: Great. It was ***a lot of*** fun. But there weren't ***many*** people there. About twenty, I suppose.
Anna: Did you know them all?
Stacey: No, I only knew (1) … of them. David and Terry, Beth and Tess, of course.
Anna: Tess is at every party I hear about. She must have (2) … friends. Or rather, she must have (3) … time. We haven't got (4) … time for parties with all these exams. Was there anybody interesting there?
Stacey: There weren't (5) … boys that I knew. Only (6) … guys from Wilton Comprehensive.
Anna: Was there any food?
Stacey: Well, there was only (7) … food left when I got there. I was late because there was (8) … traffic on Kensington Road.

c Imagine you were at the party. Tell a friend what you had to eat and drink. Use *a lot of, a few, a little, not many, not much*. Write five sentences.

4 *A letter from Bournemouth* ***every, each, any***

▶ 220

Bettina is in Bournemouth doing a language course to improve her English. She writes a letter to her penfriend in Scotland. Complete it with *every*, *each* or *any*.

Dear Angela,

Hello, here I am in Bournemouth on the English course I told you about. So far it has been great fun.

Every *morning we start with conversation to warm up.* **Each** *of us has to talk for a few minutes. We can choose* **any** *topic we like. But (1) ... single time I get nervous and make stupid mistakes. (2) ... day we have five lessons of 50 minutes (3) ..., conversation and grammar. There are a lot of different groups of students and (4) ... group has its own teacher. But the teachers change classes for one lesson (5) ... day, so we get to know other teachers too. Our teacher is called Mike. There are only eight students in my group and ten to twelve in (6) ... of the others.*

Most students are staying with a family. In my family there's another girl from our school as well. We (7) ... have our own room. The house is on the main bus route. All the buses go to town, so we can take (8) ... Last night we went to the cinema, then we had fish and chips. It was cheap compared with most other kinds of food. We paid only £6 (9) ...

If you want, you can phone me on my mobile, (10) ... evening. You can tell me if my English has improved.

Love,
Bettina

5 *Opinions* ***all***

▶ 221

People sometimes make generalizations[1] which sound intolerant or stupid. Disagree with the following statements. Use *all* and *all the* ... in your answers.

Examples: All boys are noisy.
That's not true. Not ***all boys*** *are noisy.* ***All the boys*** *I know are quiet most of the time.*
Girls are better at languages than boys.
That's not true. Not ***all the girls*** *in my class are good at languages. Some boys are better.*

1 Boys are more intelligent than girls.
2 All teenagers like to spend their parents' money.
3 Boys are better at technical things than girls.
4 Girls work harder than boys.
5 All pupils are lazy.
6 Boys know more about computers than girls.
7 Teenagers waste a lot of money with their mobiles.
8 Boys are better at sports than girls.

1 generalizations *Verallgemeinerungen, hier: Pauschalurteile*

6 *What will you have?* ***all, both, either, neither, no, none***

▶ 221-223

a James and Hannah have gone out for a meal. Complete their conversation with *all, both, either, neither, no, none*. Sometimes two words are possible.

James: ***All*** the dishes on the menu sound good, don't they? Shall we have lemon chicken? Or how about a big, juicy steak?
Hannah: Mmm. I don't mind. Is ***either*** of them with chips? I'm hungry.
James: No, (1) … of them. But I'm sure we could have (2) … meal with chips if we ask.
Hannah: Is there any wine on the menu that we can afford?
James: No, (3) … (4) … the wines are pretty expensive. Red or white?
Hannah: I don't mind. (5) … No, wait. I've changed my mind. (6) … (7) … alcohol tonight. It will make me sleepy for the disco. Which one shall we go to? To the *Nightspot* or the *Underworld*?
James: They're (8) … great. We can go to (9) … You choose.
Hannah: Well, let's choose something to eat first. I'll have the steak.
James: All right. Me too. I'll order steak for (10) … of us, with chips.

b Work with a partner. Write a dialogue similiar to a), using *all, both, either, neither, no, none*. First decide what to order in an Italian restaurant then choose between two films at the cinema. Read or act your dialogue in class.

7 *I've looked everywhere* **compounds with *some, any, every, no***

▶ 224

Pete is looking for his history project file. He needs it today for school. He asks a classmate and his mother about it. Complete the conversations with *some-*, *any-*, *every-* and *no*-combinations, i. e. *something, anybody, everything, nowhere*.

Examples: Pete has looked ***everywhere*** for his file, but ***nobody*** has seen it.

1 Pete: I've asked (1) …, but (2) … knows where it is. I thought I had put it in my locker, but it's (3) … It's bright yellow with Britney Spears stuck on it. You can't miss it.
Kate: Perhaps (4) … took it by mistake. If I see (5) … with a yellow file, I'll ask them. It must be (6) … Perhaps it's at home. Perhaps your mother knows (7) … about it. Ask her.

2 Pete: Mum, do you know (8) … about a yellow history file? Have you seen it (9) …? I've looked (10) … for it. It has just disappeared.
Mother: Now, let me see. I threw some old comics and magazines away yesterday, they were lying on the floor in your room. I put them in the dustbin[1]. Yes, I think there was (11) … yellow too.
But I know (12) … about a history file. They've just emptied the dustbins. The dustbin van has just driven round the corner.
Pete: Oh, no!
Mother: Pete? Pete? Where are you going?

1 dustbin *Mülltonne*

Pronouns and question words

A In the following sentences different kinds of pronouns are missing. Can you fill the gaps?

1 Liz saw David in a shop, but he didn't see …
2 Hi, Mrs Gordon. Jan left this message for … – Oh, thank you, Lynn.
3 We've got three cats. Two black ones and a brown …
4 The Robinson twins seem to like us, but we don't like …
5 … say that the school in Park Road is going to be pulled down[1].
6 That's my moped – the … with all the stickers on it.
7 Nobody is lucky all the time. – … have to take the good with the bad.
8 Don't buy the big peaches[2]. The small … look better.
9 … sell really cool posters at that new poster shop.

B What's missing? A reflexive pronoun (e.g. *myself*) or *each other*? Or is the sentence complete?

10 Oh dear. Have you had an accident? – Yes, I cut … with a fruit knife.
11 Jane's mum saw a mouse in the kitchen. She was too frightened to move …
12 I met Sally in town. We hadn't seen … for ages.
13 Make sure the children are careful with the fireworks. Don't let them burn …
14 What time shall we meet …? Seven-thirty?
15 Tom and Rob don't talk much. I don't think they like …

C Translate the German words in brackets into English.

16 Has Mary got *(ein eigenes Zimmer)* … ? – No, she shares her room with her sister.
17 Jeff and I have known *(uns)* … since we were about five years old.
18 I think this computer game is Selima's. – No, it isn't *(ihres)* … It might be Mark's.
19 Janet fell off her skateboard and *(brach sich das linke Bein)* …
20 How can Justin buy all that new equipment? He hasn't got any *(eigenes Geld)* …
21 Have Sasha and Louise paid for *(ihre Konzertkarten)* … yet?
22 A: Which CDs are *(deine)* …? – 23 *(Diese hier)* …?
24 B: No, *(die da drüben)* … on the table.
25 Where's the money that I gave you? – I've put it *(in die Jackentasche)* …

D *Who/What/Which/Whose?*
Choose from the four question words and use the right form of the verb given.

26 … is the quickest way to the station? – Go up Elm Street, then turn right into Station Road.
27 … Diane (meet) … at the disco last night? Is he nice? Do I know him?
28 … colour suits me best? Orange, pink or blue?
29 … is your lucky number? – Well, actually, it's thirteen.
30 … is the girl in the red T-shirt? She looks like Marion Jacobs.
31 I heard that you failed your A-levels. – … idiot told you that? It's not true.
32 … (meet) you at the station when you came back from London? – My boyfriend.
33 … dog was barking all night? – I expect it was the Watsons' poodle again.
34 … of you saw the accident? – We all did.
35 … boyfriend looks like Justin Timberlake? Janice's? Wow!
36 … of your friends has gone to live in America?

1 pull down *abreißen* 2 peach *Pfirsich*

Pronouns and question words

Correct yourself

A 1: *her.* 2: *you.* 3: *one.* 4: *them.* 5: *They* 6: *one* 7: *You* 8: *ones* 9: *They*

B 10: *myself* 11: – 12: *each other* 13: *themselves.* 14: – 15: *each other.*

C 16: *her own room/a room of her own?* 17: *each other* 18: *hers.* 19: *broke her left leg.* 20: *money of his own.* 21: *their concert tickets* 22: *yours?* 23: *These (here)?* 24: *those (over there)* 25: *in my jacket pocket.*

D 26: *Which is the quickest way to the station?* 27: *Who did Diane meet at the disco last night?* 28: *Which colour suits me best?* 29: *What is your lucky number?* 30: *Who is the girl in the red T-shirt?* 31: *What idiot told you that?* 32: *Who met you at the station when you came back from London?* 33: *Whose dog was barking all night?* 34: *Which of you saw the accident?* 35: *Whose boyfriend looks like Justin Timberlake?* 36: *Which of your friends has gone to live in America?*

Exercise finder

Sentences	CEG	Exercises
1, 4	▶ 227a/b	▶ 1
2	▶ 227b	▶ 1, 2
3, 6, 8	▶ 239a	▶ 10
5, 7, 9	▶ 229a/b	▶ 3
10, 11, 13, 14	▶ 232, 233	▶ 7
12, 15, 17	▶ 234	▶ 8
16, 20	▶ 231b	▶ 5
18, 21, 22	▶ 230, 231a	▶ 4
19, 25	▶ 231c	▶ 6
23, 24	▶ 237, 238a/b	▶ 9
26, 28, 29, 31	▶ 244a/b	▶ 14, 15, 16
27, 32	▶ 242	▶ 12, 15
30, 33, 35	▶ 241a	▶ 11, 15
34, 36	▶ 243	▶ 13, 15, 16

1 *We saw them* personal pronouns ▶ 227a/b

On their way home from school, Matt and Ali saw two people running out of a bank. They looked like robbers. Later, the boys told a police officer what they had seen. Complete their conversation with the missing personal pronouns, object form.

Ali: They ran out of the bank. We saw ***them***. The man had a kind of mask over his face, but he took ***it*** off, so then I could see (1) … properly. He was tall and dark, about thirty. There was a woman with (2) …, but I didn't see (3) … very clearly. I think she had short, brown hair.
P.O.: Did they have a bag with (4) …?
Matt: Yes, they did, a kind of rucksack. The man was carrying (5) … over his shoulder[1].
Ali: They drove off in a dark blue van. We saw (6) … clearly. It looked like a Ford. We were standing near the telephone box and they drove right past (7) … We saw (8) …, but we hope they didn't see (9) …
Matt: Well, they couldn't see (10) … because I was hiding behind the telephone box. But perhaps they saw (11) …, Ali.
Ali: No, they couldn't, because I was hiding behind (12) …

2 *A visit to an English family* the German *sie/Sie* ▶ 227b

You have been invited to tea with the Grants, an English family who lives in your town. You take small presents with you. Here's your conversation with Mr Grant when you arrive. The missing words are all translations for German *sie* and *Sie*. What are they? Count how many different translations you have. Are there four, five or six?

Mr Grant: Oh, hello. Come in. What lovely flowers!
Have you brought ***them*** for my wife?
You: Yes, (1) … are for (2) …. I hope (3) … will like (4) …
And this is a bottle of local wine. (5) … is for (6) …
Mr Grant: That's lovely. Thanks. Now, where are my glasses?
You: (7) … are there on the table. I can see (8) … under the newspaper.
And this chocolate is for the children.
Mr Grant: Oh, it's their favourite. Jenny's in her room. You can hear the music, no doubt.
(9) … always plays (10) … loud, even on Sundays. Ben's in the garden.
Oh, and this is our cat. (11) … is called Cookie. Well, come into the garden and have some tea.

1 shoulder *Schulter*

3 *The German 'man'*

229a/b

a Decide which is the most suitable word for German *man* in the following sentences. Sometimes two words may be suitable, depending on the situation.

Examples: How do (they/***you***) spell 'Tennessee'? Is this correct?
(***They***/You/One) said on the news that there has been another train accident.

1 (You/One/They) said at school that our head teacher is leaving next year.
2 Take a raincoat. (You/One/They) can never know what the weather is going to be like.
3 (One/You/They) should always be prepared for the unexpected[1] in life.
4 (They/You/One) said on the local news that there's been an explosion in a chemical factory near here.
5 The junior school is in Grove Street. (They/You) pass it on the way to the library.
6 Did (they/one/you) say on the weather forecast that it's going to be hot tomorrow?
7 (They/You) are giving away free packets of washing powder at the supermarket.
8 (You/They/One) should not rely too much on[2] others. Remember that.
9 In an emergency (they/you/one) can ring this number.
10 (They/You) say that garlic is good for colds.

b Now write four simple sentences in German with *man*. Ask a partner to translate them using *you* or *they*.

Examples:	
Welche Sprache spricht man in Peru?	*Which language do* ***they*** *speak in Peru?*
Darf man hier fotografieren?	*Can* ***you*** *take/Are* ***you*** *allowed to take photos here?*

4 *What a mix-up!* possessive determiners, possessive pronouns

230, 231a

After a big disco party at the youth club, everybody is going home. But the teenagers can't find their belongings. Can you complete their conversation with *my/mine*, *your/yours*, etc.?

Sanjay: We can't find ***our*** coats.
Alison: Look, they're here. These are ***ours***.
This dark blue anorak is (1) …, isn't it, Sanjay? And this one is (2) …
But where's (3) … scarf?
Sanjay: Bina can't find (4) … scarf either. Perhaps she's got (5) …, Alison.
Alison: Well, tell her there's a blue one here. Could it be (6) …?
Sanjay: No idea. Ask her.
Alison: Well, have we all got (7) … CDs?
Sanjay: No, Jason and Pat haven't got all (8) …
Alison: Is this one Jason's?
Pat: Let me see. *Nickelback*. Yes, I think that's (9) … Jason, is this (10) … CD?
Jason: No, (11) … CDs have a red sticker on the cover. But it could be Liam's. I'm not sure.
Alison: What a mix-up! Liam has already gone home. Well, perhaps it was (12) …, but it's one of (13) … favourites, so now it's (14) …

1 the unexpected *das Unerwartete/Unerwartetes* 2 rely on *sich verlassen auf*

5 *Happy families* possessive determiner + *own* ▶ 231b

A lot of money doesn't always make you happy ...
Complete the text about the Richmans, using phrases with *own*.

Examples: Mr Richman has got *a company*[1] *of* ***his own*** and his wife has ***her own*** *business* too.

Together Mr and Mrs Richman earn a lot of money. Their son Mark has a big flat (1) ... in the city, and he's got (2) ... sportscar too. The Richmans have a daughter, Fiona.
She also has a flat (3) ... and a car (4) ..., of course. At the weekend she likes to ride. She's got (5) ... horse, in fact. The family have got a boat (6) ... They've even got (7) ... villa in Italy.
How wonderful life is!
The problem is, Mr Richman has got no time (8) ... and Mrs Richman has hardly got any time (9) ... There isn't much family life at all. They all go on holiday – but never together.
They've got (10) ... friends and they make plans (11) ... They all go (12) ... way.

6 *Describe the pictures* possessive determiner + parts of the body, etc. ▶ 231c

a Can you describe the pictures? Make sentences with the words given in brackets.
Remember to use *my/your*, etc. and not *the* before the noun, as in the example.

Example: *He has broken* ***his leg****.*

1 (take off – shoes)

2 (bump[2] – head)

3 (put on – coats)

4 (hurt – paw)

5 (put – pocket)

6 (think – break – arm)

b Have you ever broken anything or hurt yourself? And what about your family? Write a few sentences.

Examples: *I once broke* ***my left thumb*** *when I fell off my skateboard.*
My father fell down some stairs and hurt ***his leg*** *about two months ago.*

---

1 company *Firma* 2 bump *anstoßen*

7 *Did you enjoy yourself?* **reflexive pronouns**

▶ 232, 233

a Here are some reflexive verbs. Their German equivalents are also reflexive. Can you match them?

1 Help yourself!	a) *Hat er sich verletzt?*
2 Enjoy yourselves!	b) *Bedien dich!*
3 May I introduce myself?	c) *Amüsiert euch gut!*
4 Behave yourselves!	d) *Darf ich mich vorstellen?*
5 Has he hurt himself?	e) *Benehmt euch!*

b Pat and Mel are chatting about a party that Mel went to. Add a reflexive pronoun (*myself/yourself*, etc.) where necessary, or write nothing. Remember that English reflexive verbs are not always the same as German reflexive verbs.

Pat: Did you enjoy ***yourself*** at the party last night? Was it Diane's 18th birthday?

Mel: Yes. I'm sure Diane enjoyed ***herself***, but I wasn't feeling – well. In fact, I wasn't looking forward (1) … to the party. After a difficult exam at school I felt (2) … too tired to enjoy (3) … I just wanted to sit (4) … down and relax (5) … There were too many people – all Diane's friends, and all her relatives and neighbours. I introduced (6) … to her parents and to a few aunts and uncles, just to be polite, but one of her uncles talked about (7) … for at least ten minutes.

Pat: Ughh! I hate people who talk about (8) … all the time.

Mel: And later the music was so loud. I tried to concentrate[1] (9) … on a conversation, but you could hardly hear (10) … think! There was a lovely buffet, so all the guests helped (11) … But you could hardly move (12) … In fact, Diane's cousin Tony spilt some wine on my jeans. He blamed (13) … and he apologized (14) …, of course, but it really wasn't his fault. You could hardly turn (15) … round. Anyway, because of the accident with the wine, Tony invited me out. We're meeting (16) … tomorrow evening at seven.

8 *Teach yourself* **reflexive pronoun or *each other***

▶ 234

Flo and his girlfriend Tine are on holiday in England, visiting their English friends Max and Gina. Last week they went on a bus tour of Cornwall and Devon. Back home they are telling Max and Gina about it. Put in a reflexive pronoun or *each other*.

Max: How was Cornwall? Did you enjoy ***yourselves***?

Tine: Yes, thanks. Great! We met some nice people on the bus too. We were talking German to ***each other*** and we noticed that a man and a couple opposite were listening. I saw them smile at (1) …

Flo: They said something to (2) … Then the man introduced (3) … to us, 'We're going on holiday to Germany, so we're teaching (4) … German. We've got a '*Teach* (5) …' book, but we need some practice speaking. I say the irregular verbs to (6) …, but we help (7) … with exercises.' He laughed, then they both said a few funny sentences in German. They seemed to be quite proud of (8) … because they had never spoken German to Germans before. His wife said, 'We ask (9) … vocabulary too.' Then she said all the months of the year and all the days of the week in German, plus her birthday and her age. She really seemed to be enjoying (10) … It was so funny for us.

Gina: So you really amused[2] (11) …

Tine: Yes, we did. I don't usually like people who talk about (12) … but they were really sweet. If Bill or Norah phones for us in German, you will know who it is.

1 concentrate *sich konzentrieren* 2 amuse *amüsieren*

9 *Mini-dialogues* **demonstrative determiners, demonstr. pronouns** ► 237, 238a-c

a Complete the dialogues with *this*, *that*, *these* or *those*.

Examples: Jill: Excuse me. Does ***this*** bus go to Victoria?
Man: No, it doesn't. You need ***that*** one, the 127, or any of ***those*** red ones over there.

1 At the market

Anita: (1) … strawberries over there look delicious. Shall we take some?
Lisa: What about (2) … here? They're a bit cheaper, but they're smaller.
Anita: And look at (3) … pineapple. I can hardly hold it. It's really heavy.
Lisa: Why not take (4) … one over there? It's even bigger.

2 Photos

Holly: Would you like to see (5) … photos of Washington? Here you are.
Val: Thanks. Oh, great! Where was (6) … one taken?
Holly: Which one? Oh, my penfriend took (7) … in front of the FBI building.
Val: I love (8) … trousers that you're wearing on the photo. They look great.
Holly: Look, (9) … two photos are my favourites, taken in front of the White House.

3 Finding the way

Sam: Are you sure (10) … is the right way?
Tom: Well, here's a church. Liz said it's the street opposite the church. But look, there's another church further down the road. So did she mean (11) … church or (12) … one down there?
Sam: Shall I ask (13) … people waiting for the bus over there?
Tom: We can't. We don't know which street we're looking for. I'll phone Liz on my mobile. Liz? Is (14) … you? (15) … is Tom.

b Work with a partner. Write a dialogue with the title *Shopping*. Two people are looking at clothes in a store. Make sure that you use *this*, *that*, *these*, *those* at least once each. Use your imagination.

10 *He's already got one* **the prop-word *one*** ► 201, 239a

Donna would like to buy her boyfriend a birthday present. Her friend Kay is making suggestions. Give Donna's answers with the prop-word *one* or *ones*.

Examples: Kay: How about a pen? (expensive – parents)
Donna: *No, not a pen. He's got an expensive* ***one*** *from his parents.*
Kay: Well, what about some new sunglasses? (very modern – last girlfriend)
Donna: *No, not sunglasses. He's got some very modern* ***ones*** *from his last girlfriend.*

Kay:
1 How about a new wallet[1]? (leather – sister)
2 Let's see. I know. An electric shaver[2]. (expensive German – father)
3 A pocket calculator? (new American)
4 Some headphones for his walkman? (high-quality Japanese)
5 A digital watch? (waterproof Swiss)
6 Posters of his favourite bands? (four mega-size)
7 Sweat shirts? (three new)
8 A silver ring? (valuable antique – grandmother)
It's really no fun having a boyfriend who's got everything.

1 wallet *Brieftasche* 2 electric shaver *Rasierapparat*

11 *Are you a typical teenager?* **various question words**

▶ 241

a Do you think you are a typical teenager?
First, complete the questions with question words: *where, when, which, whose, how much, how long, how often*, etc.

1 … do you go when you want to have an evening out?
2 … do you do your homework? In the afternoons or evenings?
3 … do you spend on homework every week? More than ten hours?
4 … pays your mobile phone bills?
5 … text messages do you send every day?
6 … time do you spend online every week?
7 … important are clothes to you?
8 … do you buy clothes or shoes with designer labels? More than twice a year?
9 … is the coolest designer label in the scene at the moment?
10 … do you do when you have extra money to spend?
11 … do you sometimes get angry or protest? Name the reasons.
12 … opinion or advice do you ask for, if you have a problem? (For example, a friend's advice, your parents' opinion, a teacher's advice?)

b Now write answers to the questions.

c Work in small groups. Go through the completed questions and compare your answers.
Or: Discuss everybody's answers in class. Do you think you are a typical teenager?

12 *A strange dream* ***who, what***

▶ 6, 242

A friend tells you about a strange dream, so confusing that you don't quite understand it. You ask a lot of questions. What do you want to know?

Examples: Friend: In the dream somebody was running after me.
You: ***Who** was running after you?*
Friend: I saw something terrible.
You: ***What** did you see?*
Friend: I called someone for help.
You: ***Who** did you call for help?*

Friend:
1 Something was making a terrible noise.
2 Somebody heard me shouting.
3 I was afraid of something.
4 I think I was running to someone.
5 I saw someone following me.
6 I couldn't run fast enough. Something was holding me back.
7 Someone tried to help me.
8 Someone shouted my name.
9 Then something grabbed[1] me from behind.
10 Suddenly I recognized someone.

1 grab *packen, anfassen*

13 *A computer theft* ***who, which*** ▶ 243

Some Year 10 pupils were in school one Friday evening preparing the hall for a school party the next day. There were no teachers present[1]. Two pupils heard a noise and went to see what it was. They discovered that all the new computers had been stolen from the computer room. They saw two people running away and they heard a van drive off. The police asked lots of questions. What were they? Translate the questions with *who* or *which* and use the simple past (not in sentence number 8).

Example: Wer entdeckte den Diebstahl? *(discover – theft)*
***Who** discovered the theft?*

Example: Welche Schüler waren in der Schule?
***Which** pupils were in school?*

1 Welche Tür war nicht abgesperrt? *(locked)*
2 Welche Schüler haben etwas gehört?
3 Wer wusste, dass die Schule neue Computer hatte?
4 Wen habt ihr beim Weglaufen gesehen? *(running away)*
5 Wer hat die Polizei angerufen?
6 Mit welchem Polizisten hast du gesprochen?
7 Welcher der Schüler hat die Schulleitung informiert? *(headmaster)*
8 Wer von euch kann die Männer beschreiben? *(describe)*

14 *Shoe shopping* ***what, which*** ▶ 244

a David wants to buy some new trainers[2]. In the shoe shop, the assistant is asking him some questions. Can you complete them with *what* or *which*?

Example: … kind of shoes do you want?
***What** kind of shoes do you want?*

Example: … ones do you like best?
***Which** ones do you like best?*

1 … size are you?
2 … of the shoes do you like?
3 … colour would you like?
4 … ones would you like to try on first? The black, the white or the blue ones?
5 … pair feels most comfortable?
6 … shoes fit best? These, those or the grey ones?

David also asked some questions.

7 … other colours do you have?
8 … shoes have I already tried on?
9 … pair is the cheapest?
10 … size are the grey ones?

b Write a dialogue using similar questions to the ones in a). You want to buy some new jeans in a boutique. Ask the shop assistant about size, colour, designer labels, prices, etc.

1 present *anwesend* 2 trainers *Turnschuhe*

15 *A bad connection* **question words: mixed exercise** ▶ 241-244

You are talking to a friend on your mobile, but you can't hear him/her very well. Ask questions about the things you don't understand. Sometimes more than one question word is suitable.

Examples: Friend: ???? phoned me yesterday.
You: ***Who** phoned you yesterday?*
Friend: You won't believe it, but I got ???? e-mails yesterday.
You: ***How many** e-mails did you get yesterday?*

Friend:
1 I went to ???? last night.
2 I saw ???? at the disco.
3 He didn't mention ????
4 He was with ????
5 He looked ????
6 ???? asked me for my telephone number.
7 I went home at about ????
8 When I got home I realized ????
9 I had forgotten ????
10 Then I watched ???? videos again.

16 *A local hero* **question words: mixed exercise** ▶ 241-244

a Max has written a feature on a 'local hero', a well-known person in his town, for the school magazine. He interviewed the town's best footballer, Jimmy Wild. These are Jimmy's answers. What were Max's questions? Sometimes two question words are suitable.

Example: ***When** did you join the team?*
I joined the team three years ago.

Example: ***How many** goals did you score last season?*
I scored about fifty goals last season.

1 I think my best match last season was the one against Stockdale.
2 I have been team captain for two years.
3 I train three hours a day.
4 I usually start training at eleven o'clock.
5 I normally get up at about nine o'clock.
6 I'm quite tall. I'm one metre ninety-three.
7 I weigh 85 kilos.
8 I come from Newcastle originally.
9 My girlfriend is my biggest fan.
10 I get about a hundred fan letters every week.
11 I usually go to Newcastle at the weekends, to visit my mother.
12 In my free time I go shopping, I visit friends, I answer fan mail.
13 I really don't know why I am so popular – probably because I score a lot of goals.
14 I think *Manchester United* will win the European Cup. They're a good team.

b Write down three more questions to ask Jimmy. Begin with question words.

Conditional sentences

A **Fill in the correct tenses of the verbs in brackets.**

1 If the weather is nice tomorrow, we (have) … a barbecue.
2 Would you like to live in America if you (be) … able to choose?
3 My brother would have had a car by now if he (not – fail) … his driving test twice.
4 We (not – tell) … anyone if you want to keep this information secret.
5 If I (be) … you, I would take the job offer.
6 We could have helped Jenny if we (know) … about her problems.
7 If I climb a lot of steps, I (get) … out of breath.
8 I (give) … you a fair price if you decided to sell your computer.
9 If the taxi-driver (not – get) … lost, we could have got here on time.
10 I could buy those white jeans if I (have) … ten pounds more.
11 If Leo (need) … some advice on A-level subjects, he could ask his form teacher[1].
12 Would you go out more often if you (not – have to) … do so much homework?

B **Translate the German clauses in brackets into English.**

13 You could save a lot of time *(wenn du ein Auto hättest)* …
14 *(Jane hätte die Antwort gewusst)* … if she had paid attention in class.
15 I would work harder in maths and physics *(wenn ich du wäre)* …
16 If Peter doesn't come soon, *(essen wir ohne ihn)* …
17 *(Wenn du laufen würdest)* …, you would catch the bus.
18 Tony could have passed the exam easily *(wenn er nicht so faul gewesen wäre)* …

C **Spot the mistakes. There is one mistake in each sentence (pair).**

19 If you wait a minute, I go with you.
20 Peter might be at the party. When I see him, I'll give him your message.
21 If you would go by train, it would be quicker than by bus.
22 I could have phoned you if you didn't forget to give me your new number.
23 What would you do if somebody would give you a thousand dollars?
24 If we hadn't forgotten the map, we had not got lost.
25 If you arrive in Bristol, I'll pick you up from the station.
26 I wouldn't believe everything that John says if I would be you.
27 If somebody would have stolen your money, what would you have done?
28 If I don't tidy my room on Saturdays, my mother will complain.
29 I might speak perfect English if I live in America. But I don't.
30 If I move my head to the left, I will get a sharp pain[2] in my neck.
31 If the weather will be good, we could go swimming tomorrow.
32 If I would win a lot of money, I might buy a house for my family.

1 form teacher *Klassenlehrer* 2 sharp pain *heftiger Schmerz*

Conditional sentences

? Correct yourself

A 1: *If the weather is nice tomorrow, we will have a barbecue.* 2: *Would you like to live in America if you were able to choose?* 3: *My brother would have had a car by now if he hadn't failed his driving test twice.* 4: *We won't tell anyone if you want to keep this information secret.* 5: *If I were you, I would take the job offer.* 6: *We could have helped Jenny if we had known about her problems.* 7: *If I climb a lot of steps, I get out of breath.* 8: *I would give you a fair price if you decided to sell your computer.* 9: *If the taxi-driver hadn't got lost, we could have got here on time.* 10: *I could buy those white jeans if I had ten pounds more.* 11: *If Leo needs some advice on A-level subjects, he could ask his form teacher.* 12: *Would you go out more often if you didn't have to do so much homework?*

B 13: *You could save a lot of time if you had a car.* 14: *Jane would have known the answer if she had paid attention in class.* 15: *I would work harder in maths and physics if I were you.* 16: *If Peter doesn't come soon, we'll eat without him.* 17: *If you ran, you would catch the bus.* 18: *Tony could have passed the exam easily if he hadn't been so lazy.*

C 19: *If you wait a minute, I will go with you.* 20: *Peter might be at the party. If I see him, I'll give him your message.* 21: *If you went by train, it would be quicker than by bus.* 22: *I could have phoned you if you hadn't forgotten to give me your new number.* 23: *What would you do if somebody gave you a thousand dollars?* 24: *If we hadn't forgotten the map, we wouldn't have got lost.* 25: *When you arrive in Bristol, I'll pick you up from the station.* 26: *I wouldn't believe everything that John says if I were you.* 27: *If somebody had stolen your money, what would you have done?* 28: *If I don't tidy my room on Saturdays, my mother complains.* 29: *I might speak perfect English if I lived in America. But I don't.* 30: *If I move my head to the left, I get a sharp pain in my neck.* 31: *If the weather is good, we could go swimming tomorrow.* 32: *If I won a lot of money, I might buy a house for my family.*

Exercise finder

Sentences	CEG	Exercises
1, 4, 16, 19	▶ 252a	▶ 2, 12
2, 8, 12, 17, 21, 23	▶ 253a	▶ 5, 6, 12
3, 14, 24, 27	▶ 254	▶ 9, 10, 11, 12
5, 15, 26	▶ 253b	▶ 8
6, 9, 18, 22	▶ 254	▶ 11
7, 28, 30	▶ 252b	▶ 4
10, 13	▶ 253a	▶ 7a
11, 31	▶ 252a	▶ 3
20, 25	▶ 251d	▶ 1
29, 32	▶ 253a	▶ 7b

1 *A trip to Edinburgh* ***if* or *when***

▶ 251d

Megan is going to Edinburgh to visit her relatives. Complete the mini-dialogues with *if* or *when*.

1 At the station

Megan: ***If*** the train's on time, it will leave in about ten minutes.
Mother: I'll pick you up from the station ***when*** you get back. Let me know the time.
Megan: OK. Thanks. I'll phone you (1) … I know which train I'll be on.
Mother: You didn't have much breakfast. (2) … you're hungry, get something to eat on the train.
Megan: OK. Bye, then. I'll phone you (3) … I arrive.

2 On the train

Megan: Do you mind (4) … I open the window?
Woman: No, not at all. It's too warm in here. I feel sleepy.
Megan: (5) … there's a draught[1], I'll close it again.
Woman: (6) … I fall asleep, will you wake me (7) … we get to Newcastle? I have to change there.

3 Arrival in Edinburgh

Ben: Hi, Megan! How was the journey? Give me your case. I'll carry it for you, (8) … you like.
Megan: Hi, favourite cousin! Thanks, it's heavy. How's everybody at home?
Ben: They're all looking forward to seeing you. Mum's made lots of food, so (9) … we get home, we'll have supper. And (10) … the weather's good tomorrow, we're going to have a big barbecue – specially for you. So I'm really glad you've come.

2 *What will happen if …?* **conditional sentence I**

▶ 252a

a Dan would like to go to the disco, but it's Wednesday and he's got school the next day. He is thinking about what *will/won't happen if he goes*. Write conditional sentences (type I).

Examples: *If I* ***go*** *to the disco, I'****ll come*** *home late.*
If I ***come*** *home late, I* ***won't go*** *to bed until after twelve.*
If I ***don't go*** *to bed until after twelve, …*
Continue.

~~go to the disco~~ ▪ ~~come home late~~ ▪ ~~not go to bed until after twelve~~ ▪ get up late ▪ not catch the school bus ▪ have to walk ▪ not arrive on time ▪ make the teacher angry ▪ get extra homework ▪ have to stay in tomorrow night ▪ miss the rock concert ▪ lose the fifteen pounds for the ticket

Is it a good idea to go to the disco or not? What do you think Dan will decide to do?

b What *will happen/won't happen if you don't do* these things?

1 … invite your friends to your next birthday party? *(If I don't invite …)*
2 … learn for the next school test?
3 … save enough pocket money for the rest of the month?

---

1 draught [dra:ft] *Luftzug*

3 *An exchange pupil* **conditional sentence I** ▶ 252a

a Bettina's exchange pupil from England has just arrived. Bettina is telling her what *they could do* together *if* … What are Bettina's suggestions? Write conditional sentences (type I) from the notes with *I/we/you*, etc. *could* in the main clause.

Example:

1 warm enough – weekend	go on a bike tour
2 like parties	meet all my friends – Friday night
3 weather bad – Saturday	look round the shopping mall
4 interested in history	go to the town museum
5 my best friend – time	come and meet you – this afternoon
6 understand enough German	watch some videos
7 play tennis	my brother – play with you
8 like Italian food	have a pizza at my favourite pizza restaurant – tonight

b What could you do with your friends at the weekend? Write three suggestions with an *if*-clause + *could*.

Example: *If it* ***isn't*** *too cold, we* ***could go*** *to the swimming pool on Saturday.*

4 *What parents say* **conditional sentence I** ▶ 252b

a Parents often give their teenage sons and daughters 'good advice'. Complete the general statements with a suitable main clause or with an *if*-clause, as in the examples. There are, of course, many suitable answers. Use positive or negative verb forms.

Examples: If you eat too much junk food …
If you eat too much junk food, *you* ***get*** *fat.*
…, you fail your exams.
If you ***don't do*** *any work/If you* ***don't work*** *hard enough*, you fail your exams.

1 If you don't look after your teeth, …
2 …, you always feel tired.
3 If you don't keep your room tidy, …
4 …, you ruin your eyes.
5 … if you don't listen in class.
6 You don't save any money …
7 … if you don't have breakfast before you go to school.
8 You don't have enough time for school work …

b How do *your family, friends, teachers*, etc. usually *react, if these things happen?*

Example: You play loud music on Sundays …
If I ***play*** *loud music on Sundays, my father* ***complains/gets*** *angry/****tells*** *me to turn it down.*

1 Someone leaves a mess[1] in the kitchen …
2 You arrange to meet your friends, but you arrive late …
3 Someone cheats[2] in a school test …
4 You come home later than usual …

1 mess *Unordnung, Schmutz* 2 cheat *'mogeln'*

5 *If I won the lottery …* conditional sentence II

▶ 253a

a Mike and his friends hope that they will win some money in the Saturday lottery. They are day-dreaming. What *would they do if they won* a lot of money? Make conditional sentences (type II).

Example: *If Mike **won** the lottery, he **would go** on holiday to the USA.*

1 Justin: buy – motorbike
2 Tariq: put – bank
3 Selima: go – holiday – Australia
4 Maggie: buy – presents – family
5 Pete: invite – friends – party
6 Jill: buy – horse – learn – ride

b Now you. What *would you* probably *do if you won* 1) 1000 euros 2) 10,000 euros or 3) 100,000 euros? Write a short paragraph.

6 *It would be cheaper* conditional sentence II

▶ 253a

Nick's friend Barry is planning his first trip to the States. He wants to fly to New York and Washington for ten days. Nick tells Barry that *it would be* better *if he did* things differently. Complete their conversation with the correct tenses of the verbs given, for conditional sentences (type II).

Barry: I'm planning to fly to New York and Washington in the Christmas holidays.
Nick: At Christmas? If you ***flew*** in October, it ***would be*** cheaper. And why New York and Washington in winter? If you (1 go) … to California or Florida, it would be warmer.
Barry: I know, but I'd like to see the big cities first. I think I'll fly from New York to Washington.
Nick: You (2 see) … more if you travelled overland by bus.
Barry: But it would take longer. I'm only going to stay for ten days.
Nick: If you (3 stay) … for two weeks, it wouldn't cost much more.
Barry: Well, I'll think about it. I'm going to buy some guidebooks on New York.
Nick: If you looked for travel info on the Internet, you (4 not – need) … expensive books.
Barry: That's a good idea. I'll book hotel rooms on the Internet too.
Nick: Well, if you (5 book) … hotels through a travel agency, you (6 not – pay) … the full price for the rooms.
Barry: Oh? I didn't know that. I won't book the flights until I have saved enough money.
Nick: You (7 get) … the ticket cheaper if you (8 book) … your flights as early as possible.
Barry: I've never been on holiday alone before. I hope it won't be boring.
Nick: It (9 be) … more fun if you (10 take) … someone with you.
Barry: Yes, I suppose it would. Perhaps I'll ask a friend to go with me.
Nick: Well, if you (11 ask) … me, I (12 say) … yes.

7 *Living in the USA* **conditional sentence II** ▶ 253a

a *If your family went* to live in America, what *could that mean* for you? Think of things that you and your family could do there that you can't do in Germany. Write four things. Make conditional sentences (type II) with *could*.

Example: *If we* ***lived*** *in America, I* ***could speak*** *English all day and learn it perfectly.*

b *If you* and your brothers and sisters *went* to high school in America, how *might* your daily life and your activities *be* different? What might you do? Write four things. The pictures will give you some ideas. Make conditional sentences (type II) with *might* and/or *might not*.

Examples: *If we* ***went*** *to high school in America, my sister* ***might be*** *a cheerleader.*
If I ***went*** *to high school in America, I* ***might not have*** *much free time in the evenings.*

8 *Giving advice* **conditional sentence II** ▶ 253b

Your friends sometimes ask you for advice. What advice do you think you might give in the following situations? Begin with *If I were you, …*

Example: A friend has had a quarrel with her boyfriend. They aren't talking to each other at the moment. Your friend feels really miserable.
Your advice: *If I* ***were*** *you, I* ***would talk*** *to him about the problem and tell him how you feel.*

1 Your best friend has moved to another town. He/She doesn't like the new school or the class.
2 A friend thinks he is in love with his best friend's girlfriend.
3 A friend has problems with maths. He doesn't like the maths teacher either.
4 A friend needs money for the class trip. His father is out of work, so his parents can't help.
5 A friend has lost his mobile phone. It was a present from his parents. He hasn't told his parents yet because he knows they will be angry.

9 *It wouldn't have happened if …* **conditional sentence III** ▶ 254

a Kevin never does anything stupid. If something bad happens to his classmates, he always makes comments about them to the other pupils. What did he say about his classmates? Write conditional sentences (type III).

Examples: Susan crossed the road without looking. She didn't see the cyclist.
Kevin: *If Susan* ***had looked*** *when she crossed the road, she* ***would have seen*** *the cyclist.*
Joe went out the night before the history test. He failed it.
Kevin: *If Joe* ***hadn't gone out*** *the night before the test, he* ***wouldn't have failed*** *it.*

1 Sue did her maths homework in the bus. It was full of mistakes.
2 Pete left his wallet[1] in a snack-bar. It disappeared.
3 Peggy gave in her English project late. She got a bad mark.
4 Owen forgot Julie's birthday. She didn't go to the disco with him.
5 Sanjay didn't lock his bike. It was stolen.
6 Sean didn't tell Diane the truth. She dumped[2] him.
7 Beth lost Ben's CDs. He got angry.

b Work with a partner. Write down three things that you wanted to do (but didn't do) last week and why you didn't do them. Then exchange your sentences with your partner. Your partner must write three conditional sentences (type III), as in part a) above.

Example: Your partner writes: *I didn't visit my cousin in hospital. I didn't have time.*
You write: *X* ***would have visited*** *his/her cousin in hospital if he/she* ***had had*** *time.*

10 *Friday 13th* **conditional sentence III** ▶ 254

a Jill had a really bad day last Friday. Everything went wrong. Read her story first.

When Jill left the house the sun was shining. Her mother told her to take an umbrella, but she didn't listen. It was hot in the shopping mall, so she took off her jacket. While she was looking in the stores, she met an old friend, Chrissy. They had a coffee and a long chat. Chrissy had a money problem, so Jill lent her ten pounds. On her way home, Jill realized that she had left her jacket in the café. She ran back to get it, but it had disappeared. Her return bus ticket was in the jacket pocket, and she had given Chrissy the money that she had left. Unfortunately, it started to rain heavily. Jill had no jacket, no umbrella, no bus ticket, no money. She had to walk home and she was wet to the skin when she got there. She caught a cold and on the next day – her birthday – she was ill in bed.

Examples: If Jill ***had listened*** to her mother, she ***would have taken*** an umbrella.
Jill ***wouldn't have taken off*** her jacket if it ***hadn't been*** hot in the shopping mall.

If Jill (1 not – meet) … Chrissy, she (2 not – go) … into the café. If she (3 not – leave) … her jacket in the café, it (4 not – disappear) … She (5 have) … a return bus ticket if she (6 not – lose) … her jacket. If she (7 not – give) … Chrissy ten pounds, she (8 have) … money for the bus or for a taxi. She (9 not – get) … wet if she (10 take) … an umbrella with her. If she (11 not – get) … wet, she (12 not – catch) … a cold.

b What *would you/wouldn't you have done if you had been* Jill? Find three things in the story that you would have done differently.

Example: *If I* ***had been*** *Jill, I* ***would have taken*** *an umbrella.*

1 wallet *Brieftasche* 2 dump sb *mit jdm. Schluss machen*

11 *A hundred years ago* **conditional sentence III**

▶ 254

a Imagine what *your life would have been* like *if you had lived* a hundred years ago. What *would you have done/had*, etc.? What *wouldn't you have done/had*, etc.? Write four conditional sentences (type III).

Examples: *If I **had lived** a hundred years ago, I **would have had** a different hairstyle and different clothes. … I **wouldn't have gone** to karate lessons.*

b What *couldn't you have done*? Write four sentences with *couldn't have*.

Examples: *If I **had lived** a hundred years ago, I **couldn't have phoned** my friends on a mobile phone. … I **couldn't have gone** to discos or parties.*

12 *A walking trip* **conditional sentences: mixed exercise**

▶ 252a, 253a/b, 254

Dave, his sister Pat and his friend Tom are on a walking trip in the hills. Unfortunately, there are a few problems. Put in the correct verb tense for conditional sentence types I, II or III.

Dave: It's starting to get dark. But if we ***walk*** a bit faster, we ***will be*** at the next village in ten minutes. If we ***had set off*** earlier, we ***would have arrived*** an hour ago.
Pat: I can't walk faster. I've got a blister[1] on my foot.
Dave: That's your own fault. If you (1 put on) … some sensible shoes, you wouldn't have got a blister.
Pat: There's nothing wrong with my shoes. If you (2 not – be) … such an egoist, you would carry my rucksack for me.
Tom: Be quiet, you two. Anyway, where are we?
Dave: We should soon be at the next village. But I can't see any lights.
Pat: Are we lost? You said you knew the way. If you hadn't said you knew the way, I (3 not – come) … with you on your stupid walking trip.
Tom: If we (4 not – see) … the village lights soon, we'll have to look at the map. Who's got it?
Pat: I haven't got it. Where is it? Have you lost the map, Dave? Stupid! If you (5 look after) … things better, you wouldn't lose them all the time. If we (6 not – find) … the village soon, we (7 have to) … sleep in a field.
Dave: I haven't lost the map. I didn't bring one. Anyway, we don't need a map. I know the way.
Pat: If you were intelligent, you (8 not – go) … on a walking trip without a compass and a map. I'm cold and hungry and my feet hurt. Where's the village?
Tom: Look, there's a light! I think we're almost there. Come on!
Pat: If there's a phone box, I (9 phone) … dad and ask him to pick us up. And if you ever ask me to go on another walking trip, I (10 say) … no.
Dave: If I (11 know) … what a problem you would be, I (12 ask) … someone else.
Pat: Macho!

1 blister *Blase*

Relative clauses

A **Put in the missing relative pronouns where they are necessary. Sometimes two pronouns are possible.**

1 Tom's going to the disco with the girl … used to go out with Tony.
2 I know the girl … dog got run over in that accident last night.
3 Where's the computer magazine … was lying on this chair?
4 Is there anything else … you want to tell me about what happened?
5 Look, that's the man … I told you about.
6 I don't like people … always take and never give.
7 Don't forget the present … you bought for Sheila.
8 A barometer is something … you measure[1] air pressure with, isn't it?
9 There's another thing … I want to discuss with you.
10 Alexander Fleming, the man … discovered penicillin, came from Scotland.

B **Translate the German words and clauses in brackets into English.**

11 Shall I tell you about the student *(den ich gestern beim Konzert kennengelernt habe)* …?
12 Is that the boy *(dessen Bruder gestern im Fernsehen war)* …?
13 That's the girl *(neben dem ich sitze)* … in school.
14 Where are the comics *(die ich heute Morgen gekauft habe)* …?
15 Someone's taken the magazines *(die gestern auf dem Tisch waren)* …
16 *(Das Mädchen, mit dem ich in die Disco ging,)* … comes from Australia.
17 The boy *(der gestern viermal anrief)* … is my new boyfriend.

C **Choose the correct word from the brackets.**

18 The hotel (which/where/that/–) we stayed was really big and very modern.
19 The view (that/who/what/–) we had from the top of the tower was wonderful.
20 This is the girl (whose/who/who's) sister has gone to work in Africa.
21 That's the reason (why/which) I didn't go to Rita's party.
22 I'll show you the snack-bar (where/–) we usually go to.
23 November the fourth is the day (where/which/when) children in England light fireworks and make big bonfires.

D **Spot the mistakes. There is one mistake in each sentence.**

24 All the people which were at the party were friends of Jane's.
25 That's the boy who's sister is doing a high school year in America.
26 That's the last thing what I would do.
27 That's the woman for who my brother works.
28 Which is the woman which sold you the pullover?
29 Where's the pen with that I always write?
30 That's the youth hostel where we stayed at.

1 measure *messen*

Relative clauses

? Correct yourself

A 1: *... with the girl who/that used to ...* 2: *... the girl whose dog ...* 3: *... the computer magazine that/which was lying ...* 4: *... anything else (that/which) you want to tell me ...* 5: *... the man (who/that) I told you about.* 6: *... people who/that always take ...* 7: *... the present (that/which) you bought ...* 8: *... something (that/which) you measure air pressure with ...* 9: *... thing (that/which) I want to ...* 10: *... the man who/that discovered penicillin ...*

B 11: *...(who/that) I met at the concert yesterday?* 12: *... whose brother was on TV yesterday?* 13: *... (who/that) I sit next to ...* 14: *... (that/which) I bought this morning?* 15: *... that/which were on the table yesterday.* 16: *The girl (who/that) I went to the disco with ...* 17: *... who/that phoned four times yesterday ...*

C 18: *The hotel where we stayed was really big and very modern.* 19: *The view that/ – we had from the top of the tower was wonderful.* 20: *This is the girl whose sister has gone to work in Africa.* 21: *That's the reason why I didn't go to Rita's party.* 22: *I'll show you the snack-bar (–) we usually go to.* 23: *November the fourth is the day when children in England light fireworks and make big bonfires.*

D 24: *All the people who/that were at the party were friends of Jane's.* 25: *That's the boy whose sister is doing a high school year in America.* 26: *That's the last thing (that/which) I would do.* 27: *That's the woman (who/that) my brother works for.* Or: *That's the woman for whom my brother works. (formal)* 28: *Which is the woman who/that sold you the pullover?* 29: *Where's the pen (that/which) I always write with?* 30: *That's the youth hostel where we stayed.* Or: *That's the youth hostel (that/which) we stayed at.* Or: *That's the youth hostel at which we stayed. (formal)*

Exercise finder

Sentences	CEG	Exercises
1, 3, 6, 10, 15, 17, 24, 28	▶ 260	▶ 1, 2, 7
2, 12, 20, 25	▶ 262	▶ 3
4, 7, 9, 14, 19, 26	▶ 264a	▶ 4, 6, 7
5, 11, 13, 16, 27	▶ 264	▶ 6
8, 22, 29	▶ 264b	▶ 5, 7
18, 21, 23, 30	▶ 263b	▶ 7

1 *A holiday in Italy* relative pronoun as subject: *who, which* ► 260

Read the text about the friends and their Italian holiday. Then answer the questions below.

Nicole and her friends Liz and Pat have just come back from a holiday in Italy. They stayed at a small guest house called *Azzurro* in Limone on Lake Garda. The owner was a woman called Signora Elena. She had two sons, Giorgio and Luigi. Giorgio often came home in the middle of the night on his motorbike, waking all the guests. There was also a dog. He was called Peppino, and he always barked loudly when Giorgio came home.
Tim and Markus, two young Germans, were also staying at the guest house.
There was also a restaurant called *Casa Giovanni* not far away. It served very good seafood[1].
In the evenings, the girls went to a disco called *Mamma Mia*. They met lots of other young people there. Andy and Rob, two teenagers from Ireland, went to the *Mamma Mia* every night too. During the daytime, they all went swimming, walking or shopping together.
There was an ice-cream parlour[2] called *La Fiorentina*. It sold fantastic ice-cream. Every day the teenagers looked into *Gina*'s boutique. It sold trendy teenage clothes. Of course, they spent all their pocket money.

Now answer the questions about the people and places in the text, using *who* or *which*.

Examples: Who was Signora Elena? *Signora Elena was the woman* ***who*** *owned the guest house.*
What was *Azzurro*? *Azzurro was the small guest house* ***which*** *the girls stayed at.*

1 Who are Liz and Pat?
2 Who was Giorgio?
3 What was *Casa Giovanni*?
4 Who was Peppino?
5 Who were Tim and Markus?
6 What was the *Mamma Mia*?
7 Who were Andy and Rob?
8 What was *Gina*'s?
9 What was *La Fiorentina*?

2 *I like people who …* relative pronoun as subject: *who/that, that/which* ► 260

Make ten sentences from the table which are true for you and your friends.

I *My best friend* *My girlfriend/ boyfriend*	*like* *likes* *don't like* *doesn't like*	*people* *places* *boys* *discos* *girls* *parties* *jokes* *films* *holidays*	*who/ that* *that/ which*	*really make you laugh* *are adventurous* *go on too long* *are always crowded* *make you cry* *are boring* *always tell the truth* *show off*[3] *wear too much make-up*

Examples: *I don't like people* ***who/that*** *show off.*
My best friend likes films ***that/which*** *make you cry.*

1 seafood *Meeresfrüchte, Fisch* 2 ice-cream parlour *Eisdiele* 3 show off *angeben, prahlen*

3 *People at a barbecue* ***whose, who's*** ▶ 262

You are at a barbecue with your penfriend Val from the States. Before the barbecue you told her who would be there. Now you show her who the people are. Make sentences with *whose* or *who's (who is/who has).*

Example: Jill – Her father teaches at our school.
*That's Jill, the girl **whose** father teaches at our school.*

Example: Brian – He is very good at sports.
*That's Brian, the boy **who's** very good at sports.*

1 Steve – His girlfriend has just left him.
2 Rob – He is good with computers.
3 Sarah – Her brother is often on TV.
4 Kim – She has just got a place at Oxford University.
5 Sylvia – Her moped was stolen last week.
6 Justin – He has just bought a motorbike.
7 Tariq and Sanjay – Their family comes from India.
8 Melanie and Pam – Their father has just lost his job.

4 *Where's the ketchup?* ***that* as subject; contact clauses** ▶ 260, 264a

a Dan can't find anything today. Combine his thoughts into one sentence. Use a contact clause (i.e. leave out the relative pronoun).

Example: *Where are those comics ( ) I bought this morning?*

Example: *What did I do with the CDs ( ) John lent me?*

1 Where's that red felt-tip? I found it yesterday.
2 Where's that new exercise book? I bought it for French.
3 What did I do with those e-mail addresses? Jan gave me them.

b Now Dan asks his mother and his sister where things are. They don't hear him the first time, so he repeats what he said in one sentence. What does he say the second time? Make one sentence. Leave out the relative pronoun *(that)* where possible.

Examples:
Dan: Where's the ketchup? It was in the cupboard.
Mother: I'm upstairs. What did you say?
Dan: *Where's the ketchup **that** was in the cupboard?*
Dan: Who has taken those car magazines? I left them on the table.
Sister: I'm in my room. Did you say something?
Dan: *Who has taken those car magazines ( ) I left on the table?*

Dan:
1 Where's the bottle of coke? It was in the fridge.
2 Where's the piece of apple pie? I didn't eat it at lunch.
3 Who's eaten the crisps? I bought them this morning.
4 Suzi, where are the videos? I put them on the TV.
5 Where's the new computer magazine? Dad brought it home.
6 Mum, where's my black T-shirt? It needs washing.
7 Where are the new batteries? I bought them yesterday.

5 *Write the clues* **contact clauses with prepositions** ▶ 264b

a Everybody likes crossword puzzles, but this one is different from other crosswords. The answers are done, but what were the clues? Can you write them? There is, of course, more than one way to describe the objects, but use contact clauses (ie.leave out the relative pronoun) and put the preposition at the end.

		1 c	a	r		2 g				
		h			3 p	l	a	t	4 e	
		a		5 s		a			n	
6 s	u	i	t	c	a	s	e		v	
h		r		i		s		7 b	e	d
a				s					l	
m				s		8 t			o	
p			9 j	o	k	e			p	
o				r		n		10 p	e	n
o				s		t				

Across
Examples: 1 *It is something you drive* ***in***.
3 *It is something we eat* ***from****/ something we put food* ***on***.

Now write the clues for 6, 7, 9, 10 across and 1, 2, 4, 5, 6, 8 down.

b Describe these things in the same way.

1 

2 

3 

6 *Old classmates* **relative clauses: mixed exercise** ▶ 260, 264

The twin brothers Ben and Justin are looking at an old class photo. Now they are 18. Complete their conversation about the pupils in the photo. Use *who*, a contact clause, or a contact clause with a preposition.

Examples: Ben: Do you remember Liam?
Justin: Didn't he come from Ireland?
Ben: *Yes, he was the boy* ***who*** *came from Ireland.* (*who* as subject)
And that's Jane Scott. I saw her the other day.
Justin: You used to like her best, didn't you?
Ben: *Yes, she was the girl ( ) I used to like best.* (contact clause)
Ben: Jane is still good friends with Josie Parks.
Justin: You copied your homework from her.
Ben: *Yes, she was the girl ( ) I copied my homework* ***from***. (contact clause with prep.)

1 Ben: Josie is going out with Will Marshall. He used to beat you at sports.
Justin: That's right. He was ... He's good at boxing now.

2 Ben: And do you remember Joanne Watkins?
Justin: Not very well. Nobody liked her.
Ben: Yes, she was ... But I thought she was OK.

3 Ben: That's Mick and Dennis.
Justin: They were very musical. They sang in the church choir.
Ben: Oh, yes, now I remember. They were …
4 Justin: And the girl next to Dennis must be Polly … er … can't remember. But she never stopped talking.
Ben: Yes, you're right. She was …
5 Ben: And do you remember Fiona Jackson? You often quarrelled[1] with her.
Justin: Yes, of course, Fiona. She was … Usually about nothing.
6 Ben: That's Dave. You used to sit next to him. Remember?
Justin: Yes, Dave Ashton. He was the boy … He was a good friend.
7 Ben: That's Josh Miller, I think. I helped him with maths.
Justin: Yes, he was … And he used to give you comics.
8 Ben: That's Sean. I once had a big fight with him. He thought I was you.
Justin: Oh, yes. I remember Sean. He was … You knocked his front tooth out.
9 Ben: And that's Anisha and Sarah next to Sean. They were always up for a laugh[2].
Justin: That's right. They were …, just like us.

7 *A youth hostel trip* relative clauses: mixed exercise ► 260, 262, 263b, 264, 266

a Some Year 11 pupils are chatting in the break. Complete their conversation with:

who ▪ that ▪ which ▪ whose ▪ where ▪ when ▪ why

Sometimes two words are possible. If you think you can leave out the relative pronoun, put it in brackets ( ).

Rachel: How was your youth hostel trip to Wales?

Abdul: Great. The hostel ***where*** we stayed was cool. It had been a castle. It was in the old part of town on top of a hill, and the view ***(that/which)*** we had was fantastic. Most of the rooms were a bit dark, but the room (1) … we slept was in a modern part. Clean and light[3]. Just four beds. The other two guys (2) … we shared our room with were foreigners. We tried to speak to them – a bit of French, a bit of German, but they didn't understand anything (3) … we said – (4) … isn't really surprising. It was lots of fun. We tried to guess the country (5) … they came from, but we couldn't. It was Poland. Next week you can see the photos (6) … we took. We had a lot of fun. In the evenings there was a nice disco (7) … we used to go to. It's the disco (8) … I met Sarah, my new girlfriend.

Anna: Cool. So just you and Paul went. I thought Tom was planning to go with you as well.

Abdul: Yes, but there was a problem with the girl (9) … he's going out with just now. Melissa is her name, I think.

Rachel: Oh, yes, that's the girl (10) … parents had a bad car accident last week. She has a sister (11) … goes to the same school as my brother. So that's the reason (12) … Tom didn't go with you. Poor Melissa. I remember the day (13) … my parents were hurt in a coach accident coming back from Switzerland. It was a shock (14) … I'll never forget.

b Write a short paragraph about the last youth hostel trip, class trip, etc. that you went on. Write about the place, the rooms, the people, your friends, etc. Use relative pronouns and *where, when, why* as in a).

---

1 quarrel *(sich) streiten* 2 They were always up for a laugh. *Sie waren für jeden Spaß zu haben.* 3 light *hell*

Indirect speech

A **Can you report what they say/said? Change the sentences into indirect speech.**

1 Sean: 'I go to karate classes.'	Sean says ...
2 Trish: 'Do you like Mexican food, Pat?'	Trish asked Pat ...
3 Lynn: 'Go and fetch help, Jane!'	Lynn told Jane ...
4 Abdul: 'I think the school team may win the match.'	Abdul thought ...
5 Tim: 'Can I copy your French homework, Selima?'	Tim asked Selima ...
6 Teacher: 'Don't make so much noise, Peter!'	The teacher told Peter ...
7 Jill: 'I didn't do the French homework myself.'	Jill admitted[1] that ...
8 Sarah: 'When is Beth's party?'	Sarah wanted to know ...
9 Sheila: 'I'll phone you from Glasgow, Val.'	Sheila told Val ...
10 Janice: 'I haven't been to town for over a month.'	Janice mentioned that ...
11 Layla to Chris: 'Will you help me with the maths homework?'	Layla asked Chris ...

B **Now fill in the missing forms.**

Some Year 11 pupils were talking about homework. One boy said he usually (12 do) ... homework for three hours every evening. A girl said she (13 not – go) ... to bed until eleven-thirty the night before. The pupils said they (14 already – complain) ... to the form teacher. He had said that he (15 certainly – give) ... the class less homework in future. He told the pupils (16 not – stay up) ... too late and asked them (17 tell) ... him if the situation didn't improve.

C **What did they say in direct speech?**

18 Jason said that he might go to Brighton for the weekend.	Jason:
19 His girlfriend asked him if she could go with him.	Rachel:
20 He answered that he was going on his motorbike.	Jason:
21 Rachel said he knew that she didn't like motorbikes.	Rachel:
22 She wanted to know how long the trip would take.	Rachel:
23 Jason told her to go by train instead.	Jason:

D **Spot the mistakes. There is one mistake in each sentence (pair).**

24 'Excuse me. Can you say me how to get to the library, please?'
25 Sheila asked Beth if she did usually go to the disco on Fridays or Saturdays.
26 We said to Julie to hurry up.
27 Tim: 'Serena, can I borrow your pen?' Tim asked Serena if he can borrow her pen.
28 Layla wants to know when does the film begin.
29 Richard told to James that he was saving up to buy a new computer.
30 Nicole advised Marie getting up early if she wanted to get the first train.
31 Michael says his sister was sixteen and his brother was twelve.
32 Mum told us to not walk through the park after dark.

1 admit *zugeben*

Indirect speech

? Correct yourself

A 1: *Sean says that he goes to karate classes.* 2: *Trish asked Pat if/whether she liked Mexican food.* 3: *Lynn told Jane to go and fetch help. / Lynn told Jane that she should go and fetch help.* 4: *Abdul thought (that) the school team might win the match.* 5: *Tim asked Selima if/whether he could copy her French homework.* 6: *The teacher told Peter not to make so much noise. / The teacher told Peter that he shouldn't make so much noise.* 7: *Jill admitted that she hadn't done the French homework herself.* 8: *Sarah wanted to know when Beth's party was.* 9: *Sheila told Val that she would phone her from Glasgow.* 10: *Janice mentioned that she hadn't been to town for over a month.* 11: *Layla asked Chris to help her with the maths homework. / Layla asked Chris if he would help her with the maths homework.*

B 12: *… said he usually did homework …* 13: *… said she had not gone to bed …* 14: *… said they had already complained …* 15: *… said that he would certainly give …* 16: *… told the pupils not to stay up … / told the pupils that they shouldn't stay up …* 17: *… asked them to tell him if … / asked them if they would tell him if …*

C 18: *Jason: 'I may go to Brighton for the weekend.'* 19: *Rachel: 'Can I go with you?'* 20: *Jason: 'I am going on my motorbike.'* 21: *Rachel: 'You know (that) I don't like motorbikes.'* 22: *Rachel: 'How long will the trip take?'* 23: *Jason: 'Go by train instead.'*

D 24: *'Excuse me. Can you tell me how to get to the library, please?'* 25: *Sheila asked Beth if she usually went to the disco on Fridays or Saturdays.* 26: *We told Julie to hurry up.* 27: *Tim: 'Serena, can I borrow your pen?' Tim asked Serena if he could borrow her pen.* 28: *Layla wants to know when the film begins.* 29: *Richard told James that he was saving up to buy a new computer.* 30: *Nicole advised Marie to get up early if she wanted to get the first train.* 31: *Michael says his sister is sixteen and his brother is twelve.* 32: *Mum told us not to walk through the park after dark.*

Exercise finder

Sentences	CEG	Exercises
1, 31	▶ **274d**	▶ **1**
2, 5, 19, 25	▶ **279**	▶ **10, 13**
3, 6, 16, 23, 30, 32	▶ **280a/b**	▶ **12, 13**
4, 9, 15,18, 27	▶ **273, 277**	▶ **3b, 6**
7, 10, 12, 13, 14	▶ **273, 277**	▶ **3a, 4, 5, 13**
8, 22, 28	▶ **279**	▶ **9, 10, 13**
11, 17	▶ **280b**	▶ **11**
20, 21	▶ **273, 277**	▶ **6**
24, 26, 29	▶ **274a**	▶ **2**

1 *A phone call* **changes in pronouns; reporting verb: simple present**

▶ 274d, 275

a Marcie is washing her hair. When her boyfriend Owen phones, Marcie's brother Alex answers the phone. He reports Owen's words to Marcie. Use the reporting verb *He says …* and remember to change necessary pronouns, as in the examples.

Examples: Alex: She can't come to the phone just now, Owen.
Owen: Well, **I** can't pick **her** up at eight. Tell her, please.
Alex: He says ***he** can't pick **you** up at eight.*
Owen: **My** car has broken down.
Alex: He says ***his** car has broken down.*

1 Owen: Perhaps I can borrow my brother's car.
Alex: He says perhaps …
2 Owen: If not, we will have to go to the cinema on the bus.
Alex: He says if not, …
3 Owen: The film starts at eight-thirty.
Alex: He says …
4 Owen: I'll phone again in half an hour.
Alex: He says …
5 Owen: Oh, – I'll have to borrow ten pounds from Marcie for the cinema tickets.
Alex: He says …

b Work in groups of three. Make dialogues for the following situation. In the maths lesson A wants to talk to C, but sits next to B. So A tells B what he/she is going to do after school. Then B tells C what A says. Do the exercise three times and say at least two sentences each. Here's a suggestion:

Examples: A: **I**'m hungry, so **I**'m going for a hamburger.
B: (to C) *A says **she**'s hungry, so **she**'s going for a hamburger.*
A: Afterwards **I**'m going to look round the shops. C can go with **me** if **she** wants.
B: (to C) *A says that afterwards **she**'s going to look round the shops. She says **you** can go with **her** if **you** want.*

2 *Keeping fit* ***say, tell***

▶ 274a/b

a Some teenagers were talking about fitness clubs and keeping fit. Match the sentence parts.

Examples: *Katie **said**, 'I would like to join a fitness club.'*
*Emma **told** Robbie she couldn't really afford to join a club.*

1 Leo told
2 Robbie said
3 Emma told
4 Layla said
5 Leo said,

a) that he was already a member of a club.
b) everybody that he knew a really cheap one.
c) that she was interested in bodybuilding.
d) Katie that she thought weight training was stupid.
e) 'You can easily make new friends at fitness clubs.'

b Choose the correct verb, *say* or *tell*.

1 Doug (said/told) Steve which fitness club he should join.
2 Eve (says/tells) that she hasn't got time to keep fit.
3 Marie (hasn't said/hasn't told) her friends that she's on a diet.
4 Jane (said/told) to her boyfriend, 'I think you should lose some weight.'
5 Abdul (is saying/is telling) all his friends about a fantastic girl he met at a fitness club.

3 *Weekend plans* **changes in tenses; reporting verb: simple past**

273, 277

a Trish suggested some things to do at the weekend. But most of her friends had other plans. Report what they said to Trish.
Change the verb tenses: present → past, past → past perfect, present perfect → past perfect

Examples: *Johnny said he* ***was going*** *camping with his cousin at the weekend.*
Layla said she ***had gone*** *to bed late, so she was too tired to go out.*
Karen said she ***had promised*** *to help a friend with his computer.*

b Now report what these friends said. Make the following changes: *will* → *would*, *can* → *could*, *may* → *might*

4 *A class discussion* **changes in tenses; reporting verb: simple past** ▶ 273, 277

a Year 11 had a class discussion about PE lessons. What did the pupils say? Answer the questions with *He/She said …*

Example: What did James say about running and jumping about?
*He said nobody really **enjoyed** it.*

Example: What did Carol say about an injury in the gym?
*She said she **had** once **broken** a finger jumping over the horse.*

Ben: Pupils don't take physical fitness seriously enough. Exercise and movement are important for teenagers.

Joy: I once had an accident. I fell off the parallel bars[1] and broke a tooth. I have hated gymnastics since then.

Jill: I have never had a good mark for PE, although I try really hard.

Matt: Two lessons a week aren't enough. We should have more sport.

Leo: I like outside sports in summer, but I don't like running in circles in the gym in winter.

Gina: I'll never be good at PE, so I get bad marks. But I'm the best tennis player in our club.

1 What did Ben say about physical fitness?
2 What did Joy say about an accident she once had?
3 What did James say about school sport?
4 What did Joy say about gymnastics?
5 What did Jill say about her marks for PE?
6 What did Matt say about the number of PE lessons?
7 What did Leo say about sport lessons in summer and winter?
8 What did Gina say about PE and her marks?
9 What did Ben say about exercise and movement?
10 What did Gina say about her tennis?

b Work with a partner. Ask him/her what he/she thinks about school sport, the number of lessons, the kind of activities, suggestions for better PE lessons, etc. Make notes, then report what your partner said to the class.

1 parallel bars *Barren*

5 *When do I become an adult?* **changes in tenses; rep. verb: sim. past** ▶ 273, 277

Have you ever written an e-mail to a magazine? Rachel C. wrote the following to *Teen World*. Marie found the e-mail interesting and told her friend Angela about it.

> Dear Editor,
>
> I am 14 years old and I feel confused because I don't know when I will become an adult. I hope you can help me …
> I can get married at 16, but I can't vote until I'm 18. At the cinema I already have to pay for an adult ticket, but I'm not allowed to watch adult films. I can't buy cigarettes or alcohol until I am 18, but I can drive a car at 17.
> On the bus and tube I start paying adult fares[1] at 15. I already pay the adult fare on a plane. Airlines give reductions to children under 12, which means that I'm an adult at 13 …
> In the States I can't gamble[2] in a casino until I'm 21, and I can't rent a car in my name until I'm 25! The age when I become an adult seems to depend on[3] where I'm sitting!
>
> Rachel C., Liverpool

Marie to Angela:

Examples: I read a really interesting e-mail in *Teen World* the other day. I must tell you about it. *A girl called Rachel wrote that she* ***was*** *14 and that she* ***felt*** *confused because she* ***didn't know*** *when she* ***would become*** *an adult.*

Continue.

6 *Poor Hannah* **changes in tenses; direct/indirect speech** ▶ 273, 277

On Tuesday afternoon, Hannah met Megan and told her about a problem. On Tuesday evening at home, Megan told her sister about Hannah's problem.

Examples:

Megan to her sister:
Hannah told me that (1) they had been going out for about two months. She said (2) there was just one problem, he was from Bangladesh. She added that (3) the problem would be her parents. She said (4) they would never accept him. She said (5) she didn't know how she was going to tell them because they were narrow-minded[4]. She thought (6) it could cause a lot of trouble in the family. She told me (7) she had never had a coloured boyfriend before. She said (8) her father might even tell her to stop seeing him. But she said (9) she couldn't give him up. She said (10) he was the nicest boyfriend she had ever had. Poor Hannah.

What exactly did Hannah say to Megan that afternoon?

Hannah said, '…'

1 fare *Fahrpreis* 2 gamble *Glücksspiele spielen* 3 depend on *abhängig sein von* 4 narrow-minded *engstirnig*

7 *A first meeting* **no changes in tenses** ▶ 278a

Nicole and Mark meet at a party. Later they tell their friends about the meeting. Report what they say with *He/She told me* or *He/She said*, with or without *that*. As the statements are still true when they are reported, it is not necessary to change the verb tenses. But remember to change necessary pronouns.

Example:

Nicole to Mark Later, Mark to a friend

Nicole to Mark:
1 I was born in Chicago.
2 We lived there until I was twelve.
3 I think we will go back one day.
4 I haven't lived in London very long.
5 I'm taking my driving test next week.

Mark to Nicole:
6 I have been to the States twice.
7 I went to San Francisco last year.
8 I'll probably go to New York this year.
9 I love shopping in the States.
10 I'll show you my photos tomorrow.

8 *Scenes from a soap opera* **various reporting verbs** ▶ 274a

Julie missed an episode of her favourite soap opera. Her friend Jackie saw it, so she told Julie a few things that happened. What did Jackie tell Julie about the people in the soap opera? Instead of *say* and *tell*, choose from the verbs given.

admit[1] ▪ advise ▪ explain (to someone) ▪ invite ▪ promise ▪ threaten ▪ ~~warn~~

Example: Rick ... Trish not to ...
Rick ***warned*** Trish not to *lie to him again.*

1 Donna ...
2 Jeff ... that ...
3 Troy ... Josh to ...
4 But Josh ... that ...
5 Kay ...
6 Vince ... that ...

1 admit *zugeben*

9 *The first day at work* **indirect questions with question words** ▶ 279

a Janice got a part-time office job through an agency[1]. The agency did not tell her much about the job, so on her first day she had to ask a lot of questions. What did she want to know?

Examples: *She wanted to know **what** she **was supposed to do**.*

*She asked **which** computer she **could use**.*

Janice's questions:

1 Who is the department[2] boss?	She wanted to know ...
2 Which computer system does the firm use?	She asked ...
3 Who can show me round?	She wanted to know ...
4 Where's the photocopier?	She didn't know ...
5 How do the fax machine and the scanner work?	She wanted to know ...
6 Who can I ask for help?	She didn't know ...
7 When is the lunch break?	She asked ...
8 What time does everybody go home?	She asked ...

b What would you want to know on your first day at work? Write four indirect questions with a question word.

Example: *I would want to know **what** the boss **was** like.*

10 *I asked how much the rent was* **indirect quest. with/without quest. words** ▶ 279

a Michelle has to go to London on a training course, so she needs somewhere to stay for nine months. She went to London to look at rooms. Fortunately, she found one that she liked. Later, her parents wanted to know what she had asked the owner. What does she tell her parents?

Examples: *I asked **how much** the rent **was**.*
*I asked **if** there **were** any extras for hot water and electricity.*

Michelle:

1 When do I have to pay the rent?
2 How many other students live in the house?
3 Are there any rules about visitors or noise?
4 Do I have to share the bathroom and kitchen?
5 Where's the nearest tube station?
6 Is there a telephone for students to use?
7 Can I use the washing-machine?
8 Who shall I contact if there's a problem?
9 Will I be allowed to paint or decorate the room?
10 Is there anywhere to park my bicycle?

b Imagine that there is going to be a rock concert in or near your town. Some friends who live in another town want to come to the concert and need somewhere to stay. They ask you to phone a guest house or small hotel. What would you ask? Write three things.

1 agency *Agentur* 2 department *Abteilung*

11 *What did he ask them to do?* **indirect requests** 280b

a Sam has to go into hospital to have his tonsils[1] out. He *asked* different *people to do* things for him.

Examples: Mum, will you print my e-mails for me? But Mum, don't read them.
*Sam **asked** his mother **to print** his e-mails for him. But he **asked** her **not to read** them.*

1 Suzi, will you clean the hamster's cage?
2 But don't give him too much food, Suzi.
3 Dad, will you bring me some computer magazines?
4 But Dad, don't bring me old ones.
5 Ed, will you do my paper round for me?
6 Paul, will you phone me every day and tell me all the news?
7 Dan, will you write down all the homework, please?
8 Mum, don't let anybody go into my room, please.

b Imagine that you are going on a school trip for a week. What would you *ask people* at home *to do* for you? Write four things.

Example: *I would **ask** my brother/sister **to record** my favourite programmes on the video.*

12 *What the policeman said* **indirect commands, indirect advice** 280a/b

a Millions of tourists visit Britain every year. Bad things can happen anywhere, but especially in big cities. A London policeman gave some young tourists this advice. What did the policeman *tell them/advise them to do* or *not to do?*

Examples: A young tourist: (tell, advise)
*The policeman **told us not to carry** bags over our shoulder[2]. He **advised us to put** bags round our neck and **carry** them in front of us.*

Continue.

1 Don't keep money in trouser pockets. (tell)
2 Don't walk around on your own at night. (tell) Share a taxi with someone. (advise)
3 Sit with others in the tube or train. (advise). Don't sit alone in a carriage[3] (tell)
4 Stay near crowds if you're alone. (advise)
5 Don't count money in public places. (tell)
6 Don't walk through parks or gardens after dark. (tell)
7 Watch out for pickpockets[4] in crowded places. (tell)
8 Don't put cameras in pockets. (advise)
9 Don't wear expensive jewellery[5].
10 Dial[6] 999 in an emergency. (tell)

b Work with a partner. Give each other advice on one of these things:

1 What to do (not to do) when you want to save money.
2 What to do (not to do) when your boyfriend/girlfriend dumps[7] you.

Write down what your partner *told/advised you to do* or *not to do.*

Examples: *My partner **told me to go out** with friends.*
*He/She **advised me not to sit** at home and **be** sad.*

1 tonsils *Mandeln* 2 shoulder *Schulter* 3 carriage *U-Bahnwagen* 4 pickpocket *Taschendieb/in*
5 jewellery *Schmuck* 6 dial *wählen* 7 dump sb *mit jdm. Schluss machen*

13 *Going au pair* **indirect speech: mixed exercise**

▶ 274, 277, 279, 280

Gina wants to improve her French, so she would like to go as an au pair to France for a year after school. She goes to an agency[1] to get some information.
Here's part of her conversation with Mrs Hill, an agency employee[2].

Mrs Hill: Have you been to France before, with the school perhaps?
Gina: I spent a week in Paris two years ago. I stayed with a penfriend.
Mrs Hill: How good is your spoken French?
Gina: Well, not good enough. I want to get a job in France, so I need a lot of practice.
Mrs Hill: Do you like looking after children?
Gina: Yes, I do. I have had a lot of experience with children.
Mrs Hill: What about housework? Can you cook? Would you mind cleaning?
Gina: I'm not too keen on[3] housework, but if I have enough free time, I won't mind it. I can cook a bit - a few simple things like chips and spaghetti.
Mrs Hill: Well, now, there's a family in Bordeaux that needs an au pair. There are two small boys and a baby. You see, the father is often away on business, so the mother is alone with the children and needs help – shopping, housework, babysitting, etc. I have had good reports from au pairs about the family. They'll treat[4] you well. The mother doesn't speak much English, by the way.
Gina: That doesn't matter. I want to speak French. Will I have my own room? How much free time would I get? And how old are the little boys?
Mrs Hill: You would have your own room, and you could go to school three afternoons a week. Bordeaux's a nice place. The boys are three and five. Would you be interested?
Gina: Oh, yes. It sounds perfect.
Mrs Hill: Well, could you start in August? Think about it, and let me know next week if you want the job.

Answer the questions using suitable reporting verbs: *ask, want to know, say, tell, explain, add, mention* or others. Report the most important things, not every word, and remember that you can join sentences, as in the examples.

1 What did Mrs Hill want to know about Gina?
2 What did Mrs Hill tell Gina about the French family?
3 What did Gina tell Mrs Hill about herself?
4 What did Gina ask Mrs Hill?
5 What did Mrs Hill tell Gina to do?

Examples: *Mrs Hill* ***wanted to know if*** *Gina* ***had been*** *to France before and* ***how*** *good her French* ***was****. She* ***asked*** *Gina* ***if*** *she* ***liked*** *looking after children.*

1 agency *Agentur* 2 employee *Angestellte* 3 be keen on *sehr gern mögen* 4 treat *behandeln*